Dear Jyl,

Thank you so much for the enjoyable cookbooks. My journey with your cookbooks started because my niece was concerned over her dad's health issues. My sister Rocky had joined Weight Watchers (I am a life-time member) making the commitment to healthy cooking and regular exercise. She raved about the recipes she was trying from your *Super-foods* cookbook. As soon as my order arrived I started to figure my "points" according to the nutritional information provided at the end of each recipe. It did not take long to win me over! The rest of the story: My mother, sister and I take a day off to travel to a very large holiday craft show in our area. Our day had normally been going out for breakfast, eating a not too healthy lunch and stopping for supper on the way home. I challenged Rocky and Mom to search your cookbook for a lunch we could pack along with special fruit, and told her I would decide on breakfast. As I weighed in that morning, we prepared and packed Berry Muesli and Turkey Wraps. My Weight Watchers leader asked me to bring our large RubberMaid container in with all the packed food so we could show the group. As I believe that presentation is part of the eating process, we had packed all the special things (fancy napkins, etc.) to make our day enjoyable. My WW group loved it and my leader expressed that it was the best meeting she had had. (It was a great day for her because her district manager was visiting.) They loved that we took the time and effort to make healthy living a constant part of our lives. A number of my WW friends have ordered the book and I will keep pro-moting it. Orders coming from Wisconsin and Minnesota should be growing! I e-mailed Oprah about the great books and Rocky is going to e-mail her too. We think everyone should know about your books. We hope she calls!

What most impresses me about your books, other than the great recipes:

- Easy-to-find and keep-on-hand ingredients.
- Clear and concise directions.
- Nutrition information to fit recipes into my Weight Watchers eating plan.
- *Easy—Do Ahead—Freeze* labeling.
- Variety of sections.

Jyl, being a mom of four, working 50 to 60 hours a week, and having a husband who switches shifts every two weeks, I needed a cookbook to fit MY lifestyle and I have found that in your cookbooks.

Sandy K. Kloetzke, New Richmond, Wisconsin

Dear Jyl,

I greatly appreciate your Healthy Living cookbooks. In fact, I have ordered them by the 100s and made them available to my clients. I am very glad your books have been so successful. I know they have helped thousands of people and can help a great many more in the years to come.

Daniel S. Kirschenbaum, Ph.D., Director and Professor,
Northwestern University Medical School

Dear Jyl,

I just discovered your cookbooks and I love them. I own a personal care home and these are going to help a lot with cooking healthier for my residents and myself. Yesterday we sat down and created a two-week menu using only your cookbooks and everyone is excited to start. I prepared your Garlic Chicken and Lemon Rice last night for dinner and everyone raved and was so surprised to find out it was fat-free! Thanks again.

Twana Bridges, Keysville, Georgia

Dear Jyl,

You have to know, you made this girl a happy girl! I was absolutely amazed that you even returned my phone call, to say nothing of my e-mail. I just wish I had been here to get your call. Of all people in the world, I surely did not expect yours. Thank you so very, very much. My dad had a heart attack about 17 years ago and my mother literally threw away everything that had saturated fat in it. She was bound and determined that he would live a lot longer than the 10 years the doctors predicted. He exercises hard 5 days a week and, with the help of your books, I cook fantastic meals for them without the fat. He is now 76 and I think he's healthier than he has ever been! She discovered your books several years ago, so it has been a tradition that I find newer ones or ones she doesn't have for gifts. She is a cookbook fanatic anyway, but yours are her favorites (and mine now too!). Keep up the fantastic work—I almost feel like I've made a new friend! Thank you again so much for calling and writing, and I do look forward to the new book.

Laurie Paulson, Hamilton, Montana

Dear Jyl,

Your *Superfoods Cookbook* is awesome! You have spoiled me! I don't even look at other cookbooks now. The recipes are for real food that families will eat with a nutritious twist. I am so excited! I just checked out your website and saw you have a new cookbook coming out in January. I am so anxious to get it! I have started on a weight loss plan and have lost 25 pounds so far. I have quite a bit more to go but I love your books. I have all of them so I was excited to see a new one coming out. I have talked with you on the phone a couple of times. I had the son who had terrible headaches until I changed our eating habits. You are the best! You have been wonderful when I called to order books and you were so gracious in answering my questions. I must admit I tell EVERYONE about your books. I do the Firm tapes and I tell everyone in our "e-mail" workout group that your books are the best to have! Congratulations on your new book and best wishes on the holidays to come!

Tonda Smith

Dear Jyl,

I have all of your cookbooks and I love them! My husband and I have both lost over 20 pounds using the recipes in your books. I am so excited because I never really thought fat-free or low-fat cooking would taste so good or be so easy to prepare. I also didn't think there would be such a variety. I thought that in order to lose weight I would have to eat like a rabbit and feel starved all of the time. What a pleasant surprise to have healthy, tasty dinners, as well as satisfying and low-fat or fat-free desserts. It helps a lot to not feel deprived. One of my favorite things to make is smoothies. I enjoy one almost everyday. Thank you so much for taking the time to help people like me to improve my eating habits. I am finally learning that a healthy active lifestyle is the key. I am very pleased with the lifestyle changes you have motivated me to adopt and look forward to each and every book you continue to write! I just picked up *Cook Once—Eat for a Week*. I can't wait to start cooking! God bless!

Ardith K. Frisk, Ishpeming, Michigan

Dear Jyl,

I had to write to let you know I just bought your cookbook *Fat Free Living*. I have not found a recipe I did not like. I never thought fat-free could taste so good. Each evening I look forward to a new recipe. I am going to give your cookbooks as Christmas presents.

Kathy Hall, Toano, Virginia

Dear Jyl,

Let me start by saying thank you for helping me change my life by changing my mind-set about food. When I was younger my weight fluctuated constantly but toward the end of my twenties I found that it was harder to control the weight and into my thirties I was overweight. I began to get heavier and heavier and then came the failing health; my feet, my legs, and then a brain tumor. Even though there was no medical explanation, I believe that the cancer was brought on by not eating properly and taking care of myself the way that I should have. When you get sick your body becomes more important and you search for fun ways to make yourself healthier. Knowing that certain foods have healing properties, I began to look for ways of changing my eating habits. I mentioned this to my mother and her love and concern led her to search for something to help me change my diet and myself. She sent me your first two cookbooks and that was the beginning of my drastic change. I've dieted my whole life and it never worked for me but when I started watching my saturated fat intake I lost weight so fast that my skin began to hang on me—it was a miracle! I went from 301 pounds to 140 pounds in approximately 8 months and the strangest part of it was that I did not go hungry one time. Eating three meals a day and snacking I was still losing weight. It seemed that the more good food I ate the more it helped to burn fat from my body. Since then I have gotten the rest of your cookbooks and use them daily. Even if I don't use your recipes I use your knowledge about foods, the lists and charts and incorporate them into my diet constantly. Thank you for teaching us the importance of eating healthy and taking care of ourselves the way the Lord intended.

Tanja, Douglas, Arizona

P.S. My husband says I now look like the beautiful girl he married. Thanks again!

Dear Jyl,

When my sister and I spoke this weekend I was telling her about your *Cook Once—Eat For a Week* cookbook. I received it for a Christmas present and am loving it as much as the *Superfoods* book. Both of our children are adults now but I am still very busy and love to cook several things and refrigerate/freeze them to make my week easier. My husband and I are finding more wonderful recipes for our new "healthy eating" lifestyle. I still can't believe that *every* recipe I try we love! I have never owned cookbooks like these. We try 2 to 4 new recipes every week! Sandy told me about your slow cooker book (*Countertop Cooking*) coming out soon—I can't wait to try it!! I still can't believe that my daughter found your *Superfoods* book to give us just when we were in desperate need of changing our eating habits!! I had started Weight Watchers on May 7, 2002, and we received your book in June. Your book has helped me incorporate low "point" and delicious foods into our diet. It has helped me reach my weight loss goal of 52 pounds just last week!! Thanks again for putting together these awesome cookbooks and please keep them coming!

Rocky Huber

SUPERMARKET
GOURMET

Jyl Steinback

A Perigee Book

The recipes in this book are to be followed exactly as written. Neither the author nor the publisher is responsible for your specific health or allergy needs that may require medical supervision, or for any adverse reactions to the recipes contained in this book.

A Perigee Book
Published by The Berkley Publishing Group
A division of Penguin Group (USA) Inc.
375 Hudson Street
New York, New York 10014

First Perigee edition: March 2004

ISBN: 0-399-52952-7

Visit our website at
www.penguin.com

This book has been cataloged by the Library of Congress

Printed in the United States of America

10   9   8   7   6   5   4   3   2   1

CONTENTS

❖ ❖ ❖

Acknowledgments

❖ ❖ ❖

I want to thank each and every one of you for helping and supporting me through this exciting and wonderful journey. WE DID IT! And YOU, my family and friends, made it ALL possible! Thank you from the bottom of my heart!

Gary—my gorgeous man—inside and out. Turning fifty was a positive journey for you. Cycling and challenging your body—setting goals of twenty pull-ups—you did it (I had no doubts)—and you are looking mighty handsome, my dear. Thanks as always for all of your extraordinary support in everything I venture into, and I know that's a lot! I am blessed to have you in my world and extremely grateful for your unconditional love! I love you, Gar!

Jamie—what amazes me most about you—you set your mind to something and you do it—150%—all the time! You don't look back—you just move forward with flying colors each and every time. I am so proud of your personal successes and honored and blessed to be your mom. Love radiates from my heart to yours, Jam. I love you!

Scott—you're hip, you're cool, you are my sunshine and you make me smile big. I love your white hair, but then I like it when it's blue, red, gold, brown or black. You're doing great in school—working hard, reading well, and playing lots of soccer and baseball. You are a gift in my world and I love you, Master Scott.

Mom and Dad—keep those cards and letters coming. I have to say this trip was the best! London was incredible—family time is such a beautiful gift you give to all of us—on second thought, I love all of our trips and all of our family time together. Thank you for sharing your extraordinary love for each other and with all of us. I love you both!

Jacie—congratulations on your retirement! You did it! How exciting for you. Now go out and play hard and do everything you ever dreamed of—you deserve it all! I love you!

Jeff, Diane, Alex and Casey—our visits are only too short. I love spending time with all of you. Please come play with us more often as I love to bounce off your energy and create wonderful dreams together. Journey Home is a beautiful organization and my readers can find more information on how to support this dream by logging onto Journeyhome.org.

Snooky and Harlan—thank you for always standing by me with lots of love and support!

Grandma—I love you!

I am so grateful to the following people whose help and support have made this book and dream a reality. Thank you all from the bottom of my heart. It would never happen without all of you!

Mikki Eveloff—my amazing and talented partner. I am honored and blessed to work with you each and every time. This is our eleventh book, Mikki! You are extraordinary! You are creative, gifted, and above all, a fabulous blessing in my life. Thanks for all of your hard work and special friendship.

Debra Kohh—time is never a problem with you! You make it happen. I thank you for your positive can-do attitude all the time. You are a pleasure to work with and a fabulous nutritionist. You can reach Debra at her private practice at: 602-266-0324. I highly recommend you, Deb! Thank you for everything.

Elliot—you are family! We think you're the greatest photographer there is! Thank you for always making us look fabulous! Love ya, El!

Linda Ship—you did it again, girl! I'm looking good because of your creative talent on my face and hair. Thanks, Linda!

Coleen O'Shea, Marilyn Allen and Bob Deforia— my wonderful literary agents. I thank you all from the bottom of my heart for all of your hard work, fabulous energy and support in all of our adventures together. You are a special gift in my life. Thank you!

John Duff—I appreciate you and am grateful to be working with you and all of the wonderful people at Putnam who have helped me spread the "healthy" word. Marianne Patala, my precious PR person goes the extra mile! THANK YOU! Joanne, Kenny and Courtney Prestia for getting me to the right places at the right time and never giving up on me, and the many others behind the scenes that I haven't even had the pleasure to meet. Thank you all for your time and wonderful energy to make all of this possible. I am extremely grateful to you all!

Jeanette Egan—you keep me on my toes and I like that in an editor. Thanks for all of your help, always.

Thanks so much, Bill (Wright, manager of Albertson's), and Eric Airapetias (produce manager) for your wonderful support allowing us to use Albertson's produce department for the cover of this exciting new cookbook. I appreciate all of your help!

Introduction

❖ ❖ ❖

Supermarket Gourmet is one of my all-time favorites! When I wrote *Cook Once—Eat for a Week*, I learned valuable tips for shopping efficiently and stocking my healthy kitchen. In *Supermarket Gourmet* I will share the secrets that save time, money, and energy while providing all the foods I use to prepare quick, easy and nutritious meals. You will be hooked! Did you know impulse buying accounts for 20 to 50% of the average grocery bill every time you shop? We'll give you great ideas for curbing those unnecessary, unhealthful and costly purchases. Learn the lingo of labels (page 75) and save your health. What do government-regulated labels really mean? What's in a serving (page 77)? Are there hidden ingredients that could be detrimental to your health? The answers to these questions will help you make healthful decisions when planning, shopping and cooking your meals. Along with tips for salt-free seasoning, portion control, great snacking under 100 calories and fun and fit fat-burning, you will have quick, easy recipes at your fingertips. Get ready . . . get set . . . let's go on our exciting journey from supermarket to storage to serving!

The recipes in this book were developed with an abundance of "old" and "new" foods available at most supermarkets throughout the country. Although I selected only common national brands, it is still possible that some foods are not available in certain markets. Therefore, I am providing a list of the specific foods used for testing (page 253) and possible alternatives when necessary. Cooking is an art form that requires a little creativity and innovation on the part of even the most experienced chef. If your batter's a little lumpy, add a little liquid; if your soup's a little watery, add some pureed vegetables; if you want more flavor, let loose with the salt-free seasonings. If the cake's not done in the specified baking time, then add five minutes at a time until it's properly cooked. The point is, even the most perfect recipe can suffer without a little TLC. The recipes in this book include recommended cooking/baking times, which have been successfully tested in our kitchens, but oven temperatures can vary and altitude levels will affect cooking times. Check dishes a few minutes before the indicated time and adjust cooking times according to your equipment (oven, microwave, stovetop). A few more important features of this book:

- All the recipes call for cooking spray to be used on dishes, pans and cookie sheets. Cooking spray is not included in the ingredients list unless it is to be applied to food, but should be a staple in your healthy-equipped kitchen!

- In most cases, optional ingredients or ingredients not required for recipe preparation are not included in the nutritional information or shopping list. Plan accordingly once you decide what you want to accompany the particular recipe (e.g. vegetable crudités, crackers, salsa, cheese).

- Be creative! Adapt recipes to individual preferences. If you and your family are not excited about a particular ingredient, omit or substitute with a similar ingredient and prepare as directed. The same holds true when selecting nonfat, low-fat or whole foods. You can use similar products (skim or whole milk) interchangeably but the nutritional value of the recipe will be significantly altered.

Jyl Steinback, 15202 N. 50th Place, Scottsdale, AZ 85254
1-866-LIVE-FIT

E-mail: *Jyl@AmericasHealthiestMom.com*
Website: AmericasHealthiestMom.com

STOCK YOUR HEALTHY KITCHEN WITH AN AISLE-TO-AISLE SHOPPING TRIP

❖ ❖ ❖

When the "urge to splurge" strikes, quiet your growling belly with a ready-equipped kitchen stocked with savvy food choices. Half the battle to healthy eating is having nutritious (and tasty) choices on hand. Make your kitchen a safe haven for healthy eating by making healthier choices while including small quantities of your favorite treats. According to the Food Marketing Institute, the average grocery store has over 30,000 items, but not every store has the same selection. Get the most out of your groceries with the following shopping tips:

- Make a shopping list and STICK WITH IT! You'll save fat, calories, money and time. Supermarket Challenge: Bypass your most tempting aisle and reward yourself with a favorite magazine.
- Work off a menu plan and master grocery list. Add items you need to replace or new ingredients from recipes you plan to cook.
- Outline your grocery list with the store design in mind (produce, dairy, meat, condiments).
- Write your grocery list on an envelope where coupons can be stashed for easy availability.
- Do not go grocery shopping on an empty stomach. Shopping hungry will only increase your bill and your waistline.
- Avoid food samples and "end of the aisle" marketing displays.
- Stick to the perimeter of the store as much as possible. Fresh fruit and vegetables, meat, fish, poultry, dairy products and breads are usually located in the outer aisles.
- Read the Nutrition Facts on food labels. Don't be distracted by fancy packaging or advertising.
- Select foods without added salt, sodium or sugar.
- Avoid foods with hydrogenated oil, shortening or animal fat.
- Peruse the top and bottom shelves where the best buys (and store brands) are most often located (farthest from eye level).
- Bigger is not always better; buy in bulk only if the size is practical.

Shopping Tips for Throughout the Store

Food Choices	Top Picks and Reasons to Choose Them	What to Avoid
PRODUCE Fruits and vegetables	Vibrant colors for excellent sources of vitamins and phytochemicals Purchase 4 different colors (orange, dark green, red and yellow) for a variety of vitamins and minerals. Ready-to-eat (super timesaver) Fresh produce is perishable; buy only what you need for the week. Select seasonal produce for optimal freshness and flavor. Packaged vegetable mixes	Wilted or soft fruits and vegetables Out-of-season fruits and vegetables Waxed fruits and vegetables (wax is not digestible and traps pesticides)
FREEZER Fruits Vegetables Frozen juices (concentrates)	Frozen produce is usually processed just hours after being picked, retaining high levels of nutrients. Frozen fruit and vegetable prices do not usually fluctuate with seasonal availability. May have lower pesticide residues than fresh Shorter prep time Safe storage for longer periods of time	Stained, ice-covered, wet packages that may have already been defrosted Vegetables in cream or cheese sauces
Low-fat frozen bread dough	Great for dinner Rolls, pizza crust, and calzones	
Low-fat veggie burgers or soy substitutes		
Individually frozen skinless, boneless chicken breasts or tenders		

Food Choices	Top Picks and Reasons to Choose Them	What to Avoid
Fat-free waffles		
Popsicles, sorbet, sherbet, nonfat frozen yogurt or ice cream		High-fat ice creams
DAIRY		
Skim milk or nonfat rice milk	Excellent source of calcium and protein, skim milk saves 60 calories and 8 grams of fat per 8 oz. serving of whole milk	Whole milk
Nonfat yogurt	Boosts immune system and excellent source of calcium	Yogurt made with whole milk
Nonfat sour cream		Regular sour cream
Fat-free half-and-half		Regular half-and-half
Nonfat cheeses (whole, shredded, cream, cottage)		High-fat cheeses
Egg substitute		
Whole eggs		
MEAT/POULTRY		
Extra-lean (4% fat) ground beef	Convenient, good source of iron	Ribs and other highly marbled meats
Boneless, skinless chicken breasts and tenders	High-quality protein without the fat	Bacon
White turkey tenderloins		High-sodium,-calorie and -fat sandwich meats
Low-fat ground turkey (1 gram fat per serving)		
SEAFOOD/FISH		
Shellfish (shrimp, scallops, crab, lobster)	Protects against heart disease; good source of potassium, selenium, and vitamin B_{12}; and may lower cholesterol by blocking its absorption	Breaded fish that requires deep-frying for best results
Cod Flounder Sole	Low calorie, low fat, high-protein	

Food Choices	Top Picks and Reasons to Choose Them	What to Avoid
SEAFOOD/FISH (continued)		
Halibut	Good source of selenium	
Salmon	Omega-3 fatty acids protects against heart disease, depression, endometrial cancer and diabetes	
Tuna	High protein, good source of Omega-3s	
Clams	Good source of iron	
AISLE-TO-AISLE CANS, BOXES AND BAGS		
Canned fruits and vegetables: pumpkin, squash, sweet potatoes, tomatoes (whole, diced, sauce, paste), fruit packed in juice, applesauce	Retain more Vitamin A and lycopene Good source of folate High in soluble fiber	Products with added syrups, sugar, or salt
Canned seafood and poultry: tuna packed in water; crabmeat; premium white chunk chicken		
Beans: kidney, white cannellini, Northern, navy, pinto, black, lentils, garbanzo, soy, black-eyed peas and nonfat refried	Good source of iron, zinc, and calcium (Replace a 3-oz. serving of meat with ½ cup beans and save over 100 calories and 14 grams of fat.)	Tuna in oil
Dried fruits: raisins, dates, apricots		
Nonfat or low-fat broth: chicken, beef, vegetable, Asian (where available)		
Condiments: mustard, ketchup, barbecue sauce, low-sodium teriyaki sauce, low-sodium soy sauce, salsa, nonfat salad dressings, nonfat mayonnaise, nonfat pasta sauce, vinegars, low-sugar preserves, prepared horseradish, lemon juice, lime juice, Worcestershire sauce, hot pepper sauce		

Food Choices	Top Picks and Reasons to Choose Them	What to Avoid
Baking: whole wheat flour, all-purpose flour, granulated butter substitute (e.g., Butter Buds or Molly McButter), baking soda, baking powder, sugar, brown sugar, low-fat baking mix, unsweetened cocoa powder, vanilla, almond and other extracts, fat-free brownie and muffin mixes, angel food cake and other low-fat cake mixes		
Cereals: Top picks include whole grains with at least 4 grams of fiber and less than 9 grams of sugar per serving	Arrowhead Mills Multigrain Flakes, General Mills Wheat Chex, Kashi 7 Whole Grains and Sesame, Kellogg's Complete Wheat Bran Flakes, Post Original Shredded Wheat 'n' Bran Spoon Size	
Dairy: evaporated skim milk, nonfat dry milk powder, nonfat sweetened condensed milk (where available)		
Snacks: plain popcorn for air poppers, low-sodium pretzels, raisins, flavored rice cakes, graham crackers, low-fat granola bars, dried fruit, animal crackers, nonfat fig-filled cookies, angel food cake, nonfat pudding snacks, Jell-O		
WHOLE GRAINS, RICE, PASTA, BREADS AND CEREALS Barley, cornmeal, couscous, brown rice, bulgur, flaxseed, kasha, oats, quinoa, wild rice, wheat germ, whole wheat flour	Select varieties with whole grain listed as the first ingredient	
Low-fat pasta in a variety of shapes and sizes including yolk-free egg noodles		
Low-calorie whole-wheat, rye, pumpernickel breads		Croissants, doughnuts and butter rolls

Food Choices	Top Picks and Reasons to Choose Them	What to Avoid
WHOLE GRAINS, RICE, PASTA, BREADS AND CEREALS (continued) English muffins, pita pockets, soft lahvosh, low-fat corn and flour tortillas		
REFRIGERATED Orange juice	Increase blood level of HDL cholesterol, improve arterial function, and lower blood pressure; packed with Vitamin C and other antioxidants.	
Egg substitute Whole eggs		
MISCELLANEOUS MUST-HAVES Cooking spray	Regular, butter-flavored, garlic-flavored (where available)	
Seasoned bread crumbs, cornflake crumbs or wheat germ for breading		
SEASONINGS/SPICES Basil, bay leaves, chili powder, cinnamon, cumin, garlic powder, ginger, nutmeg, onion flakes or powder, oregano, parsley, pepper, rosemary, sage, tarragon, thyme		
Seasoning blends: Cajun, Italian, Mexican, salt-free spicy seasoning, Mrs. Dash seasoning		

Impulse Buying Accounts for 20 to 50 Percent of the Average Grocery Bill Every Time You Shop. Plan Ahead And Watch Your Savings Grow!

Time- and Money-Savers for Tip-Top Shopping

1. Plan ahead. Shop with leftovers in mind. Double or triple recipes; freeze and serve later.
2. Be organized; keep a running tab of your kitchen inventory so you don't buy what you already have on hand.
3. Shop only on a full stomach; do not shop when you're hungry.
4. Plan one-dish meals that save money and time.
5. Use seasonal or on-sale fruits and vegetables. Seasonal fruits and vegetables are the least expensive and they deliver the best nutrition.
6. Stock up on frozen or canned fruits and vegetables when they go on sale. Frozen foods will keep for 3 months.
7. Don't drink your fruit servings; eat them whole instead! Whole fruits are more filling, rich in fiber and less expensive than juices.
8. Don't shy away from store brands; you can save dollars without sacrificing flavor. You can save up to $30 a week by purchasing store-brand ketchup, salad dressing, bread and milk.
9. Take advantage of pre-cut vegetables and supermarket salad bars. You'll save hours of preparation time in the kitchen while still retaining nutrients.
10. Shop the perimeter of the store instead of the inner aisles and save about 10 percent by bypassing cookies, snack foods, ultra-expensive convenience foods and pricey condiments. Staples, such as milk, bread and meat, are usually located at the back of the store. If you're just shopping for essentials, go straight to what you need and get out!
11. Walk on by the "ready-to-heat" meals.
12. Watch the register display; it's not unusual for a sale item to ring up at the regular price or for the clerk to mistakenly scan something twice.
13. Check unit pricing and price per ounce before you decide if bigger is better.
14. Check out the products on the high, middle and low shelves; more expensive brands are generally placed at eye level.
15. If you're going to freeze fresh fish, buy prepackaged frozen fish instead. It is usually better quality because it is frozen immediately after it's caught and preserved at its peak. It also costs an average of $1.50 a pound less than fresh fish.
16. Buy bagged fruit and vegetables rather than loose and save about $1.00 a pound. Weigh the bags before you select the one that offers the most for your money.

17. Stock seasonal fruits (such as berries) in the freezer to avoid spending a fortune when they're out of season.

18. Try to avoid bags of prepackaged salad greens, which can cost as much as $4 for four servings and tend to wilt more quickly than ordinary lettuce. But if time is worth more, these bags are a big bargain.

19. Buy fresh herbs and refrigerate the amount you'll use within a week. Freeze the rest on a cookie sheet, bag and store in the freezer for several months. Frozen herbs are best used in cooked dishes rather than salads and other uncooked dishes.

20. Buy milk and cheese when they are on sale and freeze for up to a month. Frozen cheese may crumble when thawed so plan to use in casseroles and other cooked dishes rather than whole.

21. Purchase bread, rolls and baked goods from the bread or snack aisle rather than the bakery.

22. Avoid individual snack packages—single servings (cookies, chips, crackers, pudding, gelatin desserts, juice) may be convenient, but you'll save money and have more control over what (and how much) your kids or you eat. Create single-serving snacks in self-sealing bags or reusable containers.

23. Buy large containers of frozen juice concentrates rather than chilled juices.

24. Buy bags of frozen vegetables instead of boxes; use what you need and freeze the rest for later use.

25. Read the newspaper on Wednesdays (or whichever day the food section is featured in your area) and plan your weekly menu around supermarket sales. Check the Internet for coupon specials.

26. Use supermarket discount cards, growing in popularity throughout the nation.

27. Don't buy foods just because you have coupons for them and avoid using coupons unless they are for a brand you normally buy. A savings on something you won't use is not a savings at all!

APPETIZERS

❖

❖ ❖ ❖

Switch and Save Starters

You and your guests will never miss the calories or fat. Serve these starters 100 percent guilt-free!

INSTEAD OF:	TRY *SUPERMARKET GOURMET* RECIPE	SAVE Calories/Fat grams
Buffalo Wings	Tortilla Chip Chicken Fingers	51 calories/ 27 grams of fat
Bloomin' Onion	Baked Onion Cheese Dip	126 calories/ 23 grams of fat
Stuffed Potato Skins	Chili Potato Skins	224 calories/ 4 grams of fat
Nachos Grande	Bell Pepper Nachos	424 calories/ 39 grams of fat
Pork Wontons (204 cal/18 g fat)	Vegetable-Cheese Wonton Wraps	139 calories/ 18 grams of fat
Regular Chili Cheese Dip (374 cal/28 g fat)	Chili-Cheese Dip	131 calories/ 27 grams of fat
Fried Potato Skins (256 cal/22 g fat)	Garlic-Cheese Potato Skins	46 cal/21 g fat
Breaded Mozzarella Sticks (698 cal/38 g fat)	Eggplant Dippers	513 cal/37 g fat
Breaded Mushrooms (305 cal/14 g fat)	Spinach-Stuffed Mushrooms	250 cal/13 g fat
Chicken Quesadilla (387 cal/19 g fat)	Quick Quesadillas	163 cal/18 g fat

Artichoke and Mushroom Pizza

Easy—Do Ahead

♦ Serves: 4

4 pita bread rounds or low-fat flour tortillas
15-oz. can seasoned tomato sauce for pizza
1½ cups shredded nonfat mozzarella cheese
13¾-oz. can quartered artichoke hearts, drained well and chopped
4-oz. can mushroom stems and pieces, drained

Preheat oven to 400°F. Line baking sheet(s) with foil and spray with cooking spray. Arrange pita rounds on baking sheet(s) in a single layer. Spread 2 to 3 tablespoons tomato sauce on each pita round; reserve remaining sauce for later use. Top with ½ cup of the cheese. Top with pita with equal amounts of artichoke hearts and mushrooms. Top with remaining cheese and bake 12 to 15 minutes, until cheese is melted and bread is golden brown.

Shopping List:

PACKAGED		DAIRY
Pita bread rounds or low-fat flour tortillas	13¾-oz. can quartered artichoke hearts (not marinated)	6 oz. shredded nonfat mozzarella cheese
CANNED	4-oz. can mushroom stems and pieces	
15-oz. can Hunt's seasoned tomato sauce for pizza		

NUTRITION PER SERVING Calories 295 • Fat 1.3 g (4%) •
Carbohydrates 47 g • Protein 25 g • Cholesterol 0 mg • Dietary Fiber 4 g •
Sodium 1019 mg
EXCHANGES 3 vegetable • 2 starch • 2 very lean meat
CARB CHOICES 3

Super Tip: Substitute any low-fat or fat-free pasta or pizza sauce for the seasoned tomato sauce for pizza if desired.

Baked Onion Cheese Dip

Easy   ◆ Serves: 8

4 cups shredded nonfat cheddar cheese
1 cup chopped onion
2 cups nonfat mayonnaise
Cocktail pumpernickel bread slices, crackers, or low-fat chips

Preheat oven to 350°F. Spray a 9-inch pie plate with cooking spray. Combine cheese, onion, and mayonnaise in a bowl and mix until blended. Spoon into pie plate and bake until puffy and lightly browned. Serve with pumpernickel bread slices.

Shopping List:

PRODUCE	PACKAGED	CONDIMENTS
1 onion (or 7-oz. container diced onion)	Cocktail pumpernickel bread slices, low-fat crackers, or baked chips	16 oz. nonfat mayonnaise
DAIRY		
1 lb. shredded nonfat cheese		

NUTRITION PER SERVING Calories 138 • Fat 0 g (0%) • Carbohydrates 14 g • Protein 16 g • Cholesterol 0 mg • Dietary Fiber <1 g • Sodium 981 mg
EXCHANGES ½ other carb • ½ starch • 2 very lean meat
CARB CHOICES 1

Super Tip: *The onion family contains both soluble and insoluble fiber, which may confer protection against high cholesterol, possible weight gain, constipation, and hemorrhoids.*

Baked Wontons with Chinese Dipping Sauce

Easy—Do Ahead   ◆ Serves: 6

12-oz. pkg. wonton squares, cut into strips
Garlic powder to taste
1 cup orange marmalade
2 tbsp. orange juice
2 tbsp. lemon juice
1 tsp. dry mustard
¼ tsp. ground ginger
2 tsp. prepared horseradish

Preheat oven to 425°F. Line baking sheet(s) with cooking spray. Arrange wonton strips in a single layer on baking sheet; sprinkle with garlic powder. Lightly spray wonton strips with cooking spray; bake 10 to 15 minutes, until golden brown and crisp. Remove from oven and cool at room temperature about 30 minutes. Combine orange marmalade, orange juice, lemon juice, mustard, ginger, and horseradish in a small bowl; mix until blended. Cover and refrigerate until ready to serve with wonton chips.

Shopping List:

PRODUCE	CANNED	SEASONINGS
12-oz. pkg. wonton squares	Orange juice	Garlic powder
Lemon or lemon juice		Dry mustard
	CONDIMENTS	Ground ginger
	8 oz. orange marmalade	
	Prepared horseradish	

NUTRITION PER SERVING Calories 314 • Fat 0 g • Carbohydrates 73 g • Protein 5 g • Cholesterol 0 mg • Dietary Fiber 1 g • Sodium 294 mg
EXCHANGES 1 starch • 4 other carb
CARB CHOICES 5

Super Tip: *For a flavor twist, substitute apricot preserves and pineapple juice for orange marmalade and orange juice.*

Bell Pepper Nachos

Easy   ◆ Serves: 8

1 green bell pepper, sliced
1 red bell pepper, sliced
1 yellow bell pepper, sliced
1½ cups shredded nonfat cheddar cheese
2 tbsp. chopped canned green chiles
Salsa

Preheat oven to 450°F. Line a baking sheet with foil and spray with cooking spray. Arrange bell pepper slices on baking sheet; top with cheese and green chiles. Bake 10 to 12 minutes, until cheese is melted. Turn broiler to high heat; broil 1 minute, until lightly browned. Serve with salsa.

Shopping List:

PRODUCE	DAIRY	CONDIMENTS
3 bell peppers (green, red, yellow, or any combination)	6 oz. shredded nonfat cheddar cheese	Salsa
	CANNED	
	4-oz. can chopped green chiles	

NUTRITION PER SERVING Calories 42 • Fat 0 g • Carbohydrates 3 g •
Protein 6 g • Cholesterol 0 mg • Dietary Fiber <1 g • Sodium 235 mg
EXCHANGES 1 vegetable • ½ very lean meat
CARB CHOICES 0

Super Tip: *Red or dark orange vegetables are loaded with antioxidant vitamins A and E, as well as bioflavonoids, which moisturize and heal your skin.*

Bruschetta with Cheese

Easy

• Serves: 8

1 lb. French baguette loaf, cut into ½-inch slices
14½-oz. can diced tomatoes with roasted garlic and onion, drained well
2½ tsp. Italian seasoning
1½ cups shredded nonfat mozzarella cheese

Preheat broiler on high. Line a baking sheet with foil and spray with cooking spray. Arrange bread slices in a single layer on baking sheet. Combine drained tomatoes and Italian seasoning and mix well. Spoon tomato mixture on bread slices and top with cheese. Broil 4 to 5 minutes, until cheese is melted and lightly browned.

Shopping List:

DAIRY	CANNED	SEASONINGS
6 oz. shredded nonfat mozzarella cheese	14½-oz. can diced tomatoes with roasted garlic and onion	Italian seasoning
		BAKERY
		1 lb. French baguette

NUTRITION PER SERVING Calories 211 • Fat 2.4 g (10%) •
Carbohydrates 32 g • Protein 13 g • Cholesterol 0 mg • Dietary Fiber 1 g •
Sodium 713 mg
EXCHANGES 1 starch • 3 vegetable • 1 very lean meat
CARB CHOICES 2

Super Tip: *Substitute 2 to 3 fresh, chopped tomatoes and ½ to 1 cup chopped fresh basil for canned tomatoes and dried Italian seasoning.*

Chicken Taquitos

Easy—Do Ahead—Freeze   • Serves: 6

2 (6-oz.) packages cooked chicken breast cuts
6 tbsp. shredded nonfat cheddar cheese
6 (6-inch) low-fat corn tortillas
1½ cups chunky-style salsa

Preheat oven to 400°F. Line a baking sheet with foil and spray with cooking spray. Divide chicken and cheese among tortillas; spoon 1 tablespoon of the salsa down center of each tortilla. Roll tortillas and place, seam side down, on baking sheet. Bake 15 to 20 minutes, until lightly browned and crisp. Serve with remaining salsa.

Shopping List:

DAIRY	MEAT	CONDIMENTS
Shredded nonfat cheddar cheese	2 (6-oz.) pkgs. cooked chicken breast cuts	12-oz. jar chunky-style salsa
	PACKAGED 6-inch low-fat corn tortillas	

NUTRITION PER SERVING Calories 180 • Fat 2.8 g (14%) •
Carbohydrates 16 g • Protein 19 g • Cholesterol 40 mg • Dietary Fiber 2 g •
Sodium 961 mg
EXCHANGES 3 very lean meat • 1 starch
CARB CHOICES 1

Super Tip: *Chicken is an excellent source of B complex vitamins, which support healthy circulation, as well as maintain normal cholesterol. A 3-oz. skinless chicken breast has 16 grams of protein and less than 1 gram of saturated fat.*

Chili-Cheese Dip

Easy—Do Ahead   • Serves: 6

15½-oz. can low-fat chili with beans
8-oz. pkg. nonfat cream cheese
1 cup shredded nonfat cheddar cheese
1 tbsp. chopped canned green chiles
6 oz. baked tortilla chips

Combine chili, cream cheese, cheddar cheese, and green chiles in microwave-safe bowl. Cover and cook on High 1 minute; stir and cook 2 to 3 minutes, until dip is bubbling hot. Serve with tortilla chips.

Shopping List:

DAIRY	PACKAGED	CANNED
8-oz. pkg. nonfat cream cheese	6 oz. baked tortilla chips	4-oz. can chopped green chiles
4 oz. shredded nonfat cheddar cheese		15½-oz. can low-fat chili with beans

NUTRITION PER SERVING Calories 243 • Fat 1 g (4%) • Carbohydrates 44 g • Protein 17 g • Cholesterol 0 mg • Dietary Fiber 3 g • Sodium 884 mg
EXCHANGES ½ very lean meat • 3 starch
CARB CHOICES 3

Super Tip: Dried beans can be stored at room temperature for one year. Once cooked, beans freeze well for up to six months. Refrigerated, cooked beans last up to five days. By cooking beans at home you avoid commercial additives such as salt, MSG, preservatives, and sugar commonly found in canned beans.

Chili Potato Skins

Easy—Do Ahead   • Serves: 6

6 medium baking potatoes, baked and cooled
1 cup cornflake crumbs
1 tbsp. chili powder
1½ tsp. ground cumin
¾ cup nonfat sour cream
Salsa

Preheat oven to 425°F. Line baking sheet(s) with foil and spray with cooking spray. Cut potatoes lengthwise into quarters and scoop out pulp, leaving ¼-inch-thick shells. (Save pulp for later use if desired.) Combine cornflake crumbs, chili powder, and cumin on paper plate and mix well. Carefully dip each potato skin in sour cream, coating lightly; roll in crumb mixture to coat on both sides and arrange on baking sheet in a single layer. Bake 20 minutes; turn potato skins over and bake 10 to 15 minutes, until crisp. Serve with salsa.

Shopping List:

PRODUCE	PACKAGED	SEASONINGS
6 medium baking potatoes	Cornflake crumbs	Chili powder Ground cumin
	CONDIMENTS	
DAIRY	Salsa	
6 oz. nonfat sour cream		

NUTRITION PER SERVING Calories 224 • Fat .4 g (2%) •
Carbohydrates 47 g • Protein 7 g • Cholesterol 0 mg • Dietary Fiber 4 g •
Sodium 202 mg
EXCHANGES 2½ starch • ½ other carb
CARB CHOICES 3

Super Tip: *Substitute bread crumbs for cornflake crumbs and nonfat mayonnaise or nonfat yogurt for sour cream.*

Eggplant Dippers

Easy

♦ Serves: 8

1 cup egg substitute
1 cup skim milk
1 cup all-purpose flour
1 cup seasoned bread crumbs
½ cup grated nonfat Parmesan cheese
2 lb. eggplant, peeled and cut into ½-inch strips
1½ cups nonfat pasta sauce

Preheat oven to 450°F. Line a baking sheet with foil and spray with cooking spray. Combine egg substitute and milk in a medium bowl and mix until blended. Combine flour, bread crumbs, and Parmesan cheese in a separate bowl and mix well. Dip eggplant strips in egg mixture; roll in flour mixture until completely coated. Arrange in a single layer on baking sheet; spray lightly with cooking spray. Bake 10 minutes; turn eggplant strips over and bake 7 to 8 minutes, until lightly browned and crisp on both sides. Heat pasta sauce on stovetop or in microwave oven and serve with eggplant dippers.

Shopping List:

PRODUCE	PACKAGED	CANNED
2 lb. eggplant	All-purpose flour	12-oz. jar nonfat pasta
	Seasoned bread crumbs	sauce
DAIRY		
8 oz. egg substitute		
8 oz. skim milk		
Grated nonfat Parmesan cheese		

NUTRITION PER SERVING Calories 185 • Fat 1 g (5%) •
Carbohydrates 34 g • Protein 10 g • Cholesterol 1 mg • Dietary Fiber 1 g •
Sodium 326 mg
EXCHANGES 3 vegetable • 1 starch • ½ very lean meat
CARB CHOICES 2

Super Tip: *A Harvard physician found that consuming tomatoes, tomato sauce, or pizza more than twice a week reduced the risk of prostate cancer by 21 to 34 percent, compared to those who never consumed any of those foods (www.healthatoz.com).*

13

Feta Cheese Soufflé with Artichoke Hearts

Easy ◆ Serves: 4

1¼ cups egg substitute
¼ cup all-purpose flour
½ tsp. baking powder
1 cup nonfat cottage cheese
2 cups shredded nonfat mozzarella cheese
4 oz. reduced-fat feta cheese crumbles
¾ cup chopped canned artichoke hearts

Preheat oven to 400°F. Spray an 8- or 9-inch baking dish with cooking spray. Combine all ingredients and mix well. Spread mixture in baking dish and bake 25 to 35 minutes, until puffy and cooked through. Cool 5 minutes; cut into squares and serve immediately.

Shopping List:

DAIRY
9 oz. egg substitute
8 oz. nonfat cottage cheese
8 oz. shredded nonfat mozzarella cheese
4 oz. reduced-fat feta cheese crumbles

CANNED
13¾-oz. can artichoke hearts

BAKING
All-purpose flour
Baking powder

NUTRITION PER SERVING Calories 207 • Fat .1 g (0%) • Carbohydrates 13 g • Protein 34 g • Cholesterol 1 mg • Dietary Fiber <1 g • Sodium 1098 mg
EXCHANGES 4 very lean meat • 1 vegetable • ½ other carb
CARB CHOICES 1

Super Tip: *Look radiant with artichokes. These green globes contain silymarin, a powerful antioxidant that keeps skin smooth by stimulating new cell growth and protecting against skin cancer.*

Garlic-Cheese Potato Skins

Easy—Do Ahead   • Serves: 4

4 medium baking potatoes, baked and cooled
Garlic-flavored cooking spray
14½-oz. can diced tomatoes with garlic and onion, drained well
½ tsp. dried basil
¾ tsp. garlic powder
½ cup grated nonfat Parmesan cheese
Nonfat pasta sauce

Preheat oven to 450°F. Line baking sheet(s) with foil and spray with cooking spray. Cut potatoes lengthwise into quarters; scoop out pulp, leaving ½-inch shell. (Save pulp for later use if desired.) Spray potato shells with garlic-flavored cooking spray. Combine tomatoes, basil, and garlic powder in a small bowl and mix well. Divide tomato mixture among potato shells and sprinkle with Parmesan cheese. Bake 15 to 20 minutes, until lightly browned and crisp. Serve with pasta sauce heated on stovetop or in microwave oven.

Shopping List:

PRODUCE	CANNED	SEASONINGS
4 medium baking potatoes	14½-oz. can diced tomatoes with garlic and onion	Dried basil Garlic powder
DAIRY Grated nonfat Parmesan cheese	Nonfat pasta sauce	**OTHER** Garlic-flavored cooking spray

NUTRITION PER SERVING Calories 210 • Fat .5 g (2%) • Carbohydrates 45 g • Protein 9 g • Cholesterol 0 mg • Dietary Fiber 4 g • Sodium 622 mg
EXCHANGES 2 starch • 2 vegetable
CARB CHOICES 3

Super Tip: *Do not use potatoes that are damaged, have turned green, or are sprouting; they may contain a toxic chemical called solanine that increases when the potatoes are exposed to light.*

Green Chile 'n' Cheese Enchiladas

Easy—Do Ahead   ◆ Serves: 6

1.5 oz. pkg. enchilada sauce mix
8-oz. can tomato sauce
1½ cups water
8-oz. pkg. nonfat cream cheese, softened
4 oz. (1 cup) shredded nonfat cheddar cheese
4 oz. (1 cup) shredded nonfat mozzarella cheese
¼ cup chopped canned green chiles
6 (8-inch) low-fat flour tortillas

Preheat oven to 350°F. Spray a 9 × 13-inch baking dish with cooking spray. Combine enchilada mix, tomato sauce, and water in a small saucepan; bring to a boil over high heat. Reduce heat to low and simmer 5 minutes. Pour ½ cup of the enchilada sauce in bottom of baking dish. Blend cream cheese with electric mixer until creamy and smooth. Add ½ cup of the cheddar cheese, ½ cup of the mozzarella cheese, and the green chiles; mix well. Divide mixture among tortillas; roll tortillas and place, seam side down, in baking dish. Pour remaining enchilada sauce over tortillas; sprinkle with remaining cheese. Bake 20 to 25 minutes, until cheese is melted and sauce is bubbly hot.

Shopping List:

DAIRY	PACKAGED	CANNED
8 oz. nonfat cream cheese	6 (8-inch) low-fat flour tortillas	4-oz. can chopped green chiles
4 oz. shredded nonfat cheddar cheese	1.5-oz. pkg. enchilada sauce mix	8-oz. can tomato sauce
4 oz. shredded nonfat mozzarella cheese		

NUTRITION PER SERVING Calories 231 • Fat .6 g (2%) •
Carbohydrates 35 g • Protein 20 g • Cholesterol 0 mg • Dietary Fiber 3 g •
Sodium 1580 mg
EXCHANGES 2 starch • 1 vegetable • 1½ very lean meat
CARB CHOICES 2

Super Tip: *Substitute low-fat canned enchilada sauce for dry mix, tomato sauce, and water.*

Mini Quiches

Easy—Do Ahead—Freeze

♦ Serves: 12

12 slices low-fat bread
1 cup frozen chopped onion, thawed
¾ cup shredded nonfat cheddar cheese
1 cup skim milk
1 cup egg substitute with vegetables
1 tbsp. prepared mustard
Pepper to taste

Preheat oven to 375°F. Spray a 12-cup muffin pan with cooking spray. Trim crust from bread and press one slice into each muffin cup. Divide onion and cheese evenly among bread-lined muffin cups. Combine remaining ingredients and mix well. Pour into muffin cups, dividing evenly, and bake 20 to 25 minutes, until toothpick inserted in center comes out clean.

Shopping List:

PACKAGED	8 oz. egg substitute with	CONDIMENTS
¾ lb. sliced low-fat	vegetables	Prepared mustard
bread	8 oz. skim milk	
		SEASONINGS
DAIRY	FROZEN	Black pepper
3 oz. shredded nonfat	12-oz. pkg. frozen	
cheddar cheese	chopped onions	

NUTRITION PER SERVING Calories 112 • Fat 1.2 g (10%) •
Carbohydrates 17 g • Protein 7 g • Cholesterol <1 mg • Dietary Fiber 1 g •
Sodium 282 mg
EXCHANGES 1 starch • 1 meat
CARB CHOICES 1

Super Tip: *Substitute any egg substitute or 8 egg whites for egg substitute with vegetables.*

17

Onion-Artichoke Dip in a Bread Bowl

Easy—Do Ahead   ◆ Serves: 8

1-lb. round loaf sourdough bread, unsliced
8-oz. pkg. nonfat cream cheese, softened
2 tsp. lemon juice
2 tbsp. nonfat half-and-half or skim milk
3 tbsp. chopped green onions
13¾-oz. can artichoke hearts, quartered and drained well

Cut the top off of bread round. Scoop out center and break into bite-size pieces. Arrange bread pieces around bread round. Combine remaining ingredients in a blender or food processor and process 30 seconds, just until artichokes and onions are minced (do not process until creamy). Spoon dip into bread bowl and serve with bread pieces.

Shopping List:

PRODUCE	PACKAGED	CANNED
Lemon or lemon juice	1-lb. whole sourdough	13¾-oz. can artichoke
Green onions	bread round	hearts, quartered
DAIRY		
8-oz. pkg. nonfat cream cheese		
Nonfat half and half or skim milk		

NUTRITION PER SERVING Calories 212 • Fat 1.8 g (8%) •
Carbohydrates 39 g • Protein 10 g • Cholesterol 0 mg •
Dietary Fiber 2 g • Sodium 553 mg
EXCHANGES 2 vegetable • 1 starch • 1 other carb
CARB CHOICES 2

Super Tip: *The dip can be served in a bowl with low-fat crackers, lahvosh, melba toast or pita chips.*

Quick Quesadillas

Easy—Do Ahead—Freeze

◆ Serves: 8

¾ cup nonfat cream cheese, softened
8 (8-inch) low-fat flour tortillas
10-oz. can chunk white chicken, drained and flaked
1 tbsp. chopped canned jalapeño chile or mild green chiles
1½ cups shredded nonfat cheddar cheese
1 cup chunky-style salsa

Preheat oven to 400°F. Line baking sheet(s) with foil and spray with cooking spray. Spread cream cheese in a thin layer on each tortilla (about 1½ tablespoons per tortilla). Combine chicken, jalapeño, and cheddar cheese in a medium bowl; mix well. Divide mixture among 4 tortillas. Top with remaining tortillas, cream cheese side down; lightly spray both sides of quesadillas with cooking spray. Arrange on baking sheet(s) and bake 6 to 7 minutes; turn quesadillas over and bake 5 to 6 minutes, until lightly browned and crisp on both sides. Cut each quesadilla into four pieces and serve with salsa.

Shopping List:

DAIRY	CANNED	CONDIMENTS
6 oz. nonfat cream cheese	10-oz. can chunk white chicken	8 oz. chunky-style salsa
6 oz. shredded nonfat cheddar cheese	4-oz. can chopped jalapeño or mild minced green chiles	
PACKAGED		
17.5-oz. pkg. low-fat flour tortillas		

NUTRITION PER SERVING Calories 224 • Fat .5 g (2%) •
Carbohydrates 29 g • Protein 23 g • Cholesterol 16 mg • Dietary Fiber 2 g •
Sodium 986 mg
EXCHANGES 2 very lean meat • 1 starch • ½ other carb • 1 vegetable
CARB CHOICES 2

Super Tip: *You can use deli-sliced chicken breast, packaged chicken breast cuts, or leftover chicken instead of canned; lower the "heat" on your quesadillas by selecting milder chiles and mild salsa.*

Salmon Roll-Ups

Easy—Do Ahead ♦ Serves: 6

8-oz. pkg. nonfat cream cheese, softened
2 tbsp. chopped green onions
1 tbsp. lemon juice
3 (10-inch) low-fat flour tortillas
14-oz. can pink salmon, drained and flaked
1 medium red onion, thinly sliced
10-oz. pkg. shredded iceberg lettuce

Combine cream cheese, green onions and lemon juice in a small bowl; mix until blended creamy and smooth. Spread cheese mixture down center of each tortilla. Top with salmon, red onion and shredded lettuce. Roll tortillas; secure with toothpicks. Cut each tortilla into 6 pieces and serve (or cover and refrigerate until ready to serve).

Shopping List:

PRODUCE	DAIRY	CANNED
Bunch green onions	8-oz. pkg. nonfat cream	14-oz. can pink salmon
Red onion	cheese	
10-oz. pkg. shredded		
iceberg lettuce	**PACKAGED**	
Lemon or lemon	10-inch low-fat flour	
juice	tortillas	

NUTRITION PER SERVING Calories 197 • Fat 4.3 g (21%) • Carbohydrates 18 g • Protein 21 g • Cholesterol 36 mg • Dietary Fiber 2 g • Sodium 778 mg
EXCHANGES 1 vegetable • 1 starch • 2 lean meat
CARB CHOICES 1

Super Tip: *Onions will keep for up to 10 days in a well ventilated, cool, dry place, not in the refrigerator or in plastic bags from the grocery store, because the humidity in these places makes the onions break down. After chopping, onions can be tightly wrapped and frozen for up to 3 months.*

Seafood-Stuffed Tomatoes

Easy—Do Ahead   • Serves: 8

8 large tomatoes
Romaine lettuce leaves
2 cups canned artichoke hearts, drained and chopped
½ cup chopped celery
½ cup chopped red onion
1 cup nonfat mayonnaise
1½ cups frozen cooked bay shrimp, thawed
2½ tbsp. bacon crumbles

Wash and dry tomatoes. Scoop out centers; place tomatoes on lettuce leaves. Combine artichoke hearts, celery, onion and mayonnaise in a medium bowl; mix well. Carefully fold in shrimp and mix; spoon seafood mixture into tomato shells. Sprinkle bacon crumbles over top. Cover and refrigerate or serve immediately.

Shopping List:

PRODUCE	FROZEN	CANNED
8 large tomatoes	12-oz. pkg. frozen	2 (13¾-oz.) cans
Whole romaine lettuce	cooked bay shrimp	artichoke hearts
or large leaves		
Celery	**PACKAGED**	**CONDIMENTS**
Small red onion	Bacon crumbles	8 oz. nonfat mayonnaise

NUTRITION PER SERVING Calories 113 • Fat 1.4 g (12%) • Carbohydrates 19 g • Protein 8 g • Cholesterol 37 mg • Dietary Fiber 3 g • Sodium 391 mg
EXCHANGES 4 vegetable • ½ very lean meat
CARB CHOICES 1

Super Tip: *Substitute cooked turkey bacon for bacon crumbles; crumble into small pieces and use as directed.*

Spicy Seafood Spread

Easy—Do Ahead ◆ Serves: 4

¼ cup nonfat mayonnaise
¼ cup diced celery
3 tbsp. finely chopped green onions
2 tsp. canned tomato paste
¼ tsp. chili powder
¼ tsp. salt-free spicy seasoning or Mexican seasoning
6-oz. can white crabmeat, drained well and flaked
Melba toast, low-fat crackers or lahvosh

Combine all ingredients, except Melba toast, in a bowl and mix well. Cover and refrigerate at least 1 hour. Serve with Melba toast.

Shopping List:

PRODUCE	PACKAGED	SEASONINGS
Celery	Melba toast, low-fat	Chili powder
Green onions	crackers or lahvosh	Salt-free spicy
		seasoning or
CANNED	CONDIMENTS	Mexican seasoning
6-oz. can white	Nonfat mayonnaise	
crabmeat		
6-oz. can tomato paste		

NUTRITION PER SERVING Calories 49 • Fat 0 g •
Carbohydrates 4 g • Protein 9 g • Cholesterol 52 mg •
Dietary Fiber <1 g • Sodium 344 mg
EXCHANGES ½ other carb • ½ other carb • 1 very lean meat
CARB CHOICES 0

Super Tip: *Carrots contain beta-carotene, which the body converts into vitamin A. It strengthens the body's immune system and reduces the risk of sun damage.*

Spicy Stuffed Shrimp

Easy—Do Ahead ◆ Serves: 8

2 tbsp. wasabi powder
1½ to 2 tbsp. cold water
8-oz. pkg. nonfat cream cheese, softened
3 lbs. large shrimp, cooked, shells on

Combine wasabi powder and water; mix to form a thick paste. Place cream cheese in a food processor; add wasabi mixture and process until smooth. Split shrimp down the center of the back, cutting almost all the way through. Using a small spoon, fill the center of each shrimp with 1½ teaspoons cream cheese–wasabi mixture. Press sides together. Cover and refrigerate until ready to serve. Serve with additional wasabi paste, if desired.

Shopping List:

DAIRY	FISH	OTHER
8-oz. pkg. nonfat cream cheese	3 lbs. large shrimp, cooked, shells on	Wasabi powder

NUTRITION PER SERVING Calories 204 · Fat 2.9 g (13%) ·
Carbohydrates 3 g · Protein 38 g · Cholesterol 262 mg ·
Dietary Fiber 0 g · Sodium 440 mg
EXCHANGES 6 very lean meat
CARB CHOICES 0

Super Tip: *To cook your own shrimp, simply bring a large pot of salted water to a boil. Add shrimp; lower heat to medium and cook 3 to 4 minutes until shrimp turn pink. Place shrimp in colander and set under running cold water for 1 minute. Remove shells but keep tails intact.*

Spinach-Stuffed Mushrooms

Easy—Do Ahead   ◆ Serves: 6

24 large white mushrooms
⅓ cup chopped green onions
1½ tsp. roasted minced garlic
2 tbsp. balsamic vinegar
¼ cup water
½ tsp. *each* dried oregano, rosemary,
   thyme and sage
1 tsp. dried basil
10-oz. pkg. frozen chopped spinach,
   thawed and drained well
¼ cup grated nonfat Parmesan cheese

Wipe mushrooms clean with paper towels. Carefully remove stems; finely chop and set aside. Preheat oven to 375°F. Line baking sheet(s) with foil and spray with cooking spray. Arrange mushroom caps on baking sheet(s). Spray medium nonstick skillet with cooking spray. Add green onions, garlic and vinegar to skillet; cook, stirring frequently, until onions are softened. Add mushroom stems, water and herbs. Cook, stirring frequently, until mushroom stems are softened. Add spinach and cook until liquid has evaporated, 5 to 8 minutes. Carefully stuff mushroom caps with spinach mixture, pressing mixture to pack compactly. Bake 10 minutes; sprinkle mushroom caps with Parmesan cheese and bake 5 to 6 minutes, until cheese is lightly browned.

Shopping List:

PRODUCE	FROZEN	SEASONINGS
24 large white mushrooms	10-oz. pkg. frozen chopped spinach	Dried oregano
Bunch green onions		Dried thyme
		Dried basil
		Dried rosemary
DAIRY		Dried sage
Grated nonfat Parmesan cheese		Roasted minced garlic

NUTRITION PER SERVING Calories 55 • Fat .4 g (7%) •
Carbohydrates 11 g • Protein 5 g • Cholesterol 0 mg • Dietary Fiber 3 g •
Sodium 480 mg
EXCHANGES 2 vegetable
CARB CHOICES 1

Super Tip: *Substitute 1 tablespoon Italian seasoning for oregano, thyme, basil, rosemary and sage.*

Stuffed Mushrooms

Easy—Do Ahead

Romaine lettuce leaves
8 large mushrooms, cleaned and stems removed
1 cucumber, finely chopped
1 tomato, finely chopped
1 cup chopped green onions, divided
¾ cup nonfat cottage cheese
Pepper, to taste
Lemon juice

Line a large plate or serving platter with romaine lettuce leaves. Arrange mushroom caps on lettuce. Combine cucumber, tomato and ¾ cup of the green onions in a medium bowl. Add cottage cheese and pepper; mix well. Sprinkle mushroom caps with lemon juice; divide cottage cheese mixture among mushrooms. Garnish with remaining green onions and serve.

Shopping List:

PRODUCE	Bunch green onions	SEASONINGS
Romaine lettuce leaves	Lemon or lemon juice	Black pepper
8 large mushrooms		
(1½–1¾ lb.)	DAIRY	
1 tomato	6 oz. nonfat cottage	
1 cucumber	cheese	

NUTRITION PER SERVING Calories 42 • Fat .5 g (11%) • Carbohydrates 8 g • Protein 3 g • Cholesterol 1 mg • Dietary Fiber 3 g • Sodium 42 mg
EXCHANGES 1 vegetable • ½ meat
CARB CHOICES 1

Super Tip: *Calcium may be able to protect you from colon cancer. Experts think that bile and fatty acids inside your colon can trigger abnormal cell growth, the first step to cancer. Calcium seems to lock onto those toxic chemicals and render them harmless, allowing you to safely "eliminate" them.*

Sweet 'n' Sour Scallops

Easy—Do Ahead   • Serves: 8

1 lb. bay scallops
1 cup nonfat French or Catalina salad dressing

Bring a medium pot of water to a boil; add scallops, reduce heat to low and simmer until scallops turn white and are cooked through, 4 to 5 minutes. Drain well; immediately place in bowl with tight-fitting lid. Pour dressing over scallops; toss to coat, cover and refrigerate at least 4 hours or overnight. Drain scallops and serve with toothpicks.

Shopping List:

FISH	CONDIMENTS
1 lb. bay scallops	8 oz. nonfat French or Catalina salad dressing

NUTRITION PER SERVING Calories 84 • Fat .4 g (4%) • Carbohydrates 9 g • Protein 10 g • Cholesterol 19 mg • Dietary Fiber 0 g • Sodium 221 mg
EXCHANGES 1 very lean meat • ½ other carb
CARB CHOICES 1

Super Tip: *According to* Roper Reports Survey, *almost 7 in 10 adults eat at fast food restaurants just to save time, but what price do their waistlines pay?*

Sun-Dried Tomato Pita Pizza Bites

Easy—Do Ahead—Freeze • Serves: 4

4 low-fat pita pockets, cut in half
1½ cups shredded nonfat mozzarella cheese
3-oz. pkg. dry-pack sun-dried tomatoes, sliced or chopped
½ cup tomato sauce for pizza

Preheat oven to 450°F. Line baking sheet(s) with foil and spray with cooking spray. Arrange pita halves on baking sheet in a single layer; sprinkle half the cheese over pitas; top with sun-dried tomatoes and remaining cheese. Bake 10 to 15 minutes, until crust is crisp and cheese is lightly browned. Pour tomato sauce into microwave-safe bowl; cook on High 30 to 45 seconds, until warmed. Cut each pizza into 4 slices and serve with heated sauce.

Shopping List:

PRODUCE	PACKAGED	CANNED
3-oz. pkg. sun-dried tomatoes (dry-pack)	Low-fat pita pockets	15-oz. can tomato sauce for pizza or any nonfat pasta sauce
DAIRY		
6 oz. shredded nonfat mozzarella cheese		

NUTRITION PER SERVING Calories 241 • Fat .6 g (2%) • Carbohydrates 37 g • Protein 20 g • Cholesterol 0 mg • Dietary Fiber 2 g • Sodium 631 mg
EXCHANGES 1½ very lean meat • 4 vegetable • 1 starch
CARB CHOICES 2

Super Tip: *Substitute 12-inch prepared pizza crust or low-fat flour tortillas for pita pockets, if desired.*

Three-Cheese Pita Pizzas

Easy   • Serves: 4

4 low-fat pita pockets
2 tsp. minced roasted garlic
1 tsp. Italian seasoning
2 cups canned diced tomatoes with basil, garlic, and oregano, drained well
1 cup shredded nonfat mozzarella cheese
2 oz. reduced-fat feta cheese crumbles
¼ cup grated nonfat Parmesan cheese

Preheat oven to 400°F. Line baking sheet(s) with foil and spray with cooking spray. Arrange pita pockets on baking sheet(s). Spread each pita with ½ teaspoon of the roasted garlic and sprinkle with ¼ teaspoon of the Italian seasoning. Divide drained tomatoes among pitas. Sprinkle with mozzarella, feta and Parmesan cheeses. Bake 8 to 10 minutes, until cheese is melted and pita is lightly browned.

Shopping List:

DAIRY	PACKAGED	SEASONINGS
4 oz. shredded nonfat mozzarella cheese	Low-fat pita pockets	Minced roasted garlic
4 oz. reduced-fat feta cheese crumbles		Italian seasoning
Grated nonfat Parmesan cheese	CANNED	
	28-oz. can diced tomatoes with basil, garlic and oregano or 2 (14½-oz.) cans	

NUTRITION PER SERVING Calories 223 • Fat 1.1 g (5%) •
Carbohydrates 32 g • Protein 20 g • Cholesterol 0 mg • Dietary Fiber 1 g •
Sodium 1,300 mg
EXCHANGES 1 starch • 3 vegetable • 1½ very lean meat
CARB CHOICES 2

Super Tip: *Basil often turns up in Shakespeare's plays as a remedy for colds and headaches. More recently, studies have shown that fresh leaves aid digestion and lower blood sugar levels.*

Tortilla Chip Chicken Fingers

Easy—Do Ahead ♦ Serves: 6

½ cup skim milk
½ cup egg substitute
12-oz. package baked tortilla chips, crushed
½ tsp. Mexican seasoning
2 lbs. boneless, skinless chicken breast tenders
Salsa or barbecue sauce (optional)

Preheat oven to 400°F. Line a baking sheet with foil and spray with cooking spray. Combine milk and egg substitute in a medium bowl and mix well. Combine tortilla chips and Mexican seasoning on a paper plate or in a medium bowl and mix well. Dip chicken tenders in milk mixture; roll in tortilla crumbs and arrange in a single layer on baking sheet. Spray lightly with cooking spray. Bake 10 minutes; turn tenders over. Bake 8 to 10 minutes, until cooked through and crisp. Serve with salsa if desired.

Shopping List:

DAIRY	PACKAGED	SEASONINGS
4 oz. skim milk	12-oz. pkg. baked	Mexican seasoning
4 oz. egg substitute	tortilla chips	
MEAT		
2 lbs. boneless, skinless chicken tenders		

NUTRITION PER SERVING Calories 384 • Fat 2.6 g (6%) •
Carbohydrates 57 g • Protein 42 g • Cholesterol 76 mg • Dietary Fiber 0 g •
Sodium 717 mg
EXCHANGES 3 starch • 4½ very lean meat
CARB CHOICES 3

Super Tip: *Milk is good for your gums. You can save your teeth by strengthening your gums with calcium. State University of New York researchers found that men who got more than 800 mg of calcium a day had half the risk of periodontal (gum) disease than men who consumed 500 mg of calcium or less a day.*

Vegetable-Cheese Wonton Wraps

Easy—Do Ahead   • Serves: 6

12 large wonton or egg roll skins
2 cups finely chopped mixed vegetables (carrots, celery, broccoli, cauliflower, onions)
½ cup shredded nonfat cheddar cheese

Preheat oven to 350°F. Line a baking sheet with foil and spray with cooking spray. Fill each wonton or egg roll skin with chopped vegetables and cheese; fold carefully, seal and place, seam side down, on baking sheet. Spray on both sides with cooking spray. Bake wonton wraps 20 to 25 minutes, until golden brown and crisp.

Shopping List:

PRODUCE	16-oz. pkg. mixed	DAIRY
Large wonton or egg roll skins	vegetables	Shredded nonfat cheddar cheese

NUTRITION PER SERVING Calories 65 • Fat 0 g • Carbohydrates 11 g •
Protein 4 g • Cholesterol 0 mg • Dietary Fiber 1 g • Sodium 172 mg
EXCHANGES ½ starch • ½ very lean meat • ½ vegetable
CARB CHOICES 1

Super Tip: *Keep the root end intact as you slice onions; it will prevent you from crying.*

Vegetable Fajita Nachos

Easy

♦ Serves: 6

7-oz. container sliced bell peppers and onions
½ tsp. Mexican seasoning
9-oz. bag baked tortilla chips
1 cup shredded nonfat cheddar cheese
½ cup canned diced tomatoes with green chiles
1 cup southwestern salsa (contains beans and corn)

Spray a medium nonstick skillet with cooking spray; add peppers and onions. Sprinkle with Mexican seasoning and cook over medium-high heat until softened and lightly browned, 5 to 6 minutes. Preheat oven to 450°F. Line a baking sheet with foil and spray with cooking spray. Arrange baked tortilla chips in a single layer on baking sheet; top with peppers and onions. Sprinkle cheese over peppers and onions; top with tomatoes and green chiles. Bake 10 to 15 minutes, until cheese is browned and melted. Serve with salsa.

Shopping List:

PRODUCE
7-oz. container sliced bell peppers and onions or 16-oz. pkg. frozen pepper stir-fry

DAIRY
4 oz. shredded nonfat cheddar cheese

PACKAGED
9-oz. bag baked tortilla chips

CANNED
10-oz. can diced tomatoes and green chiles

CONDIMENTS
8 oz. Southwestern salsa

SEASONINGS
Mexican seasoning

NUTRITION PER SERVING Calories 251 • Fat 1.6 g (6%) •
Carbohydrates 50 g • Protein 11 g • Cholesterol 0 mg • Dietary Fiber <1 g •
Sodium 816 mg
EXCHANGES 3 starch • ½ very lean meat • 1 vegetable
  CARB CHOICES 3

Super Tip: *Substitute 1½ cups frozen pepper stir-fry or small bell pepper and onion, sliced, for 7-oz. container prepared bell peppers and onions. Substitute ½ cup chopped tomatoes and 2 tablespoons chopped canned green chiles for the canned tomatoes and chiles.*

SUPER SALADS, DRESSINGS AND SPECTACULAR SANDWICHES

❖

❖ ❖ ❖

Turn Salad Sabotage into Salad Savvy

Modern-day salads are no longer stuck in the rut of boring and nutritionally-lacking chopped iceberg lettuce with tomatoes and cucumbers. Salads have worked their way from warm-up course to main dish fare, taking salads out of the side dish arena into the entrée class. Their versatility can satisfy cravings, provide healthy fast-food meals and wow guests with spectacular flavors and presentations. Nutritionally prepared and packed with antioxidant rich ingredients, salads contribute to cancer prevention. There are unlimited salad combination possibilities. Mix colors, textures and flavors with an array of greens, vegetables, fruits, meat, legumes and grains.

- Combine textures such as wilted greens with crunchy celery or grains with toasted nuts.
- Combine flavors such as bitter greens with sweet fruit or tart dressings.
- Add protein (meat, fish, poultry, tofu, hard-cooked egg whites) for a hearty meal.
- Spark your salad with flavor enhancers including dry-packed sun-dried tomatoes, sweet onions, pickled vegetables, roasted red peppers, fresh chopped herbs or shredded nonfat sharp cheddar cheese.

RATING YOUR GREENS: NUTRIENTS IN A 2-CUP SERVING

	Fiber	Iron	Calcium	Vitamin K	Vitamin A	Vitamin E	Vitamin C
Arugula	10 g	0 mg	.6 mg	64 mg	148 RE*	95 mg	0 mg
Butter lettuce	15 g	1 mg	.3 mg	36 mg	288 RE*	109 mg	.5 mg
Endive	17 g	2 mg	.8 mg	52 mg	314 RE*	205 mg	.9 mg
Iceberg lettuce	14 g	1 mg	.5 mg	21 mg	177 RE*	37 mg	.5 mg
Radicchio	18 g	1 mg	10 mg	25 mg	242 RE*	2 mg	0 mg
Romaine lettuce	18 g	1 mg	1 mg	40 mg	325 RE*	291 mg	.5 mg
Superstar spinach	25 g	3 mg	3 mg	111 mg	625 RE*	752 mg	2 mg
Watercress	7 g	1 mg	.1 mg	82 mg	224 RE*	320 mg	.7 mg

*Retinol equivalent: The amount that a vitamin A compound will yield after conversion to the active vitamin in the body; plants do not contain already formed vitamin A.

SUGGESTED SUBSTITUTIONS

INSTEAD OF:	SELECT:	PROVIDES:
Iceberg lettuce	**Arugula, spinach or watercress**	Antiaging antixodiants 8 times more calcium than iceberg lettuce Iodine (watercress), contributing to healthy thyroid function, which regulates metabolism and contributes to weight control Carotenoids, lutein and zeaxanthin (spinach), which protect the eyes
Coleslaw	**Shredded red cabbage**	16 calories and 0 grams of fat (compared to 100 calories and 7 grams of fat per ½ cup coleslaw) Anthocyanins (red pigments credited with lowering cholesterol)

INSTEAD OF:	SELECT:	PROVIDES:
Deli meats	Cooked beans	Excellent source of protein while low in fat
		High in folate, which protects against Alzheimer's and Parkinson's diseases
		Vitamin B$_6$, which helps relieve PMS symptoms
Bacon bits	Seeds (e.g., sunflower seeds, pumpkin seeds)	Magnesium, to keep blood pressure in check
		Polyunsaturated fat that may lower total cholesterol
		Reduced sodium intake
Cheddar cheese	Grated Parmesan cheese	Calcium with half the calories and 30 percent less fat
Chinese noodles	Nonfat croutons	

STORAGE SAVVY FOR FRUITS AND VEGGIES!

The average household throws out more than $300 worth of spoiled fruits and vegetables every year. Cut back on waste of valuable nutrients; they contribute to your health.

Food	Proper Storage Technique	Length of Storage for Optimal Freshness	Valuable Info for Fruit and Veggie Freshness	What to Do with Overripe Fruits and Veggies
Asparagus	Cut ends of spears and submerge cut ends in water; refrigerate.	1 to 2 days	Select thin or fat shoots with tight buds and firm, smooth stalks without wrinkles.	
Avocados	Ripen at room temperature; refrigerate.	1 to 2 weeks	Refrigerating avocados before they ripen can cause internal browning.	

Food	Proper Storage Technique	Length of Storage for Optimal Freshness	Valuable Info for Fruit and Veggie Freshness	What to Do with Overripe Fruits and Veggies
Bananas	Store at room temperature away from vegetables and citrus fruits.	1 to 2 weeks	Chilling bananas turns the skin black; the ethylene gas produced by bananas causes fruits and vegetables to spoil.	Mash and use in breads, cookies, cakes or pancakes.
Bell Peppers	Refrigerate.	1 week	Select smooth, heavy peppers; shake peppers to see if seeds rattle. If they rattle, peppers are past their prime.	Dice and add to omelets, casseroles, stir-fries, soups or stews.
Berries	Spread out in single layer in perforated plastic bag and refrigerate. Wash just before eating. Fresh berries can be frozen; lay in single layer on baking sheet, freeze and store in freezer bags. Do not wash berries before freezing.	7 to 10 days	Select firm, plump, fully-colored berries; avoid mushy berries and packages that show signs of leakage. Select firm strawberries with stems attached. Avoid those with large, uncolored seedy areas.	Use for smoothies, muffins and other quick breads.
Broccoli	Refrigerate.	1 week	Select bright, compact heads with unopened buds.	

Food	Proper Storage Technique	Length of Storage for Optimal Freshness	Valuable Info for Fruit and Veggie Freshness	What to Do with Overripe Fruits and Veggies
Cabbage	Refrigerate.	1 to 2 weeks	Select dense, heavy heads of cabbage with red or green leaves.	
Cantaloupe	Store whole at room temperature.	2 to 3 days	Select cantaloupe with sweet scent; avoid those with pronounced yellow color or moldy aroma indicating overripeness.	Use for cold soup.
	Refrigerate whole.	1 week		
	Refrigerate cut-up melon.	2 to 3 days		
Carrots	Refrigerate (unpeeled).	2 to 3 weeks	Select firm carrots with rich orange color; avoid those with soft or flabby roots.	Use in soups, stews, cakes, muffins or other quick breads.
Cauliflower	Refrigerate in perforated plastic bag.	1 week	Select compact cauliflower heads with green outside leaves.	Puree, heat and serve.
Corn	Best eaten within a few hours of purchase.	1 to 2 days	Select green, moist looking husks with plump kernels that squirt out juice when lightly pressed.	Add to casseroles and Southwestern dishes (burritos, quesadillas, chilis).
	Refrigerate in husks.			
	Remove husks and silk only when ready to cook.		Avoid brownish husks.	
Cucumbers	Refrigerate.	1 week	Select hard cucumbers that have a natural sheen. Avoid yellowed or softened cucumbers.	

Food	Proper Storage Technique	Length of Storage for Optimal Freshness	Valuable Info for Fruit and Veggie Freshness	What to Do with Overripe Fruits and Veggies
Grapefruit	Refrigerate.	2 weeks		
Lettuce	1. Soak in cold water. 2. Spin in salad spinner. 3. Wrap in paper towel in plastic bag. 4. Refrigerate.	3 weeks	Soaking slows wilting and draining and wrapping in absorbent paper discourages mold.	
Mushrooms	Refrigerate. Freeze if cooked first.	4 to 5 days	Select light-colored mushrooms with closed gills (underside of mushrooms).	
Onions	Store in well-ventilated, cool, dry place. Chop and freeze in tightly wrapped packaging.	10 days Up to 3 months	Do not store in refrigerator or in plastic bags from the grocery store because humidity makes onions break down.	
Oranges	Store at room temperature. Refrigerate.	Up to 1 week 2 weeks	Avoid oranges with thick, coarse or spongy skin.	Squeeze juice and use in sauces or salad dressings.
Peaches	Store at room temperature. Refrigerate.	Few days 1 week	Peaches bruise easily, so handle them carefully.	Puree and use in sauces.
Pears	Ripen at room temperature; refrigerate.	3 days		Bake, sprinkled with sugar and cinnamon, until softened.

Food	Proper Storage Technique	Length of Storage for Optimal Freshness	Valuable Info for Fruit and Veggie Freshness	What to Do with Overripe Fruits and Veggies
Potatoes	Store in cool, dry place in a plastic bag poked with holes so air can circulate properly.	2 weeks		
Spinach	Refrigerate (wash spinach as needed; do not wash before storing).	1 to 2 weeks	Select spinach with dark-green leaves; avoid wilted and discolored leaves.	
Tomatoes	Store in uncovered bowl on countertop.	1 to 3 weeks	Chilling tomatoes destroys a major chemical compound, leading to loss of flavor.	
Watermelon	Store whole at room temperature. Refrigerate after cutting. Remove seeds and skins.	2 to 3 days 2 to 3 days	Select whole, symmetrical watermelon with smooth surface, pale green color and well-rounded ends. If watermelon is cut, look for rich-colored flesh, dark seeds and no white streaks.	

GET THE MOST OUT OF EVERY SEASON

Season	Fruits	Vegetables
Winter	Bananas · Citrus fruits · Cranberries · Kiwi fruit · Kumquat · Pears · Red grapes · Rhubarb	Artichokes · Avocados · Bok choy · Broccoli · Brussels sprouts · Cabbage · Cauliflower · Celery root · Chicory · Fennel · Greens · Mushrooms, wild · Parsnips · Radishes · Snow Peas · Spinach · Sweet Potatoes · Turnips
Spring	Apricots · Blueberries · Cantaloupe · Cherries · Figs · Mangoes · Nectarines · Oranges · Papayas · Pineapple · Raspberries · Strawberries	Asparagus · Avocados · Basil · Beans · Beets · Broccoli · Cabbage · Carrots · Cucumbers · Fennel · Garlic · Head or iceberg lettuce · Okra · Onions · Peas · Peppers · Shallots · Spinach · Summer squash · Swiss chard · Turnips
Summer	Apricots · Berries (blackberries, raspberries, strawberries) · Cantaloupe · Cherries · Dates · Figs · Grapes · Guava · Mangoes · Melons · Nectarines · Papayas · Peaches · Plums · Watermelon	Arugula · Beans · Beets · Collards · Corn · Cucumbers · Eggplant · Garlic · Kohlrabi · Mushrooms · Okra · Onions · Peas · Peppers · Potatoes · Summer squash · Swiss chard · Tomatoes · Zucchini
Fall	Apples · Bananas · Cranberries · Dates · Grapes · Grapefruit · Kiwi fruit · Oranges · Pears · Persimmons · Pomegranates · Starfruit · Tangerines	Avocados · Beets · Broccoli · Brussels sprouts · Cabbage · Carrots · Cauliflower · Celery root · Chicory · Cucumbers · Fennel · Garlic · Greens · Head or iceberg lettuce · Kale · Leaf lettuce · Leeks · Mushrooms · Okra · Parsnips · Pumpkin · Peppers · Shallots · Spinach · Sweet potatoes · Swiss chard · Turnips · Winter squash

Apple-Raisin Coleslaw

Easy—Do Ahead • Serves: 6

3 apples, peeled and shredded
3 tbsp. lemon juice
16-oz. pkg. shredded cabbage
½ cup diced celery
¾ cup shredded carrots
¼ cup golden raisins
½ cup nonfat sour cream
¼ cup nonfat mayonnaise
¾ tsp. celery salt

Place apples in a medium bowl; sprinkle with lemon juice and toss until coated. Add cabbage, celery, carrots and raisins and toss lightly. Combine sour cream, mayonnaise and celery salt in a small bowl; mix until completely blended. Spoon dressing over cabbage mixture and toss until coated. Cover and refrigerate 30 minutes before serving.

Shopping List:

PRODUCE	DAIRY	CONDIMENTS
3 apples	4-oz. nonfat sour cream	Nonfat mayonnaise
16-oz. pkg. shredded cabbage		
Celery	PACKAGED	SEASONINGS
8-oz. pkg. shredded carrots	6-oz. pkg. golden raisins	Celery salt
Lemon or lemon juice		

NUTRITION PER SERVING Calories 109 • Fat .4 g (3%) • Carbohydrates 25 g • Protein 3 g • Cholesterol 0 mg • Dietary Fiber 4 g • Sodium 368 mg
EXCHANGES 2 vegetable • ½ other carb • ½ fruit
CARB CHOICES 2

Super Tip: *Buyer beware: According to ConsumerReports.org, many seemingly heart-healthy foods made with vegetable oils containing little saturated fat and no cholesterol, contain the most heart-unfriendly fat of all—trans fat, which currently is not labeled.*

Apple Spinach Salad

Easy—Do Ahead   • Serves: 4

16-oz. pkg. baby spinach leaves
2 medium apples, unpeeled, chopped
2 tbsp. minced red onion
4½ tbsp. nonfat sour cream
3 tbsp. lemon juice
3 tbsp. honey
½ tsp. pepper
2 tbsp. low-fat bacon crumbles

Combine spinach, apples and onion in a large bowl; toss to mix. Combine sour cream, lemon juice, honey and pepper in a medium bowl; mix until blended. When ready to serve, pour dressing over salad; toss to mix until coated. Sprinkle with bacon crumbles and serve.

Shopping List:

PRODUCE	DAIRY	SEASONINGS
16-oz. pkg. baby spinach leaves	8-oz. carton nonfat sour cream	Black pepper
2 medium apples		OTHER
Small red onion or 7-oz. container chopped red onion	PACKAGED 1.3-oz. pkg. low fat bacon crumbles	Honey
Lemon or lemon juice		

NUTRITION PER SERVING Calories 146 • Fat 1.4 g (9%) •
Carbohydrates 30 g • Protein 6 g • Cholesterol 0 mg • Dietary Fiber 5 g •
Sodium 222 mg
EXCHANGES ½ fruit • 2 vegetable • ½ other carb
CARB CHOICES 2

Super Tip: Keep bagged salad mixes or vegetables fresh longer: once the package has been opened, gently push out any excess air. Clip or wrap a rubber band and store in the refrigerator to keep your produce moist and fresh until reuse.

Berry Delicious Coleslaw

Easy—Do Ahead • Serves: 6

⅓ cup nonfat mayonnaise
2 tbsp. honey
1½ tbsp. red wine vinegar
2 (10-oz.) pkgs. shredded cabbage for coleslaw
⅓ cup dried cranberries

Combine mayonnaise, honey and vinegar in a small bowl; mix until blended. Combine cabbage and cranberries in a large bowl; pour dressing over top and toss until coated. Cover and refrigerate until ready to serve.

Shopping List:

PRODUCE	PACKAGED	CONDIMENTS
2 (10-oz.) pkgs. shredded cabbage for coleslaw (angel hair coleslaw or 3-color deli coleslaw)	Dried cranberries	Nonfat mayonnaise Honey Red wine vinegar

NUTRITION PER SERVING Calories 75 · Fat .1 g (1%) · Carbohydrates 18 g · Protein 1 g · Cholesterol 0 mg · Dietary Fiber 2 g · Sodium 111 mg
EXCHANGES ½ fruit · 1 vegetable · ½ other carb
CARB CHOICES 1

Super Tip: *Cabbage is one the cheapest, yet best sources of vitamin C.*

Berry Salad Dressing

Easy—Do Ahead

• Yields: 2 cups

1 cup strawberries or raspberries, sliced
¼ cup red wine vinegar
1 tsp. sugar
¼ tsp. pepper

Combine all ingredients in a food processor or blender and process until smooth. Cover and refrigerate up to 24 hours. Serve over mixed greens or favorite salad mix.

Shopping List:

PRODUCE	PACKAGED	SEASONINGS
½ pint strawberries or raspberries	Sugar	Black pepper
	CONDIMENTS	
	Red wine vinegar	

NUTRITION PER SERVING Calories 30 • Fat .2 g (6%) • Carbohydrates 9 g •
Protein <1 g • Cholesterol 0 mg • Dietary Fiber 2 g • Sodium 1 mg
EXCHANGES • ½ fruit
CARB CHOICES 1

Super Tip: *When strawberries or raspberries are not in season, simply substitute frozen no-sugar-added varieties.*

Caesar Salad–Stuffed Sandwiches

Easy—Do Ahead

• Serves: 4

10-oz. can chunk white chicken in water, drained
10-oz. pkg. romaine lettuce or romaine salad mix
½ cup fat-free Caesar salad dressing
4 low-fat pita pockets

Combine chicken, lettuce and salad dressing in a bowl; toss until completely coated and mixed. Stuff into pita pockets and serve.

Shopping List:

PRODUCE	CANNED	CONDIMENTS
10-oz. pkg. romaine lettuce or romaine salad mix	10-oz. can chunk white chicken in water	12.5-oz. bottle fat-free Caesar salad dressing
PACKAGED		
4 low-fat pita pockets		

NUTRITION PER SERVING Calories 237 • Fat .7 g (3%) • Carbohydrates 29 g • Protein 24 g • Cholesterol 32 mg • Dietary Fiber 2 g • Sodium 718 mg
EXCHANGES 2½ very lean meat • 1 starch • ½ other carb • 1 vegetable
CARB CHOICES 3

Super Tip: *According to research by the American Heart Association, eating fatty fish (i.e., tuna and salmon) just once a week reduces the chances of suffering a fatal heart attack by 44 percent compared to eating leaner fish (i.e., cod and snapper).*

SALADS & SANDWICHES

Chicken and Artichoke Salad

Easy—Do Ahead

SALADS &
SANDWICHES

18 oz. cooked chicken breast cuts
6 oz. sliced fresh mushrooms
3-oz. pkg. julienne-cut, dry-pack sun-dried tomatoes
14-oz. can artichokes, drained and chopped
¾ cup nonfat Catalina, French or Dorothy Lynch salad dressing
¼ cup fresh chopped basil
1 large red onion, sliced into rings or strips
2 (10-oz.) pkgs. romaine lettuce or romaine salad mix

Combine all ingredients except lettuce; toss until mixed. Divide lettuce among 6 plates or bowls. Top with chicken/artichoke mixture.

Shopping List:

PRODUCE	MEAT	CANNED
6 oz. sliced mushrooms	3 (6-oz.) pkgs. cooked	15-oz. can artichoke
Fresh basil	chicken breast cuts	hearts
Red onion		
2 (10-oz.) pkgs. romaine	**PACKAGED**	**CONDIMENTS**
lettuce or romaine	3-oz. pkg. julienne-cut,	Nonfat Catalina, French
salad mix	dry-pack sun-dried	or Dorothy Lynch
	tomatoes	salad dressing

NUTRITION PER SERVING Calories 216 • Fat 2.9 g (13%) •
Carbohydrates 24 g • Protein 26 g • Cholesterol 24 mg • Dietary Fiber 3 g •
Sodium 943 mg
EXCHANGES 3 very lean meat • 3 vegetable • ½ other carb
CARB CHOICES 2

Super Tip: *Research indicates that onions are most powerful when eaten raw and freshly peeled. Of course, raw onions can do a number on your breath; follow up with fresh parsley.*

Chicken Pasta Salad à l'Orange

Easy—Do Ahead

½ cup orange juice
1 cup nonfat mayonnaise
¾ tsp. dried basil
¾ tsp. dried thyme
¼ tsp. ground cinnamon
1½ lbs. cubed, cooked chicken breast
11-oz. can mandarin orange segments, drained
½ cup canned sliced water chestnuts, chopped
2 cups cooked rotini

Combine orange juice, mayonnaise, basil, thyme and cinnamon in a blender; process until completely blended. Combine remaining ingredients in a large bowl and toss lightly. Spoon dressing over top; toss to mix. Cover and refrigerate 1 to 2 hours before serving.

Shopping List:

MEAT	PACKAGED	CONDIMENTS
1½ lbs. boneless, skinless chicken breasts or tenders or 3 (6-oz.) pkgs. cubed, cooked chicken breast cuts	8 oz. rotini pasta	8 oz. nonfat mayonnaise
	CANNED	**SEASONINGS**
	11-oz. can mandarin orange segments	Dried basil
	6-oz. can sliced water chestnuts	Dried thyme
DAIRY		Ground cinnamon
4 oz. orange juice		

NUTRITION PER SERVING Calories 286 • Fat 3.4 g (11%) • Carbohydrates 29 g • Protein 32 g • Cholesterol 79 mg • Dietary Fiber <1 g • Sodium 1335 mg
EXCHANGES 3 very lean meat • 1 starch • ½ fruit • ½ other carb
CARB CHOICES 2

Super Tip: *Eating citrus and drinking orange juice can cut the risk of stroke by nearly a third.*

Chopped Salad with Cucumber Dressing

Easy—Do Ahead

• Serves: 4

1 cup finely chopped, peeled cucumber
½ cup chopped green bell pepper
½ tsp. roasted minced garlic
⅓ cup plain nonfat yogurt
⅓ cup nonfat mayonnaise
1 tbsp. prepared horseradish
10-oz. pkg. shredded lettuce
½ cup diced red onion
2 (7-oz.) containers finely chopped vegetable salad mix

Combine cucumber, bell pepper, garlic, yogurt, mayonnaise and horseradish in a food processor or blender; process until smooth and creamy. Cover and refrigerate 30 to 45 minutes.

Combine lettuce, onion and salad mix in a medium bowl; pour dressing over salad and mix until coated.

Shopping List:

PRODUCE		CONDIMENTS
1 large or 2 medium cucumber	Red onion or 7-oz. container diced red onion	Nonfat mayonnaise Prepared horseradish
1 green bell pepper or 7-oz. container diced tri-colored peppers	2 (7-oz.) containers finely chopped vegetable salad mix	**SEASONINGS** Roasted minced garlic or regular minced garlic
10-oz. pkg. shredded lettuce	**DAIRY** 6 oz. plain nonfat yogurt	

NUTRITION PER SERVING Calories 86 • Fat .5 g (5%) • Carbohydrates 17 g • Protein 5 g • Cholesterol .5 mg • Dietary Fiber 4 g • Sodium 230 mg
EXCHANGES 2 vegetable • ½ other carb
CARB CHOICES 1

Super Tip: *You can substitute 2 to 2½ cups diced vegetables (broccoli, carrots, celery, cauliflower) for finely chopped salad mix.*

Creamy Cucumber Salad

Easy—Do Ahead

1 cup nonfat sour cream
1 tbsp. plus 2 tsp. prepared horseradish
1 tbsp. plus 1 tsp. lemon juice
1 tsp. dried dill
4 medium cucumbers, thinly sliced
16-oz. pkg. salad mix

Combine sour cream, horseradish, lemon juice and dill in a medium bowl; mix until blended smooth. Add cucumbers and toss until coated. Cover and refrigerate several hours before serving. Serve cucumber salad on a bed of salad mix.

Shopping List:

PRODUCE	DAIRY	CONDIMENTS
16-oz. pkg. salad mix of choice	8-oz. carton nonfat sour cream	Prepared horseradish
4 medium cucumbers		**SEASONINGS**
Lemon or lemon juice		Dried dill

NUTRITION PER SERVING Calories 67 • Fat .4 g (5%) • Carbohydrates 11 g • Protein 5 g • Cholesterol 0 mg • Dietary Fiber 3 g • Sodium 74 mg
EXCHANGES ½ other carb • 1 vegetable
CARB CHOICES 1

Super Tip: *Select firm cucumbers with a dark, green wrinkle-free skin. They will stay fresh for up to about 1 week if stored properly in the refrigerator.*

Creamy Herb Salad Dressing or Dip

Easy—Do Ahead   • Serves: 6

SALADS & SANDWICHES

½ cup nonfat mayonnaise
⅓ cup nonfat sour cream
4 tsp. dried parsley
1 tbsp. chopped green onion
1 tbsp. lemon juice
1 tbsp. Dijon mustard
Pepper to taste

Combine all ingredients in a medium bowl and mix until blended. Cover and refrigerate several hours before serving as salad dressing or vegetable dip.

Shopping List:

PRODUCE	CONDIMENTS	SEASONINGS
Bunch green onions	Nonfat mayonnaise	Dried parsley
Lemon or lemon juice	Dijon mustard	Black pepper
DAIRY		
Nonfat sour cream		

NUTRITION PER SERVING Calories 31 • Fat .2 g (6%) • Carbohydrates 5 g • Protein 1 g • Cholesterol 0 mg • Dietary Fiber 0 g • Sodium 187 mg
EXCHANGES ½ other carb
CARB CHOICES 0

Super Tip: *Substitute ¼ cup fresh chopped parsley for the 4 teaspoons dried, if desired.*

Curried Rice Salad with Chicken and Fruit

Easy—Do Ahead   • Serves: 6

1 cup cooked brown rice
2 cups cooked white rice
2 (6-oz.) pkgs. cooked chicken breast cuts
½ cup sliced celery
¼ cup diced red onion
8-oz. can pineapple chunks in juice, diced and drained
¼ cup raisins
½ cup canned mandarin orange segments, drained
½ cup nonfat mayonnaise
½ cup nonfat sour cream
1 tsp. lemon juice
½ tsp. curry powder
Whole romaine or iceberg lettuce leaves

Combine brown and white rice, chicken, celery, onion, pineapple, raisins and orange segments in a large bowl; toss to mix. Combine mayonnaise, sour cream, lemon juice and curry powder in a small bowl; mix and blend until smooth. Pour dressing over rice mixture and toss until ingredients are coated. Line 6 plates with lettuce leaves and top with rice salad.

Shopping List:

PRODUCE
Celery
Red onion
Lemon or lemon juice
Whole head romaine or iceberg lettuce

DAIRY
4 oz. nonfat sour cream

MEAT
2 (6-oz.) pkgs. chicken breast cuts

PACKAGED
Brown rice
White rice
Raisins

CANNED
8-oz. can pineapple chunks in juice
8-oz. can mandarin orange segments

CONDIMENTS
Nonfat mayonnaise

SEASONINGS
Curry powder

NUTRITION PER SERVING Calories 284 • Fat 2 g (6%) •
Carbohydrates 46 g • Protein 19 g • Cholesterol 40 mg • Dietary Fiber 1 g •
Sodium 690 mg
EXCHANGES 2 starch • 1 fruit • 2 very lean meat
CARB CHOICES 3

Super Tip: When using fresh pineapple, select plump, firm ones. The stem end should have a sweet, aromatic fragrance and leaves should be crisp and deep green.

Fruit and Chicken Salad
on Red Leaf Lettuce

Easy—Do Ahead   ◆ Serves: 4

½ lb. cooked boneless chicken breast cuts
½ cup golden raisins
¾ cup sliced celery
¾ cup sliced jicama
¾ cup seedless grapes, cut in half
1 tart apple, unpeeled, coarsely chopped
1 cup nonfat mayonnaise
2 tbsp. lemon juice
10-oz. pkg. red leaf lettuce or salad mix

Combine chicken, raisins, celery, jicama, grapes and apple in a large bowl; mix well. Combine mayonnaise and lemon juice in a small bowl; mix until blended. Toss with chicken mixture until all ingredients are well coated. Serve over salad mix.

Shopping List:

PRODUCE	MEAT	PACKAGED
Celery sticks	2 (6-oz.) pkgs. cooked	Golden raisins
Jicama sticks	chicken breast cuts	
½ lb. seedless grapes		
Apple	**CONDIMENTS**	
10-oz. pkg. red leaf	8 oz. nonfat mayonnaise	
lettuce or salad mix	Lemon juice	

NUTRITION PER SERVING Calories 234 • Fat 2.2 g (8%) •
Carbohydrates 41 g • Protein 17 g • Cholesterol 40 mg • Dietary Fiber 2 g •
Sodium 976 mg
EXCHANGES 1½ fruit • 2 vegetable • ½ other carb • 1 very lean meat
CARB CHOICES 3

Super Tip: *Pound for pound, the best whole food to eat during extended workouts is raisins. They contain more of the vital electrolytes (potassium, calcium and sodium) than a banana.*

Garlic-Dijon Salad Dressing

Easy—Do Ahead

1 cup nonfat mayonnaise
1½ tsp. garlic powder
2 tbsp. Dijon mustard
⅓ cup sugar
½ tsp. celery seeds

SALADS & SANDWICHES

Combine all ingredients in a food processor or blender and process until smooth. Store dressing in an airtight container in the refrigerator up to 2 weeks. Serve as a salad dressing, sandwich spread or dip.

Shopping List:

PACKAGED	CONDIMENTS	SEASONINGS
Sugar	8 oz. nonfat mayonnaise	Garlic powder
	Dijon mustard	Celery seeds

NUTRITION PER SERVING Calories 38 • Fat .2 g (5%) • Carbohydrates 8 g • Protein <1 g • Cholesterol 0 mg • Dietary Fiber 0 mg • Sodium 208 mg
EXCHANGES ½ other carb
CARB CHOICES 1

Super Tip: *Celery seed contains a potent chemical called butyl phthalide that lowers blood pressure as well as some medicines. When researchers gave a daily dose to animals their blood pressure was slashed by 15 percent in just 4 weeks.*

Greek Chicken Salad

• Serves: 4

2 (6-oz.) pkgs. cooked chicken breast cuts
1 carrot, thinly sliced
1 small cucumber, thinly sliced
2 tbsp. chopped black olives
2 tbsp. reduced-fat feta cheese crumbles
⅓ cup nonfat Italian salad dressing
16-oz. pkg. salad mix of choice

Combine chicken, carrot, cucumber, olives and feta cheese in a large bowl;
add salad dressing and toss until ingredients are coated. Cover and refrigerate at least 1 hour before serving. Divide packaged salad mix among 4 dinner plates and top with prepared chicken salad.

Shopping List:

PRODUCE	MEAT	CONDIMENTS
16-oz. pkg. salad mix of choice	2 (6-oz.) pkgs. chicken breast cuts	Nonfat Italian salad dressing
1 carrot		
1 cucumber	CANNED	
	4-oz. can chopped black olives	
DAIRY		
Reduced-fat feta cheese crumbles		

NUTRITION PER SERVING Calories 165 • Fat 3 g (16%) •
Carbohydrates 11 g • Protein 24 g • Cholesterol 60 mg • Dietary Fiber 3 g •
Sodium 969 mg
EXCHANGES 2 vegetable • 3 very lean meat
CARB CHOICES 1

Super Tip: *Bake or broil a batch of your favorite boneless, skinless chicken
breasts; cool, wrap them individually and freeze. Substitute cooked chicken
breasts for packaged and prepared varieties.*

Grilled Cheese and Tomato Sandwiches

Easy

SALADS &
SANDWICHES

8 slices low-fat honey whole wheat bread
1½ tbsp. fat-free margarine
4 slices nonfat American, Swiss or cheddar cheese
1 large tomato, cut into 8 slices

Preheat oven to 450°F. Line a baking sheet with foil and spray with cooking spray. Spread 4 slices of bread with margarine; top each slice with 1 slice of the cheese and tomato. Place remaining bread on top; spread with remaining margarine. Bake 6 to 8 minutes; turn sandwich over and bake 5 to 8 minutes, until cheese is melted and bread is golden brown.

Shopping List:

PRODUCE	DAIRY	PACKAGED
Large tomato	4 oz. nonfat American, Swiss or Cheddar cheese slices	8 slices low-fat honey whole wheat bread slices
	Fat-free margarine	

NUTRITION PER SERVING Calories 240 • Fat 4 g (15%) • Carbohydrates 27 g • Protein 21 g • Cholesterol 0 mg • Dietary Fiber 3 g • Sodium 684 mg
EXCHANGES 2 starch • 2 very lean meat
CARB CHOICES 2

Super Tip: What's a sandwich without cheese? According to a study conducted by the Opinion Research Corporation, Americans eat more than 4.07 billion Kraft ® Singles each year, 11.1 million slices a day and 129 slices per second.

You can substitute butter-flavored cooking spray, Butter Buds or low-fat margarine for fat-free margarine on the bread slices.

Honey Dijon Salad
with Chicken Tenders

Easy—Do Ahead

SALADS &
SANDWICHES

1 lb. boneless, skinless chicken breast
  tenders
⅓ cup plus 6 tbsp. nonfat honey Dijon
  salad dressing
14½-oz. can diced tomatoes with
  garlic, oregano and basil,
  drained

13¾-oz. can quartered artichoke
  hearts, drained and cut in half
15-oz. can cannellini (white kidney
  beans), rinsed and drained
1 bell pepper, thinly sliced
7-oz. pkg. salad mix with baby lettuce
  and greens

Preheat broiler on high heat. Line a baking sheet with foil and spray with
cooking spray. Arrange chicken tenders on baking sheet; brush with 3 tablespoons of the dressing. Broil 6 to 7 minutes; turn chicken tenders over.
Brush with remaining 3 tablespoons dressing and broil 6 to 7 minutes, until
cooked through. Combine tomatoes, artichoke hearts, beans and bell pepper in a large bowl; pour ⅓ cup salad dressing over top and toss until ingredients are coated. Arrange salad mix on a large platter or in a large bowl;
spoon bean mixture over salad mix and top with cooked chicken tenders.

Shopping List:

PRODUCE	CANNED	CONDIMENTS
7-oz. pkg. salad mix with baby lettuce and greens or salad mix of choice	14½-oz. can diced tomatoes with garlic, oregano and basil	Nonfat honey-Dijon salad dressing
1 bell pepper (green, red, yellow or orange)	15-oz. can cannellini (white kidney beans)	
	13¾-oz. can quartered artichoke hearts	
MEAT		
1 lb. boneless, skinless chicken tenders		

NUTRITION PER SERVING Calories 332 • Fat 1.3 g (4%) •
Carbohydrates 45 g • Protein 36 g • Cholesterol 57 mg • Dietary Fiber 7 g •
Sodium 1181 mg
EXCHANGES 3 very lean meat • 3 vegetable • 1½ starch • ½ other carb
CARB CHOICES 3

Super Tip: *Bell peppers are available in many colors: green, red, yellow and
even orange. The color depends on the variety and stage of ripeness. As green
bell peppers ripen on the vine, they turn redder and sweeter, boosting the
amount of vitamins A and C.*

Italian Pasta Salad

Easy—Do Ahead

10 oz. fusilli or angel hair pasta
14½-oz. can diced tomatoes with roasted garlic and onions, drained
7-oz. container finely chopped vegetable salad mix
¾ cup fat-free cheese and garlic Italian salad dressing
¼ cup grated nonfat Parmesan cheese

Cook pasta according to package directions; drain well and place in a large bowl. Immediately toss with tomatoes, vegetables and salad dressing. Sprinkle with Parmesan cheese; toss lightly and serve.

Shopping List:

PRODUCE	PACKAGED	CONDIMENTS
7-oz. container finely chopped vegetable salad mix	10 oz. fusilli or angel hair pasta	10 oz. fat-free cheese Garlic Italian salad dressing
	CANNED	
DAIRY Grated nonfat Parmesan cheese	14½-oz. can diced tomatoes with roasted garlic and onions	

NUTRITION PER SERVING Calories 239 · Fat 1 g (4%) ·
Carbohydrates 48 g · Protein 8 g · Cholesterol 0 mg · Dietary Fiber 3 g ·
Sodium 418 mg
EXCHANGES 3 vegetable · 2 starch
CARB CHOICES 3

Super Tip: *Chop cauliflower, carrots, bell peppers, celery and cabbage and substitute for 7-oz. container of finely chopped vegetable salad mix or pick up prepared vegetables at the supermarket salad bar.*

Leaf Lettuce with Pears and Feta Cheese

Easy—Do Ahead

• Serves: 4

SALADS &
SANDWICHES

7-oz. pkg. red leaf lettuce mix
7-oz. pkg. salad mix with escarole, endive and radicchio
7-oz. pkg. salad mix with romaine, endive and radicchio
1 cup diced pear
2 oz. reduced-fat feta cheese crumbles
½ cup fat-free red raspberry vinegar salad dressing

Combine salad greens, pear and cheese in a large bowl; toss lightly to mix. Pour dressing over top, toss and serve.

Shopping List:

PRODUCE	DAIRY	CONDIMENTS
7-oz. pkg. red leaf lettuce mix	4 oz. reduced-fat feta cheese crumbles	Fat-free red raspberry vinegar salad dressing or red wine vinegar salad dressing
7-oz. pkg. salad mix with escarole, endive and radicchio		
7-oz. pkg. salad mix with romaine, endive and radicchio		
1 large pear		

NUTRITION PER SERVING Calories 93 • Fat .5 g (5%) • Carbohydrates 18 g • Protein 5 g • Cholesterol 0 mg • Dietary Fiber 3 g • Sodium 367 mg
EXCHANGES ½ fruit • 2 vegetable • ½ very lean meat
CARB CHOICES 1

Super Tip: *Each medium pear boasts about 4 grams of fiber, making it as potent a constipation cure as the legendary prune.*

Lentil Salad

Easy—Do Ahead ◆ Serves: 4

4 cups nonfat vegetable broth
2 cups lentils
¾ cup frozen chopped onion
½ cup sliced roasted red bell peppers, drained well
½ cup canned diced tomatoes with garlic and onions, drained well
½ cup balsamic vinegar
3 tbsp. sugar
2 tbsp. roasted minced roasted garlic
¼ cup grated nonfat Parmesan cheese
¼ tsp. black pepper

Combine vegetable broth, lentils and onion in a medium saucepan; bring to a boil over high heat. Reduce heat to low and cook, stirring occasionally, until lentils are tender, 20 to 25 minutes. Drain lentils and onion (save broth for later use or discard) and place in a large bowl. Add bell peppers and tomatoes. Combine vinegar, sugar and garlic in a small bowl; stir to mix. Pour dressing over lentil mixture; sprinkle with cheese and black pepper. Toss carefully and serve.

Shopping List:

DAIRY	**CANNED**	**SEASONINGS**
Grated nonfat	3 (14½-oz.) cans nonfat	Roasted minced garlic
Parmesan cheese	vegetable broth	or regular minced
	14½-oz. can diced	garlic
FROZEN	tomatoes with garlic	Black pepper
12-oz. pkg. frozen	and onions	
chopped onions	12-oz. jar roasted red	
	peppers	
PACKAGED		
Lentils	**CONDIMENTS**	
Sugar	Balsamic vinegar	

NUTRITION PER SERVING Calories 442 • Fat 1.2 g (2%) •
Carbohydrates 78 g • Protein 33 g • Cholesterol 0 mg • Dietary Fiber 1 g •
Sodium 896 mg
EXCHANGES 5 starch • 1 vegetable • 1 very lean meat
CARB CHOICES 5

Super Tip: What is a lentil? A member of the legume family and a cousin of the bean, lentils are an excellent source of fiber. One-quarter cup cooked lentils provides 11 grams of fiber.

Oriental Chicken Salad

Easy   • Serves: 4

¼ cup lemon juice
2 tbsp. honey
1 tbsp. chili sauce
2 tbsp. oyster sauce
10-oz. pkg. shredded cabbage or angel hair coleslaw mix
12-oz. cooked chicken breast cuts
1½ cups shredded carrots

Combine lemon juice, honey, chili sauce and oyster sauce in a bowl or blender; mix until completely blended. Combine cabbage, chicken and carrots in a large bowl; toss to mix. Pour dressing over top, toss and serve.

Shopping List:

PRODUCE	MEAT	CONDIMENTS
6- to 8-oz. pkg. shredded carrots	2 (6-oz.) pkgs. cooked chicken breast cuts	Lemon juice
10-oz. pkg. shredded cabbage or angel hair coleslaw mix		Honey
		Chili sauce
		Oyster sauce

NUTRITION PER SERVING Calories 197 • Fat 2.6 g (13%) •
Carbohydrates 22 g • Protein 24 g • Cholesterol 60 mg • Dietary Fiber 3 g •
Sodium 1149 mg
EXCHANGES 3 vegetable • 2½ very lean meat • ½ other carb
CARB CHOICES 1

Super Tip: *Dark honey has more antioxidants than light honey. However, all varieties contain an impressive array of antioxidants.*

Penne Salad with Peppers and Peas

Easy—Do Ahead

½ cup nonfat sour cream
½ cup skim milk
½ cup nonfat mayonnaise
¼ cup sugar
½ cup red wine vinegar
4 tsp. dried minced parsley
½ tsp. black pepper
¼ cup sugar
12-oz. pkg. penne pasta, cooked, drained and cooled
10-oz. pkg. frozen peas, cooked
2 bell peppers (yellow, red or orange), thinly sliced

Combine sour cream, milk, mayonnaise, sugar, vinegar, parsley and black pepper in a food processor or blender; process until smooth and creamy. Cover and refrigerate 30 to 45 minutes.

Combine pasta, peas and bell peppers in a large bowl; pour dressing over top and toss lightly until ingredients are coated. Serve immediately or cover, refrigerate and serve within 2 days.

Shopping List:

PRODUCE	FROZEN	CONDIMENTS
2 bell peppers	10-oz. pkg. frozen peas	Nonfat mayonnaise
		Red wine vinegar
DAIRY	PACKAGED	
4 oz. nonfat sour cream	12-oz. pkg. penne pasta	SEASONINGS
4 oz. skim milk	Sugar	Dried minced parsley
		Black pepper

NUTRITION PER SERVING Calories 321 • Fat 1 g (3%) •
Carbohydrates 66 g • Protein 12 g • Cholesterol <1 mg • Dietary Fiber <1 mg •
Sodium 171 mg
EXCHANGES 3 starch • ½ other carb • 2 vegetable
CARB CHOICES 5

Super Tip: *Time Savers: Purchase cooked peas and sliced bell peppers from the supermarket salad bar.*

Salmon Caesar Salad

Easy • Serves: 6

SALADS & SANDWICHES

2 (10-oz.) pkgs. hearts of romaine
¾ cup sliced roasted red bell peppers, drained
2 (6-oz.) cans salmon, drained and flaked
1 cup seasoned nonfat croutons
¾ cup nonfat Caesar salad dressing
1 tbsp. grated nonfat Parmesan cheese or cheese topping

Combine all ingredients except salad dressing and cheese in a large bowl and mix well. Pour salad dressing over top; sprinkle with Parmesan cheese. Toss salad and serve.

Shopping List:

PRODUCE	PACKAGED	CONDIMENTS
2 (10-oz. pkgs. hearts of romaine or romaine lettuce leaves	12-oz. pkg. nonfat seasoned croutons (or flavor of choice)	Nonfat Caesar salad dressing
		12-oz. jar roasted red bell peppers
DAIRY	**CANNED**	
Grated nonfat Parmesan cheese or cheese topping	2 (6-oz.) cans salmon	

NUTRITION PER SERVING Calories 142 • Fat 3.3 g (21%) •
Carbohydrates 13 g • Protein 14 g • Cholesterol 22 mg • Dietary Fiber 2 g •
Sodium 613 mg
EXCHANGES ½ other carb • 2 lean meat • 1 vegetable
CARB CHOICES

Super Tip: *Canned salmon, comprised only of salmon sections and a little salt, is one of the healthiest and purest processed foods.*

Seafood Pasta Salad

Easy—Do Ahead   • Serves: 6

12-oz. pkg. angel hair pasta, cooked, drained and rinsed under cold water
9 oz. cooked bay shrimp
9 oz. cooked bay scallops
1 cup chopped green onions
1½ cups nonfat ranch salad dressing
Grated nonfat Parmesan cheese (optional)

Combine all ingredients except Parmesan cheese and toss carefully until well mixed. Sprinkle with Parmesan cheese before serving, if desired.

Shopping List:

PRODUCE	SEAFOOD	CONDIMENTS
Bunch green onions	9 oz. cooked bay shrimp	12 oz. nonfat ranch
	9 oz. cooked bay	salad dressing
DAIRY	scallops	
Grated nonfat Parmesan cheese (optional)		

NUTRITION PER SERVING Calories 368 • Fat 2 g (5%) •
Carbohydrates 58 g • Protein 26 g • Cholesterol 106 mg • Dietary Fiber 2 g •
Sodium • 748 mg
EXCHANGES 3 starch • 1 other carb • 2 very lean meat
CARB CHOICES 4

Super Tip: *How long will noodles stay fresh? Dried noodles, stored in a cool, dry place, will keep indefinitely; fresh noodles will last 2 to 3 days in the refrigerator.*

Spiced Turkey Salad

◆ Serves: 6

¼ cup nonfat mayonnaise
¼ cup nonfat sour cream
½ tsp. ground nutmeg
½ tsp. ground cinnamon
Pepper to taste
2½ cups cubed, cooked turkey breast
2 cups chopped celery
2 apples, unpeeled, chopped
¼ cup golden raisins

Combine mayonnaise, sour cream, nutmeg, cinnamon and pepper in a small bowl; mix until smooth and creamy. Combine remaining ingredients in a large bowl; toss to mix. Spoon dressing over top and toss until ingredients are coated. Cover and refrigerate until ready to serve.

Shopping List:

PRODUCE	MEAT	CONDIMENTS
1 small bunch celery	¾ lb. cooked turkey	Nonfat mayonnaise
2 medium apples	breast	
		SEASONINGS
DAIRY	PACKAGED	Ground nutmeg
Nonfat sour cream	Golden raisins	Ground cinnamon
		Black pepper

NUTRITION PER SERVING Calories 126 • Fat .5 g (4%) •
Carbohydrates 16 g • Protein 15 g • Cholesterol 32 mg • Dietary Fiber 2 g •
Sodium 137 mg
EXCHANGES ½ fruit • ½ other carb • 2 very lean meat
CARB CHOICES 1

Super Tip: *For shortcut cooking, use cooked chicken breast cuts available in the meat section of your supermarket.*

Spinach-Orange Salad

Easy

16-oz. pkg. baby spinach leaves
11-oz. can mandarin orange segments, drained well
6-oz. can sliced water chestnuts, drained well
½ cup nonfat honey bacon French salad dressing

Combine spinach leaves, orange segments and water chestnuts in a large bowl. Pour dressing over top and toss to mix.

Shopping List:

PRODUCE	CANNED	CONDIMENTS
16-oz. pkg. baby spinach leaves	11-oz. can mandarin orange segments	Nonfat honey bacon French salad dressing
	6-oz. can sliced water chestnuts	or other nonfat salad dressing of choice

NUTRITION PER SERVING Calories 138 • Fat .2 g (1 %) •
Carbohydrates 31 g • Protein 4 g • Cholesterol 0 mg • Dietary Fiber 2 g •
Sodium 237 mg
EXCHANGE 3 vegetable • ½ fruit • ½ other carb
CARB CHOICES 2

Super Tip: *The water chestnut, also called the Chinese water chestnut or the water caltrop, is a tuber vegetable that resembles a chestnut in color and shape, but not in flavor or texture.*

Spring Mix with Yogurt–Poppy Seed Dressing

Easy—Do Ahead   ◆ Serves: 6

½ cup plain nonfat yogurt
1 tbsp. lemon juice
¼ tsp. dried rosemary leaves
1 tsp. dried basil
1 tsp. mustard powder
½ tsp. poppy seeds
1 tbsp. chopped fresh parsley
2 (10-oz.) pkgs. salad mix with baby lettuce and greens

Combine all ingredients except salad mix in a blender or jar; blend or shake until well combined. Pour over salad mix; toss and serve.

Shopping List:

PRODUCE	DAIRY	SEASONINGS
2 (10-oz.) pkgs. baby lettuce and greens salad mix	4 oz. plain nonfat yogurt	Dried rosemary
Parsley		Dried basil
Lemon or lemon juice		Mustard powder
		Poppy seeds

NUTRITION PER SERVING Calories 29 • Fat .3 g (1%) • Carbohydrates 4 g • Protein 2 g • Cholesterol <1 g • Dietary Fiber 1 g • Sodium 34 mg
EXCHANGES 1 vegetable
CARB CHOICES 0

Super Tip: *The flavonoid doismin, an active ingredient in rosemary, is a natural brain stimulant and memory enhancer.*

Superb Salad Supper

Easy—Do Ahead

SALADS &
SANDWICHES

1¾ cups nonfat chicken broth
2 cups instant brown rice
16-oz. can black-eyed peas, drained and rinsed
1 cup diced bell pepper (red, green or yellow)
1 cup diced celery
¾ cup sliced green onions
2 cups diced oven-roasted chicken or turkey breast
½ cup nonfat Italian salad dressing

Pour chicken broth into a medium saucepan; bring to a boil over high heat. Stir in rice. Reduce heat to low, cover and simmer 5 minutes. Combine black-eyed peas, bell pepper, celery, green onions, chicken and rice in a large bowl; add salad dressing and toss carefully until mixed.

Shopping List:

PRODUCE	MEAT/DELI	CANNED
Large bell pepper or 7-oz. container diced tri-pepper mix	2 (6 oz.) pkgs. cooked chicken or turkey breast slices (smoked, honey-roasted or oven-roasted)	16-oz. can black-eyed peas
Celery or 7-oz. container diced celery		14½-oz. can nonfat chicken broth
Bunch green onions		
	PACKAGED	**CONDIMENTS**
	14-oz. box instant brown rice	Nonfat Italian salad dressing

NUTRITION PER SERVING Calories 196 • Fat 1.9 g (9 %) •
Carbohydrates 27 g • Protein 17 g • Cholesterol 30 mg • Dietary Fiber 1 g •
Sodium 954 mg
EXCHANGES 1 vegetable • 1 starch • 2 very lean meat • ½ other carb
CARB CHOICES 2

Super Tip: *Black-eyed peas are soft, creamy beans that originated in Asia. Featured in many southern or soul food dishes, the most popular is hoppin' John, a traditional New Year's dish thought to bring good luck.*

Tuna-Mac Salad

Easy—Do Ahead   ♦ Serves: 6

4 cups shredded lettuce
1⅓ cups medium shell pasta, cooked, rinsed and drained
1 large cucumber, chopped
1 cup grape tomatoes, cut in half
9½-oz. can tuna packed in water, drained well and flaked
1 cup frozen peas, thawed
¾ cup nonfat ranch salad dressing
¾ cup shredded nonfat cheddar
    cheese
3 tbsp. sliced green onions

Place lettuce in bottom of a 3-quart glass bowl; top with pasta, cucumber, tomatoes, tuna and peas. Spread salad dressing in one layer over the top; sprinkle with cheese and green onions. Cover tightly and refrigerate at least 4 hours or overnight. Toss salad just before serving.

Shopping List:

PRODUCE	FROZEN	CONDIMENTS
16-oz. pkg. shredded iceberg lettuce	10-oz. pkg. frozen peas	12 oz. nonfat ranch salad dressing
Large cucumber	**PACKAGED**	
1 pint grape tomatoes	8 oz. medium shell pasta	
Bunch green onions		
DAIRY	**CANNED**	
Shredded nonfat cheddar cheese	9½-oz. can tuna packed in water	

NUTRITION PER SERVING Calories 244 · Fat 1 g (4 %) ·
Carbohydrates 34 g · Protein 23 g · Cholesterol 8 mg · Dietary Fiber 2 g ·
Sodium 604 mg
EXCHANGES 4 vegetable · 2 very lean meat · 1 starch
CARB CHOICES 2

Super Tip: *Use Creamy Herb Salad Dressing (page 52) in place of ranch dressing desired.*

Turkey Taco Salad

Easy—Do Ahead

1½ lbs. low-fat ground turkey
1¼-oz. pkg. taco seasoning mix
14½-oz. can diced tomato sauce for tacos
15-oz. can pinto, black or kidney beans, drained well
14½-oz. can diced tomatoes with green chiles, drained well

1 cup nonfat mayonnaise
1 cup chunky-style salsa
2 (10-oz.) pkgs. shredded iceberg lettuce
¾ cup chopped red onion
2 cups shredded nonfat cheddar cheese
6 oz. baked tortilla chips, slightly crumbled

Spray a large nonstick skillet with cooking spray and heat over medium-high heat. Add turkey and cook, stirring frequently, until meat is browned. Remove from heat and drain. Add taco seasoning according to package directions. Stir in beans and tomatoes; cook until heated through. Combine mayonnaise and salsa in a medium bowl; mix until blended. Place shredded lettuce in bottom of a large bowl; top with turkey mixture, red onion and cheese. Spoon mayonnaise mixture over top and mix lightly. Garnish with tortilla chips.

Shopping List:

PRODUCE	PACKAGED	CONDIMENTS
2 (10-oz.) pkgs. shredded iceberg lettuce	6 oz. baked tortilla chips	8 oz. chunky-style salsa
Red onion		8 oz. nonfat mayonnaise
	CANNED	
DAIRY	14½-oz. can diced tomato sauce for tacos	**SEASONINGS**
8 oz. shredded nonfat cheddar cheese	15-oz. can low-fat pinto, black or kidney beans	1¼-oz. pkg. taco seasoning mix
MEAT	14½-oz. can diced tomatoes with green chiles	
1½ lbs. low-fat ground turkey		

NUTRITION PER SERVING Calories 463 • Fat 3.2 g (6%) • Carbohydrates 59 g • Protein 47 g • Cholesterol 46 mg • Dietary Fiber 6 g • Sodium 2491 mg
EXCHANGES 5 very lean meat • 3 vegetable • 2 starch • 1 other carb
CARB CHOICES 4

Super Tip: *For a great spicy flavor, use Southwest chunky-style salsa as a dressing in place of the mayonnaise-salsa mixture. Make your own taco seasoning with a blend of 1½ tsp. chili powder, ¼ tsp. dried oregano, ¼ tsp. cumin powder, ½ tsp. garlic powder, ½ tsp. onion powder, 1 tsp. salt and ¼ tsp. pepper.*

QUICK BREADS
AND MUFFINS

❖ ❖ ❖

Label Lingo: Nutrition Facts

It pays to read between the lines! What do those labels really mean? What constitutes a serving? What's really inside that package? Understanding FDA regulated labels can save you from the diet danger zone and help you make healthful decisions.

LABEL LINGO	WHAT IT REALLY MEANS
SERVING SIZE (See One Serving = How Much?, page 77)	The amount of food in one serving (based on cups, tablespoons or teaspoons with equivalent weight in grams, ounces or pounds)
CALORIES	Amount of energy from carbohydrates, protein and fat
FAT	Includes saturated, polyunsaturated and monounsaturated fats
CARBOHYDRATE	Includes complex carbohydrates, simple sugars, as well as fiber
VITAMINS and MINERALS	Aim for foods containing at least 20% of the daily value
Ingredients List	Ingredients are listed in descending order by weight, so the first few ingredients are the main product components
% Daily Value (DV)	Indicates how much of each nutrient one serving provides (based on a 2000-calorie daily intake)
Nutrients	Food labeled "excellent source of" indicates the food contains 20% or more of the Daily Value per serving; a "good source of" contains 10 to 19% and any nutrients listed as 5% or less of Daily Value are low in that nutrient
FREE	Product contains .5 or fewer grams of fat, saturated fat, cholesterol, sodium, sugar or calories per serving
FAT-FREE (NONFAT)	Less than .5 grams of fat per serving
SUGAR-FREE	Less than .5 grams of sugar per serving
CALORIE-FREE	Less than 5 calories per serving

LABEL LINGO	WHAT IT REALLY MEANS
CHOLESTEROL FREE	Less than 2 milligrams of cholesterol and 2 grams (or less) of saturated fat per serving
LOW	7% or less of the RDA for a nutrient such as calorie, fat, cholesterol or sugar
LOW FAT	Less than 3 grams of fat per serving
LOW CALORIE	Less than 40 calories per serving
LOW CHOLESTEROL	Less than 20 milligrams cholesterol per serving and 2 g (or less) of saturated fat per serving
LOW SODIUM	Less than 140 milligrams of sodium per serving
VERY LOW SODIUM	35 milligrams (or less) of sodium per serving
LEAN	Less than 10 grams of fat, 4 grams of saturated fat and 95 milligrams of cholesterol per serving (100 grams)
EXTRA-LEAN	Less than 5 grams of fat, 2 grams of saturated fat and 95 milligrams of cholesterol per serving (100 grams)
LITE	Product contains 1/3 fewer calories or 1/2 the fat or sodium content of the "regular" or full-fat variety
HIGH	Any food that contains 20% or more of the guidelines for a particular nutrient (high sodium, high calcium, etc.)
REDUCED	Products are nutritionally altered to contain 25% less of an undesirable nutrient (fat, sodium, cholesterol, sugar) or calories than the "standard" item (i.e., reduced-fat cheese)
LESS	Products contain 25% less of an undesirable nutrient or calories with or without alteration than the "standard" item (i.e., contains 50% less sodium)
MORE	Product, with or without alteration, contains a minimum of 10% more of the guidelines for a desired nutrient (i.e., more fiber)
ORGANIC	Must contain at least 95% organically produced ingredients (produced without synthetic pesticides, herbicides, fungicides, fertilizers, antibiotics, hormones, genetically modified ingredients and irradiation)
"MADE WITH" Organic Ingredients	Must have no less than 70% organic ingredients

LABEL LINGO	WHAT IT REALLY MEANS
FRESH	Product is minimally processed and can include anything that isn't canned or frozen, including everything from a head of lettuce packed 6 days ago to kiwi that took 6 months to reach the United States
GOOD SOURCE	Product contains 10 to 19% of the daily value of a certain nutrient

ONE SERVING = HOW MUCH?

Food Group	One Serving Size
Vegetables and Fruit	½ cup chopped fruit ½ cup cooked or raw vegetables 1 cup raw green leaves ¾ cup vegetable or fruit juice 1 medium whole piece of fruit 1 small baked potato
Whole Grains	1 slice whole wheat bread ½ cup brown rice or bulgur ½ cup whole wheat pasta
High-Calcium Foods	1 cup skim or 1% milk 1 cup nonfat or low-fat yogurt 1 cup calcium-fortified orange juice 1 oz. nonfat or low-fat hard cheese
Meat, Fish and Poultry	3 ounces cooked
Other High-Protein Foods	Peanut butter = 2 tablespoons ½ cup cooked dried beans or lentils 2 tablespoons chopped nuts

Understanding the Lingo

- Ingredients are listed from highest to lowest percentage in each product. If "wheat" bread lists "whole wheat" after a multitude of other ingredients, the percentage of actual "whole wheat" in the bread is very minimal. The first five ingredients make up the bulk of the food.
- Compare carbohydrate grams to sugar grams; if the numbers are very close, all those carbohydrates come from sugar!
- Compare the amount of saturated fat, total fat and cholesterol provided per serving. Choose products low in all these areas.
- Beware of "healthy" claims; some items, as "healthy granola," are loaded with nuts, seeds, coconut and oil.

Pay Attention to Portion Sizes

A 7-ounce package of caramel popcorn is labeled fat-free, indicating that the product has .5 or less grams of fat per serving. A 7-ounce bag is fairly typical for a snack-size bag, but if you eat the whole thing, you've consumed 7 servings! How does that all add up? One serving contains 100 calories (reasonable for snacking), but . . . eat the whole bag and you've munched down 700 calories! And the fat falls under the free labeling codes, but what about the hydrogenated vegetable oil listed as one of the ingredients? When servings are doubled, tripled or "you can't believe you ate the whole thing" your fat consumption increases dramatically. It's no longer a fat-free food. The USDA recommends the following "eyeball checks" for portion sizes:

- Bagel = hockey puck
- ½ cup fruit, vegetables, pasta or rice = small fist
- 3 oz. cooked meat, poultry or fish = deck of cards
- 1 ounce of cheese = 4 dice
- 1 teaspoon margarine or butter = thumb tip
- 1 serving snack foods = small handful
- 1 muffin = large egg
- 2 tablespoons peanut butter = golf ball
- 1 baked potato = computer mouse

Ramen noodles marketed in single-serving packages actually contain 2 servings, doubling the calories, sodium and fat content.

Can you spray "nonfat cooking spray" for one-third of a second and will that really prevent sticking? Probably not, but the nutritional information provided is based on a one-third of a second spray.

If a label advertises a product as 95 percent fat free, does that mean it's ultra-low in fat? Not necessarily! Some low-fat claims are based on the percentage of a food's weight rather than total calories. For example, 99 percent fat-free milk contains 27 calories of fat per 1-cup serving, so 27 percent of the calories are from fat, not 5 percent.

"Organic," "all-natural" and "high energy" do not translate to low calorie or low fat.

According to a report in *Psychological Science* (2002), a new study reported that subjects were more likely to interpret yogurt as healthy if it was labeled 95 percent fat-free as opposed to "contains 5 percent fat" even though their fat contents were the same. Misleading labels can pack on unwanted pounds; don't be fooled by label lingo. Learn the language and save!

Apple-Oat Bread

Easy—Do Ahead—Freeze

1 cup quick-cooking rolled oats
½ cup whole wheat flour
½ cup all-purpose flour
½ tsp. baking soda
½ tsp. baking powder
1½ tsp. ground cinnamon
½ tsp. ground allspice
½ cup packed brown sugar
¼ cup skim milk
¼ cup cinnamon-flavored applesauce
2 egg whites
2 cups diced apples

Preheat oven to 350°F. Spray a 9 × 5-inch loaf pan with cooking spray. Combine oats, flours, baking soda, baking powder, cinnamon and allspice in a large bowl; mix well. Add remaining ingredients, except apples, and mix until moistened. If batter is too thick, add additional applesauce, 1 tablespoon at a time, until desired consistency is reached. Fold in apples. Spoon batter into loaf pan; bake 45 to 55 minutes until toothpick inserted in center comes out clean. Cool slightly, slice and serve.

Shopping List:

PRODUCE	PACKAGED	BAKING
2 medium apples	Quick-cooking rolled oats	Whole wheat flour
		All-purpose flour
DAIRY	Cinnamon-flavored applesauce	Brown sugar
Skim milk		Baking soda
2 eggs		Baking powder
	SEASONINGS	
	Ground cinnamon	
	Ground allspice	

NUTRITION PER SERVING Calories 140 • Fat .8 g (5%) • Carbohydrates 31 g • Protein 4 g • Cholesterol <1 mg • Dietary Fiber 2 g • Sodium 76 mg
EXCHANGES 1 starch • 1 fruit
CARB CHOICES 2

Super Tip: *Substitute 2 cups chopped canned apples for fresh apples.*

Baking Mix Muffins

Easy—Do Ahead—Freeze ♦ Serves: 6

2 cups reduced-fat baking mix
½ cup granulated sugar
¼ cup packed light brown sugar
1 tbsp. baking powder
1 tsp. ground cinnamon
½ cup egg substitute
½ cup skim milk
¾ tsp. vanilla extract
Cinnamon-sugar mixture

BREADS AND MUFFINS

Preheat oven to 350°F. Spray 6 muffin cups with cooking spray. Combine baking mix, sugars, baking powder and cinnamon in a large bowl and mix well. Add egg substitute, milk and vanilla; stir until completely blended and smooth, but do not overbeat. Fill muffin cups three-fourths full; sprinkle with cinnamon-sugar mixture. Bake 15 minutes, until toothpick inserted in center comes out clean.

Shopping List:

DAIRY	SEASONINGS	BAKING
4 oz. egg substitute	Ground cinnamon	Reduced-fat baking mix
4 oz. skim milk	Vanilla extract	(Bisquick or store
	Cinnamon-sugar mixture	brand)
		Granulated sugar
		Light brown sugar
		Baking powder

NUTRITION PER SERVING Calories 255 • Fat 3 g (9%) • Carbohydrates 55 g • Protein 5 g • Cholesterol <1 mg • Dietary Fiber 1 g • Sodium 705 mg
EXCHANGES 2½ other carb
CARB CHOICES 3

Super Tip: *Reduced-fat baking mixes have 50% less fat than original versions. You'll never miss the fat; the overall flavor and texture remain the same.*

Beer Bread

Easy—Do Ahead—Freeze • Serves: 12

3 cups all-purpose flour
1 tbsp. baking powder
1 tsp. salt
12-oz. can lite beer

Preheat oven to 375°F. Spray a 9 × 5-inch loaf pan with cooking spray. Combine all ingredients and mix well. Press dough into pan; bake 55 to 60 minutes, until knife inserted in center comes out clean.

Shopping List:

SEASONING	BAKING	OTHER
Salt	All-purpose flour	12-oz. can lite beer
	Baking powder	

NUTRITION PER SERVING Calories 184 • Fat .5 g (2%) •
Carbohydrates 37 g • Protein 5 g • Cholesterol 0 mg • Dietary Fiber 1 g •
Sodium 392 mg
EXCHANGES 2 starch • ½ other carb
CARB CHOICES 2½

Super Tip: *If more Americans reduced their fat intake, ate 5 to 9 servings of fruits and vegetables a day, limited alcohol and exercised regularly, the number of cancers in America could be cut by one third or more. (Source: Food and Nutrition Science Alliance.)*

Biscuits with Herbs

Easy

• Serves: 12

2 cups all-purpose flour
2 tsp. baking powder
½ tsp. baking powder
1 tsp. salt
1 tsp. Italian seasoning
1 cup skim milk
¼ cup nonfat mayonnaise

Preheat oven to 400°F. Spray a 12-cup muffin pan with cooking spray. Combine flour, baking powder, baking soda, salt and Italian seasoning in a medium bowl; mix well. Add milk and mayonnaise and mix until ingredients are combined. Spoon batter into muffin cups; bake 12 to 15 minutes, until lightly browned.

Shopping List:

DAIRY	CONDIMENTS	SEASONINGS
8 oz. skim milk	Nonfat mayonnaise	Salt
		Italian seasoning
PACKAGED		
All-purpose flour		
Baking powder		
Baking soda		

NUTRITION PER SERVING Calories 87 • Fat .2 g (2%) • Carbohydrates 18 g • Protein 3 g • Cholesterol <1 mg • Dietary Fiber 1 g • Sodium 313 mg
EXCHANGES 1 starch
CARB CHOICES 1

Super Tip: *Getting 1,000 to 1,200 mg of Calcium per day can ease the symptoms of premenstrual syndrome. (Source: PMS study conducted by Susan Thys-Jacobs, M.D., of St. Luke's Roosevelt Hospital in New York City.)*

BREADS AND MUFFINS

Blueberry Muffins

Easy—Do Ahead—Freeze

2 cups reduced-fat baking mix
¾ cup granulated sugar
½ cup egg substitute
½ cup skim milk
¾ tsp. vanilla extract
½ cup blueberries
1 tbsp. powdered sugar

Preheat oven to 350°F. Spray a 12-cup muffin pan with cooking spray. Combine baking mix, sugar, egg substitute, milk and vanilla in a large bowl and mix until blended and smooth. Add blueberries; sprinkle with powdered sugar and carefully fold into batter. Fill muffin cups three-fourths full; bake 15 to 18 minutes, until toothpick inserted in center comes out clean.

Shopping List:

DAIRY	PRODUCE/FROZEN	BAKING
4 oz. skim milk	Fresh or frozen	Reduced-fat baking mix
4 oz. egg substitute	blueberries	(Bisquick or store
		brand)
		Granulated sugar
		Powdered sugar
		Vanilla extract

NUTRITION PER SERVING Calories 129 • Fat 1.5 g (10%) •
Carbohydrates 28 g • Protein 3 g • Cholesterol <1 mg • Dietary Fiber <1 g •
Sodium 269 mg
EXCHANGES 1 starch • 1 fruit
CARB CHOICES 2

Super Tip: *Save! Save! Save! Store-bought blueberry muffins can weigh in at almost 6 ounces with a whopping 480 calories and 20 grams of fat, as compared to home-baked muffins.*

Carrot-Cheese Bread

Easy—Do Ahead—Freeze ◆ Serves: 10

½ cup nonfat cream cheese, softened
½ cup sugar
¾ cup egg substitute
1 tsp. vanilla extract
1½ cups all-purpose flour
1½ tsp. baking powder
1 tsp. ground cinnamon
4 tbsp. skim milk
2 cups shredded carrots
¼ cup raisins

BREADS AND MUFFINS

Preheat oven to 350°F. Spray a 9 × 5-inch loaf pan with cooking spray. Combine cream cheese and sugar in a large bowl; beat with electric mixer until creamy and smooth. Add egg substitute and beat well. Add ¾ cup of the flour, baking powder, cinnamon and 2 tablespoons of the milk; mix well. Add remaining flour and milk; mix until smooth. Fold in carrots and raisins. Spoon batter into loaf pan; bake 35 to 40 minutes, until a knife inserted in center comes out clean.

Shopping List:

PRODUCE	DAIRY	BAKING
6-oz. pkg. shredded carrots	Skim milk	All-purpose flour
	6 oz. egg substitute	Sugar
	4 oz. nonfat cream cheese	Vanilla extract
		Baking powder
		Ground cinnamon
	PACKAGED	
	Raisins	

NUTRITION PER SERVING Calories 146 • Fat .2 g (1%) •
Carbohydrates 31 g • Protein 6 g • Cholesterol <1 mg • Dietary Fiber 1 g •
Sodium 165 mg
EXCHANGES 2 other carb
CARB CHOICES 2

Super Tip: *One problem with cooking carrots is some of the nutrients remain in the water. To get the nutrients into your body rather than pouring them down the drain, try reusing the cooking water in your recipe.*

Chili-Cheese Bread

Easy—Do Ahead—Freeze

¾ cups reduced-fat baking mix
1 cup shredded nonfat cheddar cheese
1½ cups skim milk
¼ cup Southwest-flavor egg substitute
2 tbsp. chopped canned green chiles, drained well

Preheat oven to 350°F. Spray a 9 × 5-inch loaf pan with cooking spray. Combine all ingredients and mix until blended. Spoon batter into pan; bake 40 to 45 minutes, until a knife inserted in center comes out clean.

Shopping List:

DAIRY	CANNED	BAKING
4 oz. shredded nonfat cheddar cheese	4-oz. can chopped green chiles	Reduced-fat baking mix (Bisquick or store brand)
12 oz. skim milk		
Southwest-flavor egg substitute		

NUTRITION PER SERVING Calories 239 • Fat 4.3 g (16%) •
Carbohydrates 41 g • Protein 10 g • Cholesterol 1 mg • Dietary Fiber 1 g •
Sodium 902 mg
EXCHANGES 3 other carb • 1 fat
CARB CHOICES 3

Super Tip: *Storing chili powder at room temperature will eventually deplete its beta-carotene. Keep chili powder in a dark, cool place, such as the freezer.*

Chocolate Chip Muffins

Easy—Do Ahead—Freeze   • Serves: 12

2 cups reduced-fat baking mix
¼ cup granulated sugar
⅔ cup packed light brown sugar
1 tbsp. baking powder
½ cup egg substitute
½ cup skim milk
¾ tsp. vanilla extract
½ cup miniature chocolate chips

Preheat oven to 350°F. Spray a 12-cup muffin pan with cooking spray. Combine baking mix, sugars and baking powder in a large bowl; add egg substitute, milk and vanilla; mix until completely blended. Fold in chocolate chips. Fill muffin cups three-fourths full; bake 15 to 18 minutes, until toothpick inserted in centers comes out clean.

Shopping List:

DAIRY	BAKING	
4 oz. egg substitute	Reduced-fat baking mix	Light brown sugar
4 oz. skim milk	(Bisquick or store	Baking powder
	brand)	Vanilla extract
	Granulated sugar	Miniature chocolate
		chips

NUTRITION PER SERVING Calories 173 • Fat 3 g (16%) •
Carbohydrates 35 g • Protein 3 g • Cholesterol <1 mg • Dietary Fiber <1 g •
Sodium 359 mg
EXCHANGES 2 other carbs • ½ fat
CARB CHOICES 2

Super Tip: *Some ongoing research at the Cleveland Clinic claims that the fat in chocolate has no ill effects on cholesterol. Chocolate lovers will be happy about this!*

Choc-o-lot Chip Zucchini Bread

Easy—Do Ahead—Freeze

• Serves: 16

1½ cups all-purpose flour
⅓ cup unsweetened cocoa powder
1 tsp. baking soda
¼ tsp. baking powder
1 tsp. ground cinnamon
½ cup granulated sugar

½ cup packed light brown sugar
½ cup egg substitute
½ cup unsweetened applesauce
1 tsp. vanilla extract
2 cups shredded zucchini
¼ cup miniature chocolate chips

Preheat oven to 350°F. Spray a 9 × 5-inch loaf pan with cooking spray. Combine flour, cocoa, baking soda, baking powder and cinnamon in a large bowl; mix well. Add sugars, egg substitute, applesauce, vanilla and zucchini; mix until ingredients are combined. Fold in chocolate chips. Spoon batter into loaf pan; bake 40 to 45 minutes, until toothpick inserted in center comes out clean. Cool slightly before removing from pan; slice and serve.

Shopping List:

PRODUCE	SEASONINGS	Light brown sugar
2 to 3 zucchini	Ground cinnamon	Baking soda
(depending on size)	Vanilla extract	Baking powder
		Miniature chocolate
DAIRY	**BAKING**	chips
4 oz. egg substitute	All-purpose flour	
	Unsweetened cocoa	
PACKAGED	powder	
Applesauce	Granulated sugar	

NUTRITION PER SERVING Calories 119 • Fat 1 g (8%) •
Carbohydrates 27 g • Protein 3 g • Cholesterol 0 mg • Dietary Fiber 1 g •
Sodium 72 mg
EXCHANGES 1½ other carb
CARB CHOICES 2

Super Tip: *Research presented in February 2002 at the American Association for the Advancement of Science's annual meeting revealed preliminary evidence that cocoa and other chocolates may keep high blood pressure down, your blood flowing and your heart healthy.*

Cinnamon Apple Muffins

Easy—Do Ahead—Freeze   • Serves: 12

2 cups reduced-fat baking mix
½ cup granulated sugar
⅓ cup packed light brown sugar
1 tbsp. baking powder
1 tsp. ground cinnamon
½ cup egg substitute
⅓ cup skim milk
½ cup cinnamon-spice apple slices

Preheat oven to 350°F. Spray a 12-cup muffin pan with cooking spray. Combine baking mix, sugars, baking powder and cinnamon in a large bowl; mix well. Add egg substitute and milk; beat until smooth. Fold in apple slices. Fill muffin cups three-fourths full; bake 15 to 18 minutes, until toothpick inserted in centers comes out clean.

Shopping List:

CANNED	SEASONINGS	
20-oz. can cinnamon-spice apple slices	Ground cinnamon	Granulated sugar
		Light brown sugar
		Baking powder
	BAKING	
	Reduced-fat baking mix (Bisquick or store brand)	

NUTRITION PER SERVING Calories 136 • Fat 1.5 g (10%) •
Carbohydrates 30 g • Protein 3 g • Cholesterol <1 mg • Dietary Fiber 1 g •
Sodium 351 mg
EXCHANGES 2 other carb
CARB CHOICES 2

Super Tip: *Numerous studies over the past quarter century have shown that a diet rich in apples can help lower blood cholesterol. Pectin, a soluble fiber found in apples at a rate of .78 grams per 100 grams of edible fruit, is thought to play a significant role in that relationship. Other fruits and vegetables also contain pectin, but apples are a handy and excellent means toward cholesterol reduction.*

Creamed Corn Cornbread

Easy

1 cup cornmeal
½ cup all-purpose flour
1 tbsp. baking powder
3 tbsp. sugar
⅓ cup unsweetened applesauce
¾ cup skim milk
¼ cup Southwestern-flavor egg substitute
15-oz. can low-fat creamed corn
Honey (optional)

Preheat oven to 425°F. Spray an 8- or 9-inch square baking dish with cooking spray. Combine cornmeal, flour, baking powder and sugar in a large bowl; mix well. Add applesauce, milk, egg substitute and corn; mix until ingredients are moistened and blended. Place empty baking dish in oven for 5 minutes; remove from oven and immediately pour batter into dish. Bake 18 to 20 minutes, until toothpick inserted in center comes out clean. Cool slightly; cut into squares and serve with honey, if desired.

Shopping List:

DAIRY	PACKAGED	CANNED
6 oz. skim milk	Cornmeal	15-oz. can low-fat
4 oz. Southwestern egg	All-purpose flour	creamed corn
substitute or plain egg	Sugar	Unsweetened
substitute	Baking powder	applesauce
		CONDIMENTS
		Honey (optional)

NUTRITION PER SERVING Calories 223 • Fat .8 g (3%) •
Carbohydrates 50 g • Protein 6 g • Cholesterol 1 mg • Dietary Fiber 2 g •
Sodium 207 mg
EXCHANGES 3 other carb
CARB CHOICES 3

Super Tip: *Lutein and zeaxanthin are carotenoids that may help prevent certain eye conditions such as age-related macular degeneration, one of the leading causes of blindness in older adults. Corn is high in lutein; 1 cup has 3 milligrams.*

Honey-Glazed Rolls

Easy—Do Ahead—Freeze

• Serves:16

1 lb. frozen bread dough, thawed
3 tbsp. honey
3 tsp. water
2 tsp. sesame seeds

Thaw frozen bread dough in refrigerator overnight. Line a baking sheet with foil and spray with cooking spray. Cut dough into 16 equal pieces; roll each piece into a ball. Place rolls on baking sheet; cover with towel and let rise in warm place until doubled in size, about 2 hours. Preheat oven to 375°F. Combine honey and water in a small bowl and mix well; brush rolls with honey mixture and sprinkle with sesame seeds. Bake 15 to 18 minutes, until lightly browned.

Shopping List:

FROZEN	CONDIMENTS	SEASONINGS
1 lb. frozen bread dough	Honey	Sesame seeds

NUTRITION PER SERVING Calories 107 • Fat 1 g (8%) •
Carbohydrates 19 g • Protein 3 g • Cholesterol 0 mg • Dietary Fiber 1 g •
Sodium 187 mg
EXCHANGES 1 starch • ½ other carb
CARB CHOICES 1

Super Tip: *Honey is sweeter than sugar, so you can substitute 1 cup honey for 1¼ cups sugar, but you must reduce the liquid in the recipe by ¼ cup.*

Honey-Orange Cornbread

Easy—Do Ahead—Freeze   ♦ Serves: 12

14.5-oz. pkg. fat-free honey cornbread mix
12-oz. can whole-kernel corn, drained well
¼ cup grated orange zest
1¼ cups water

Preheat oven to 400°F. Spray an 8-inch baking dish with cooking spray. Combine cornbread mix, corn, orange zest and water in a medium bowl; mix well. Spread batter into prepared pan; bake 20 to 25 minutes, until knife inserted in center comes out clean and bread is golden brown.

Shopping List:

PACKAGED	CANNED	OTHER
14.5-oz. pkg. Krusteaz fat-free honey cornbread mix or any regular nonfat or low-fat cornbread mix	12-oz. can whole-kernel corn	Orange zest

NUTRITION PER SERVING Calories 143 • Fat 0 g • Carbohydrates 33 g • Protein 3 g • Cholesterol 0 mg • Dietary Fiber 2 g • Sodium 490 mg
EXCHANGES 2 starch
CARB CHOICES 2

Super Tip: *To get the most juice out of an orange, warm the fruit to room temperature and roll it on the counter with your palm before squeezing.*

Lemon-Berry Muffins

Easy—Do Ahead—Freeze

19-oz. pkg. fat-free blueberry muffin mix with blueberries
1¼ cups water
2 tsp. grated lemon zest
⅓ cup sugar
3 tbsp. lemon juice

Preheat oven to 350°F. Spray a 12-cup muffin pan with cooking spray. Combine muffin mix, water and lemon zest in a medium bowl; mix well. Fold in blueberries (provided with mix). Spoon batter into muffin cups; bake 18 to 20 minutes, until toothpick inserted in centers comes out clean.

While muffins are baking, prepare lemon glaze: Combine sugar and lemon juice in small microwave-safe cup and mix well. Microwave on High 2 to 3 minutes. Remove muffins from oven. Pierce tops of muffins with a fork; immediately drizzle hot lemon glaze over top and let stand 25 to 30 minutes. Remove muffins from pan and serve or wrap for freezer.

Shopping List:

PRODUCE	BAKING
Lemon	19-oz. pkg. fat-free blueberry muffin mix
	Sugar

NUTRITION PER SERVING Calories 198 • Fat 0 g • Carbohydrates 57 g • Protein 1 g • Cholesterol 0 mg • Dietary Fiber 3 g • Sodium 435 mg
EXCHANGES 4 other carb
CARB CHOICES 4

Super Tip: *Preliminary research indicates that 8 to 10 glasses of water a day could significantly ease back and joint pain for up to 80 percent of sufferers.*

Lemon–Poppy Seed Muffins

Easy—Do Ahead—Freeze

◆ Serves: 12

2 cups reduced-fat baking mix
¾ cup sugar
1 tbsp. baking powder
1 tbsp. grated lemon zest
½ cup egg substitute
½ cup skim milk
½ tsp. lemon extract
1 tsp. poppy seeds

Preheat oven to 350°F. Spray a 12-cup muffin pan with cooking spray. Combine baking mix, sugar, baking powder and lemon zest in a medium bowl; mix well. Stir in egg substitute, milk and lemon extract until blended; fold in poppy seeds. Fill muffin cups three-fourths full; bake 15 to 18 minutes, until toothpick inserted in centers comes out clean.

Shopping List:

PRODUCE	BAKING	Lemon extract
Lemon	Reduced-fat baking mix (Bisquick or store brand)	Poppy seeds
DAIRY		
4 oz. egg substitute	Sugar	
4 oz. skim milk	Baking powder	

NUTRITION PER SERVING Calories 126 • Fat 1.6 g (11%) •
Carbohydrates 27 g • Protein 3 g • Cholesterol <1 mg • Dietary Fiber <1 g •
Sodium 351 mg
EXCHANGES 1½ other carb
CARB CHOICES 2

Super Tip: *Poppy seeds that are commonly sold in supermarkets do not contain the natural alkaloids that serve as painkillers, because they are lost when the seed ripens, leaving only trace amounts. Poppy seeds are excellent sprinkled on salads, bread and rolls.*

Orange Cranberry Bread

Easy—Do Ahead—Freeze

• Serves: 16

¼ cup mixed berry applesauce
¾ cup orange juice
¼ cup egg substitute
¾ cup sugar
¾ tsp. vanilla extract
1 tbsp. grated orange zest
2 cups all-purpose flour
1½ tsp. baking powder
½ tsp. baking soda
1½ cups chopped fresh or dried cranberries

BREADS AND MUFFINS

Preheat oven to 350°F. Spray a 9 × 5-inch loaf pan with cooking spray. Combine applesauce, orange juice, egg substitute, sugar and vanilla in a large bowl; blend with electric mixer until creamy and smooth. Add orange zest; stir to combine. Add flour, baking powder and baking soda to applesauce mixture and mix until ingredients are blended. Fold in cranberries. Spoon batter into loaf pan; bake 45 to 50 minutes, until toothpick inserted in center comes out clean. Cool slightly before removing from pan and slicing.

Shopping List:

PRODUCE	DAIRY	BAKING
16-oz. pkg. fresh cranberries or 12-oz. pkg. dried cranberries)	Egg substitute	All-purpose flour
		Sugar
Orange	CANNED	Baking powder
	6-oz. can orange juice	Baking soda
	Mixed berry applesauce	Vanilla extract

NUTRITION PER SERVING Calories 107 • Fat .2 g (2%) •
Carbohydrates 25 g • Protein 2 g • Cholesterol 0 mg • Dietary Fiber 1 g •
Sodium 62 mg
EXCHANGES 1½ other carb
CARB CHOICES 2

Super Tip: *You can substitute raisins or dates for chopped cranberries.*

Sour Cream–Herb Bread

Easy—Do Ahead

• Serves: 8

2½ cups all-purpose flour
1½ tsp. baking powder
2½ tbsp. sugar
⅛ tsp. dried basil
⅛ tsp. dried rosemary
⅛ tsp. dried thyme
¾ tsp. salt
¾ cup nonfat sour cream
¾ cup lite beer

Preheat oven to 350°F. Spray a 9 × 5-inch loaf pan or 9-inch square baking dish with cooking spray. Combine flour, baking powder, sugar, basil, rosemary, thyme and salt in a large bowl; add sour cream and beer and mix until ingredients are blended. Spoon batter into prepared pan; bake 45 to 60 minutes, until browned on top and hollow-sounding when tapped.

Shopping List:

DAIRY	SEASONINGS	OTHER
6 oz. nonfat sour cream	Dried basil	12-oz. can lite beer
	Dried rosemary	
PACKAGED	Dried thyme	
All-purpose flour	Salt	
Sugar		
Baking powder		

NUTRITION PER SERVING Calories 178 • Fat .3 g (2%) •
Carbohydrates 36 g • Protein 6 g • Cholesterol 0 mg • Dietary Fiber 1 g •
Sodium 278 mg
EXCHANGES 2 starch • ½ other carb
CARB CHOICES 2

Super Tip: *Thyme tea makes an excellent remedy for sore throats and hangovers. Lightly crush 5 fresh or dried leaves in a cup and fill with water cooled to just below boiling. Cover the cup and infuse for 5 minutes. Remove leaves and drink.*

Southwest Honey Cornbread

Easy—Do Ahead—Freeze   ◆ Serves: 12

14.5-oz. package fat-free honey cornbread mix
1 cup water
½ cup Southwest-style salsa with corn and beans
1½ tbsp. canned chopped jalapeño chiles

Preheat oven to 400°F. Spray an 8-inch square baking pan with cooking spray. Combine cornbread mix, water, salsa and chiles in a medium bowl. Pour batter into prepared pan; bake 20 to 25 minutes, until knife inserted in center comes out clean.

BREADS AND MUFFINS

Shopping List:

PACKAGED	CANNED	CONDIMENTS
14.5-oz. pkg. Krusteaz fat-free honey cornbread mix or any nonfat or low-fat cornbread mix	4-oz. can chopped jalapeño chiles	4 oz. Southwest-style salsa with corn and beans

NUTRITION PER SERVING Calories 121 • Fat 0 g • Carbohydrates 27 g • Protein 2 g • Cholesterol 0 mg • Dietary Fiber 1 g • Sodium 432 mg
EXCHANGES 2 starch
CARB CHOICES 2

Super Tip: *Drinking at least 5 glasses of water daily decreases the risk of colon cancer by 45%, breast cancer by 79% and bladder cancer by 50%.*

Vegetable-Cheese Cornbread

Easy

• Serves: 8

14.5-oz. package fat-free cornbread mix
1¼ cups water or amount recommended on cornbread mix package
2 cups shredded nonfat cheddar cheese
10-oz. pkg. frozen chopped broccoli, thawed and well drained

Preheat oven to 350°F. Spray a 9-inch baking dish with cooking spray. Combine cornbread mix and water according to package directions. Stir in cheese and broccoli; mix well. Spread batter in baking dish; bake 20 to 25 minutes, until toothpick inserted in center comes out clean. Serve warm.

Shopping List:

DAIRY	FROZEN	PACKAGED
8 oz. shredded nonfat cheddar cheese	10-oz. pkg. frozen chopped broccoli	14.5-oz. pkg. Krusteaz fat-free cornbread mix or fat-free honey cornbread mix

NUTRITION PER SERVING Calories 237 • Fat 0 g • Carbohydrates 45 g • Protein 12 g • Cholesterol 0 mg • Dietary Fiber 3 g • Sodium 908 mg
EXCHANGES 2½ starch • 1 vegetable • ½ very lean meat
CARB CHOICES 3

Super Tip: *What makes broccoli a superfood? It is a good source of folic acid, vitamin K, Vitamin C, riboflavin (vitamin B₂) and and niacin (vitamin B₃).*

Walnut–Dried Cranberry Bread

Easy—Do Ahead—Freeze　　　　　　　　　　　　　⬧ Serves: 16

1 lb. frozen bread dough
¾ cup dried cranberries
2 tbsp. chopped walnuts
Cinnamon sugar for topping

Thaw bread dough in refrigerator overnight. Spray a 9 × 5-inch loaf pan with cooking spray. Knead dried cranberries and walnuts into bread dough until well combined. Shape into loaf and place in loaf pan. Spray a piece of plastic wrap with cooking spray. Cover dough with plastic wrap, sprayed side down; let dough rise about 2 hours, until doubled in size.

　　Preheat oven to 375°F. Sprinkle top of bread with cinnamon sugar mixture; spray lightly with cooking spray. Bake 30 to 35 minutes; cover with foil. Bake 10 to 15 minutes, until loaf is lightly browned and sounds hollow when tapped. Remove bread from pan and place on wire rack. Cool 10 to 15 minutes before slicing.

Shopping List:

FROZEN	PACKAGED	BAKING
1 lb. frozen bread dough	Dried cranberries	Cinnamon sugar mixture
	Chopped walnuts	or cinnamon plus
		sugar

NUTRITION PER SERVING Calories 230 · Fat 3 g (12%) ·
Carbohydrates 41 g · Protein 6 g · Cholesterol 0 mg · Dietary Fiber 3 g ·
Sodium 373 mg
EXCHANGES 2 starch · 1 fruit
CARB CHOICES 3

Super Tip: *Walnuts contain ellagic acid, an antioxidant that helps fight cancer by getting rid of the free radicals that reduce the body's ability to protect itself from harmful diseases.*

FAST-FIX FISH AND SEAFOOD WITH SALSAS AND SAUCES

❖

❖ ❖ ❖

Fish Facts for Selecting, Storing and Serving

How much fish should I figure per person?
Allow ⅓ to ½ pound for steaks or fillets, ¾ pound for fish with fins and skin.

What's the difference between a fish steak and a fish fillet?
A fillet generally comes with the skin on and is a section of a full-size fish. A fish steak is a cross-section of the whole fish, is usually skinless, and tends to be thicker than fillets.

How long can I refrigerate or freeze fish?
Fresh fish is best eaten on the day of purchase but can be refrigerated up to 2 days before using. Fish wrapped in freezer paper can be frozen for up to 3 months. Allow 1 day to thaw frozen fish in the refrigerator. Frozen fish can also be placed in a resealable plastic bag and immersed in cold water until thawed.

What's the best way to cook fish?
Cook quickly on high heat.

How can I tell when fish is done cooking?
Fish should reach an internal temperature of 145°F. As a general rule, cook fish at 450° for 10 minutes per inch of thickness, turning the fish halfway through cooking time. Add 5 minutes if you are cooking the fish in a foil packet or sauce. Double the cooking time for fish that is frozen (20 minutes per inch). Fish is done when it flakes easily when tested with a fork and loses its translucent or raw appearance.

Do I cook stuffed and unstuffed fish for the same length of time?
Measure fish at its thickest part after it is stuffed or rolled; cook 10 minutes per inch until fish flakes easily with a fork.

What about fish that is less than ½ inch thick?
Cook as directed but do not turn fish while cooking.

What are the best cooking methods for fish?
- Bake at 450°F (10 minutes per inch): best for whole fish, whole stuffed fish, fillets, stuffed fillets, steaks and fish chunks.

- Broil 2 to 4 inches from heat source; thicker cuts of fish, 5 to 6 inches from heat source (10 minutes per inch): best for steaks, whole fish.
- Grill over moderately hot fire; spray grill with cooking spray to prevent sticking; (10 minutes per inch): best for fish steaks, including salmon, halibut, swordfish and tuna.
- Microwave with thicker parts of fillets pointing outward and thinner parts toward center (3 minutes per pound of boneless fish cooked on High).
- Poach in fish stock or water; bring to a boil; add fish and return to boiling; reduce heat to low and simmer until cooked through (10 minutes per inch.)
- Steam fish on a steamer rack in a large saucepan filled with one inch of water; cover tightly, bring water to a boil and steam until cooked through (10 minutes per inch): best for whole fish, chunks, steaks and stuffed fillets.
- Stir-fry in a small amount of stock, tossing gently to coat on all sides (3 to 5 minutes): best for sliced or cut pieces cooked with variety of vegetables.

Are there special safety precautions when cooking fish?
- Before cooking, rinse fish under running cold water to remove surface bacteria and pat dry with paper towels.
- Always marinate fish in the refrigerator, never at room temperature. Discard marinade after use.
- Thoroughly wash countertops, utensils, cutting surfaces, sponges and hands after handling raw fish.

Super Marinades for Fish Fillets, Steaks and Seafood

Combine 1 cup dry white wine or nonfat vegetable broth, 2 tablespoons drained capers and 2 teaspoons chopped fresh thyme. Use with light fish such as flounder, red snapper, sea bass, trout, cod and Dover sole.

Combine ½ cup dry white wine or water, ¼ cup honey, ¼ cup Dijon mustard and ½ teaspoon dried ginger. Use with firm-textured fish such as tuna, shark and swordfish.

Combine 1 cup pineapple juice, ½ cup crushed juice-packed pineapple and ¼ cup packed light brown sugar. Use with shrimp, tuna steaks and orange roughy.

Baked Halibut on Spinach Leaves

Easy   • Serves: 4

1 lb. halibut fillets
2 (10-oz.) pkgs. fresh spinach leaves
1½ cups tropical salsa

Preheat oven to 450°F. Spray a 9 × 13-inch baking dish with cooking spray; arrange spinach leaves on the bottom of dish. Top with fish fillets. Spoon ¾ cup of the salsa on fish, cover with foil and bake 12 to 15 minutes, until fish flakes easily with a fork. Place remaining salsa in a shallow dish; cover with plastic wrap and microwave on High 45 seconds, until warm. Serve with fish.

Shopping List:

PRODUCE	FISH	CONDIMENTS
2 (10-oz.) pkgs. fresh spinach leaves	1 lb. halibut fillets	12-oz. jar tropical salsa (see Super Tip)

NUTRITION PER SERVING Calories 179 • Fat 3.1 g (16%) •
Carbohydrates 10 g • Protein 28 g • Cholesterol 36 mg • Dietary Fiber 4 g •
Sodium 566 mg
EXCHANGES 2 vegetable • 3½ very lean meat
CARB CHOICES 1

Super Tip: If tropical salsa is not available at your local supermarket, substitute 1 cup of your favorite salsa combined with 8-oz. can pineapple tidbits (drained). Try this recipe with sea bass, grouper, flounder, cod, orange roughy or red snapper.

FISH & SEAFOOD

Baked Halibut with Sesame Coating

Easy—Do Ahead
❖ Serves: 6

1½ lbs. halibut fillets, cut into 6 pieces
3 tbsp. nonfat ranch salad dressing
1½ tsp. lemon pepper
2 tbsp. sesame seeds

Preheat oven to 425°F. Spray a baking dish with cooking spray; arrange fish fillets in a single layer in dish. Drizzle fillets with ranch dressing; sprinkle each fillet with lemon pepper and sesame seeds. Cover with foil; bake 30 to 35 minutes, until fish flakes easily with a fork.

Shopping List:

FISH	CONDIMENTS	SEASONINGS
1½ lbs. halibut fillets	Nonfat ranch salad dressing	Sesame seeds Lemon pepper

NUTRITION PER SERVING Calories 149 • Fat 4 g (24%) •
Carbohydrates 2 g • Protein 24 g • Cholesterol 36 mg • Dietary Fiber <1 g •
Sodium 220 mg
EXCHANGES 4 very lean meat
CARB CHOICES 0

Super Tip: *Halibut is the largest flat fish and can weigh as much as 300 pounds. Mild with a sweet flavor, it has dense, tender, firm flakes. A 4-ounce serving has approximately 110 calories, 23 grams of protein, less than 1 gram of saturated fat and 35 milligrams cholesterol.*

Barbecued Fish Fillets

Easy—Do Ahead

1 lb. fish fillets
1 tsp. garlic powder
¼ cup ketchup
3 tbsp. lemon juice
1 tbsp. Worcestershire sauce
2 tsp. sugar
1 dash hot pepper sauce
2 tsp. onion powder

Spray a 9 × 13-inch baking dish with cooking spray. Arrange fish fillets in dish; sprinkle on both sides with garlic powder. Combine remaining ingredients in a blender; process until smooth. Pour sauce over fish; turn to coat fish on both sides. Cover and refrigerate 30 to 60 minutes. Preheat oven to 400°F. Bake, uncovered, 10 to 15 minutes (10 minutes per 1-inch thickness), until fish flakes easily with a fork. Serve fish with pan juices.

FISH & SEAFOOD

Shopping List:

PRODUCE	CONDIMENTS	SEASONINGS
Lemon	Ketchup	Garlic powder
	Worcestershire sauce	Onion powder
FISH	Hot pepper sauce	
1 lb. fish fillets		
PACKAGED		
Sugar		

NUTRITION PER SERVING Calories 158 • Fat 2.6 g (15%) •
Carbohydrates 9 g • Protein 24 g • Cholesterol 36 mg • Dietary Fiber 0 g •
Sodium 256 mg
EXCHANGES 3 very lean meat • 1 other carb
CARB CHOICES 2

Super Tip: *The American Heart Association has revised its recommendations for healthy eating plans by including 2 weekly servings of fatty fish such as tuna or salmon, including canned tuna and canned salmon.*

Barbecued Salmon

Average—Do Ahead   • Serves: 4

1 mango, peeled, pitted and cut into small cubes
1 cup mango chutney
1 tbsp. minced onion
1 tbsp. roasted minced garlic
28-oz. can crushed tomatoes in juice
2 tbsp. white wine vinegar
1 tbsp. light brown sugar
Dash red pepper flakes
1 lb. salmon fillets
¾ tsp. garlic powder

FISH & SEAFOOD

Combine mango cubes, chutney, onion, garlic, tomatoes with juice, vinegar, brown sugar and red pepper flakes in a medium saucepan. Cover and cook over low heat 20 to 25 minutes, until sauce thickens. Cool 10 to 15 minutes. Pour sauce into a food processor or blender and process until smooth. Cover and refrigerate until ready to use.

Preheat broiler on high heat. Line a baking sheet with foil and spray with cooking spray. Arrange salmon fillets in single layer on baking sheet; sprinkle with garlic powder. Generously brush salmon on both sides with mango barbecue sauce. Broil 8 to 10 minutes; turn salmon over. Brush with sauce; broil 8 minutes, until fish flakes easily with a fork. Microwave remaining sauce on High until boiling and serve with salmon.

Shopping List:

PRODUCE	CANNED	SEASONINGS
Mango	28-oz. can crushed tomatoes	Instant minced onion
FISH		Roasted minced garlic or regular minced garlic
1 lb. salmon fillets	**CONDIMENTS**	
	9-oz. bottle mango chutney	Red pepper flakes
PACKAGED		Garlic powder
Light brown sugar	White wine vinegar	

NUTRITION PER SERVING Calories 393 • Fat 4.3 (10%) •
Carbohydrates 65 g • Protein 25 g • Cholesterol 59 mg • Dietary Fiber 3 g •
Sodium 598 mg
EXCHANGES 3 fruit • 2 vegetable • 1 other carb • 2½ lean meat
CARB CHOICES 4

Super Tip: *Try this recipe with tuna or mahi-mahi fillets.*

Breaded Grouper

Easy

½ cup cornflake crumbs
½ cup all-purpose flour
1 tsp. Old Bay seasoning
½ tsp. garlic powder
½ tsp. dried oregano
¼ tsp. pepper
4 (4-oz.) grouper fillets
½ cup egg substitute

Combine cornflake crumbs, flour, Old Bay seasoning, garlic powder, oregano and pepper in a resealable plastic bag; shake until blended. Spray a large nonstick skillet with cooking spray and heat over medium-high heat. Dip grouper in egg substitute; place in bag with crumb mixture and shake to coat on both sides. Add fish to skillet and cook 3 to 5 minutes; turn fish over and cook 3 to 5 minutes, until lightly browned and cooked through.

FISH & SEAFOOD

Shopping List:

DAIRY	PACKAGED	SEASONING
Egg substitute	Cornflake crumbs	Old Bay seasoning
	All-purpose flour	Garlic powder
FISH		Dried oregano
1 lb. grouper fillets		Black pepper

NUTRITION PER SERVING Calories 215 • Fat 1.3 g (5%) • Carbohydrates 21 g • Protein 27 g • Cholesterol 41 mg • Dietary Fiber <1 g • Sodium 220 mg
EXCHANGES 3 very lean meat • 1½ starch
CARB CHOICES 1

Super Tip: *Substitute tilapia or catfish for grouper.*

Cheese "Tun-a-toes"

Easy   • Serves: 4

4 large baking potatoes, scrubbed
2 (6-oz.) cans tuna packed in water, drained well
2 tbsp. chopped red onion
½ cup nonfat sour cream and onion salad dressing
1 cup shredded nonfat cheddar cheese

Pierce potatoes with a fork in several places. Microwave on High 8 to 9 minutes per potato. Preheat oven to 400°F. Place potatoes in oven 15 minutes to
crisp the skins. Remove potatoes from oven; slice potatoes open and fluff
potato flesh. Combine tuna, onion and salad dressing in a medium bowl;
toss to mix. Divide mixture among potatoes; top with cheddar cheese and
bake 6 to 7 minutes, until cheese is melted and browned.

Shopping List:

PRODUCE	DAIRY	CONDIMENTS
4 large baking potatoes	4 oz. shredded nonfat cheddar cheese	Nonfat sour cream and onion salad dressing
Red onion or 7-oz. container diced red onions	**CANNED** 2 (6-oz.) cans water-pack tuna	

NUTRITION PER SERVING Calories 412 • Fat 2 g (4%) •
Carbohydrates 60 g • Protein 35 g • Cholesterol 36 mg • Dietary Fiber 6 g •
Sodium 895 mg
EXCHANGES 3½ starch • ½ other carb • 3 very lean meat
CARB CHOICES 4

Super Tip: *Substitute nonfat ranch or any creamy salad dressing for the sour
cream and onion dressing.*

Creole-Style Flounder
on a Bed of Rice

Easy   ◆ Serves: 4

1 lb. flounder, cut into 4 pieces	8-oz. can tomato sauce
1½ tsp. garlic powder	½ tsp. dried thyme
1 tbsp. nonfat vegetable broth	⅛ tsp. pepper
16-oz. pkg frozen pepper stir-fry	1 bay leaf
14½-oz. can diced tomatoes with garlic and onion	2 cups cooked rice

Preheat oven to 375°F. Spray a 9 × 13-inch baking dish with cooking spray. Arrange flounder fillets in dish; sprinkle on both sides with garlic powder. Spray a large nonstick skillet with cooking spray; add broth and heat over medium-high heat. Add stir-fry mix and cook, stirring frequently, until vegetables are softened. Add tomatoes, tomato sauce, thyme, black pepper and bay leaf. Bring to a boil over medium-high heat; reduce heat to low and simmer, uncovered, 15 minutes. Pour sauce over flounder and bake 10 to 15 minutes, until fish flakes easily with a fork. Discard bay leaf. Serve over cooked rice.

FISH & SEAFOOD

Shopping List:

FISH	CANNED	SEASONING
1 lb. flounder	14½-oz. can diced tomatoes with garlic and onion	Garlic powder
		Dried thyme
FROZEN		Black pepper
16-oz. pkg. frozen pepper stir-fry mix	8-oz. can tomato sauce	Bay leaf
	Nonfat vegetable broth	
PACKAGED		
Rice		

NUTRITION PER SERVING Calories 352 • Fat 2.5 g (6%) •
Carbohydrates 47 g • Protein 34 g • Cholesterol 77 mg • Dietary Fiber 3 g •
Sodium 981 mg
EXCHANGES 3 very lean meat • 3 vegetable • 2 starch
CARB CHOICES 2

Super Tip: *Tomatoes are packed with the antioxidants beta-carotene, vitamin C and lycopene, all known to protect against sun damage and skin cancer. Cooking tomatoes makes the lycopene more readily available.*

Fish Fillets with Fresh Herbs

Easy

• Serves: 4

1 lbs. fish fillets (halibut, orange roughy, grouper, sole, flounder or red snapper)
¾ cup white wine or nonfat vegetable broth
1 tbsp. finely chopped fresh parsley
1 tbsp. finely chopped fresh chives
1 tbsp. finely chopped fresh thyme
4 green onions, finely chopped

Preheat oven to 375°F. Line a baking pan with cooking spray; arrange fish fillets in a single layer on baking sheet. Pour wine over fish; sprinkle with fresh herbs and green onions. Spray another sheet of foil and lay loosely on top of fish. Bake 15 to 20 minutes, until fish flakes easily with a fork.

Shopping List:

PRODUCE	FISH	OTHER
Parsley	1 lb. fish fillets	White wine or vegetable
Chives		broth
Thyme		
Bunch green onions		

NUTRITION PER SERVING Calories 112 • Fat .8 g (7%) • Carbohydrates 1 g •
Protein 17 g • Cholesterol 23 mg • Dietary Fiber <1 g • Sodium 75 mg
EXCHANGES 2½ very lean meat • ½ other carb
CARB CHOICES 0

Super Tip: *A 4-ounce serving of flounder has 133 calories and 1.7 grams of fat. It is a good source of selenium, a disease-fighting antioxidant.*

Fish Fillets with Onions, Mushrooms and Peppers

Easy

• Serves: 6

1½ lbs. fish fillets, cut into 6 pieces
2 tsp. garlic powder
14½-oz. can diced tomatoes with garlic, oregano and basil, lightly drained
1 cup sliced fresh mushrooms
½ cup diced green bell pepper
½ cup diced onion
½ cup diced celery

Preheat oven to 350°F. Spray a baking dish with cooking spray; arrange fish fillets in a single layer and sprinkle on both sides with garlic powder. Combine remaining ingredients in a medium bowl and mix well. Pour sauce over fish; cover with foil and bake 10 minutes. Remove foil and bake 5 to 10 minutes, until fish flakes easily with a fork.

FISH & SEAFOOD

Shopping List:

PRODUCE	FISH	SEASONINGS
4 oz. sliced mushrooms	1½ lbs. fish fillets	Garlic powder
Green bell pepper or packaged diced peppers		
	CANNED	
Onion or packaged diced onion and celery	14½-oz. can cut tomatoes with garlic, oregano and basil	
Celery		

NUTRITION PER SERVING Calories 131 • Fat 1.1 g (8%) •
Carbohydrates 8 g • Protein 22 g • Cholesterol 49 mg • Dietary Fiber 1 g •
Sodium 403 mg
EXCHANGES 3 very lean meat • 1 vegetable
CARB CHOICES 1

Super Tip: *Two to 3 small mushrooms or 1 reasonable-size white mushroom will supply all of the Vitamin B$_{12}$ you need for an entire day.*

Fish Tostadas

Easy ◆ Serves: 6

1¼-oz. pkg. taco seasoning mix
1 lb. cod fillets
½ cup nonfat sour cream
½ cup nonfat mayonnaise
¼ cup fresh cilantro, chopped fine
12 (6-inch) low-fat corn tortillas
Shredded lettuce, chopped tomatoes and salsa

Preheat broiler on high heat. Line a baking sheet with foil and spray with cooking spray. Remove 2 tablespoons taco seasoning from package and set aside. Sprinkle fish with half of the remaining seasoning. Broil 8 minutes; turn fish over, sprinkle with reserved 2 tablespoons seasoning and broil 5 to 8 minutes, until fish flakes easily with a fork. Combine sour cream, mayonnaise and cilantro in a small bowl; mix well. Preheat oven to 400°F. Heat tortillas in oven 1 to 1½ minutes, until crisp. To serve: Place a tortilla on a plate. Top each tortilla with some of the fish, sour cream mixture, lettuce, tomatoes and salsa, as desired.

FISH &
SEAFOOD

Shopping List:

PRODUCE	FISH	CONDIMENTS
Fresh cilantro	1 lb. cod fillets	Nonfat mayonnaise
Shredded lettuce		Salsa
Tomatoes	**PACKAGED**	
	12 (6-inch) low-fat corn	
DAIRY	tortillas	
4 oz. nonfat sour cream	1¼-oz. pkg. taco	
	seasoning mix	

NUTRITION PER SERVING Calories 273 • Fat 1 g (3%) •
Carbohydrates 40 g • Protein 21 g • Cholesterol 23 mg • Dietary Fiber 3 g •
Sodium 1185 mg
EXCHANGE 2 starch • ½ other carb • 2 very lean meat
CARB CHOICES 3

Super Tip: *The truth about salt: Cutting back on this one little mineral could be the way to stronger bones, a healthier heart and a lot less bloat. Two teaspoons of taco seasoning contain about 410 milligrams of sodium.*

Flounder with Quick Hollandaise Sauce

Easy—Do Ahead

1 lb. flounder fillets
¾ tsp. garlic powder
¾ tsp. Mrs. Dash seasoning
1 cup nonfat sour cream
1 cup nonfat mayonnaise
2 tbsp. lemon juice

Preheat broiler on high heat. Line a baking sheet with foil and spray with cooking spray. Arrange flounder fillets in a single layer on baking sheet; sprinkle with garlic powder and Mrs. Dash seasoning. Broil 6 to 8 minutes; turn fish over and broil 6 to 8 minutes, until fish flakes easily with a fork. Combine sour cream, mayonnaise and lemon juice in a blender and process until smooth. Cover and microwave on High 30 to 45 seconds, until warmed. Serve with cooked fish.

FISH & SEAFOOD

Shopping List:

PRODUCE	FISH	SEASONING
Lemon or lemon juice	1 lb. flounder fillets	Garlic powder
		Mrs. Dash seasoning
DAIRY	CONDIMENTS	
8-oz. container nonfat sour cream	8 oz. nonfat mayonnaise	

NUTRITION PER SERVING Calories 175 • Fat 1.2 g (6%) •
Carbohydrates 13 g • Protein 23 g • Cholesterol 53 mg • Dietary Fiber 0 g •
Sodium 542 mg
EXCHANGES 1 other carb • 3 very lean meat
CARB CHOICES 1

Super Tip: *Try Quick Hollandaise Sauce with broiled, baked or grilled orange roughy, cod or sole.*

Halibut Fillets with Pineapple Salsa

Easy   • Serves: 4

1 lb. halibut steaks
½ cup egg substitute
¾ cup Cajun-style coating mix for fish or chicken
1 cup salsa
1 cup canned crushed pineapple in juice, well drained

Spray a large nonstick skillet with cooking spray and heat over medium heat. Dip halibut in egg substitute and roll in coating mix to coat; place in skillet and cook until browned, 5 minutes. Spray skillet with cooking spray; turn fish and cook 3 to 4 minutes, until browned and fish flakes easily with a fork. Combine salsa and pineapple in bowl; mix well. Place halibut on plates and top with pineapple salsa.

Shopping List:

DAIRY	PACKAGED	CANNED
4 oz. egg substitute	10-oz. pkg. Cajun-style coating for fish or chicken	8-oz. can crushed pineapple in juice
FISH		
1 lb. halibut fillets		**CONDIMENTS**
		8 oz. salsa

NUTRITION PER SERVING Calories 268 • Fat 2.6 g (9%) •
Carbohydrates 27 g • Protein 27 g • Cholesterol 36 mg • Dietary Fiber 1 g •
Sodium 980 mg
EXCHANGES 3 very lean meat • 2 vegetable • ½ fruit • ½ other carb
CARB CHOICES 2

Super Tip: *You can substitute bread crumbs and Cajun seasoning or cornflake crumbs and Cajun seasoning for Cajun-style coating mix.*

Hawaiian Swordfish

Easy

1 lb. swordfish steaks
1 tsp. garlic powder
¾ cup canned crushed pineapple in juice, undrained
1½ tbsp. light brown sugar
⅛ tsp. onion powder
3 tbsp. low-sodium soy sauce

Preheat broiler on high heat. Line a baking sheet with foil and spray with cooking spray. Arrange fish on baking sheet and sprinkle with garlic powder. Combine remaining ingredients in a food processor or blender and process until smooth. Broil fish 6 to 7 minutes; turn fish and spread with pineapple sauce. Broil 3 to 4 minutes, until fish flakes easily with a fork.

FISH & SEAFOOD

Shopping List:

FISH	CONDIMENTS	SEASONINGS
1 lb. swordfish or tuna steaks	Low-sodium soy sauce	Garlic powder
		Onion powder
	BAKING	
CANNED	Light brown sugar	
8-oz. can crushed pineapple in juice		

NUTRITION PER SERVING Calories 194 • Fat 4.6 g (21%) • Carbohydrates 14 g • Protein 23 g • Cholesterol 44 mg • Dietary Fiber <1 g • Sodium 554 mg
EXCHANGES ½ fruit • ½ other carb • 3 very lean meat • ½ fat
CARB CHOICES 1

Super Tip: *A 4-ounce serving of swordfish has 176 calories and 5.9 grams of fat with small amounts of omega-3s.*

Hot 'n' Spicy Barbecue Shrimp

Easy   • Serves: 4

1 lb. uncooked shrimp, peeled and deveined
⅓ cup barbecue sauce
3 tbsp. chunky-style salsa

Preheat broiler on high heat. Line a baking sheet with foil and spray with cooking spray. If using frozen shrimp, thaw first under cold water. Arrange shrimp in a single layer on baking sheet. Combine barbecue sauce and salsa in a small bowl; mix well. Broil shrimp 3 to 4 minutes. Turn shrimp and spread with sauce. Broil 2 to 4 minutes, until shrimp turn pink and curl. Do not overcook.

FISH & SEAFOOD

Shopping List:

FISH	CONDIMENTS
1 lb. uncooked shrimp, peeled and deveined	Barbecue sauce Chunky-style salsa

NUTRITION PER SERVING Calories 140 • Fat 2.3 g (15%) •
Carbohydrates 4 g • Protein 23 g • Cholesterol 175 mg • Dietary Fiber <1 g •
Sodium 398 mg
EXCHANGES 3 very lean meat • ½ other carb
CARB CHOICES 0

Super Tip: *Contrary to popular belief, shrimp does not dramatically raise blood cholesterol levels. A 4-ounce serving has 112 calories and only 1.2 grams of fat.*

Mahi-Mahi with Kiwi-Orange Salsa

Easy—Do Ahead   ◆ Serves: 4

1 lb. mahi-mahi fillets
1 tsp. salt-free spicy seasoning
3 kiwifruit, peeled, sliced and quartered
1 cup canned mandarin orange segments, drained
2 tbsp. canned chopped jalapeño chiles
1 cup chopped onion

Preheat broiler on high heat. Line a baking sheet with foil and spray with
cooking spray. Arrange fish on baking sheet; sprinkle with seasoning. Broil 7
to 8 minutes; turn fish over and broil 7 to 8 minutes, until fish flakes easily
with a fork. While fish is cooking, combine remaining ingredients in bowl
and mix well. Serve over cooked fish.

Shopping List:

PRODUCE	CANNED	SEASONINGS
3 kiwifruit	11-oz. can mandarin	Salt-free spicy
7-oz. container chopped	orange segments	seasoning
onions or whole onion	4-oz. can chopped	
	jalapeño chiles	
FISH		
1 lb. mahi-mahi fillets		

NUTRITION PER SERVING Calories 192 • Fat 1.3 g (7%) •
Carbohydrates 22 g • Protein 22 g • Cholesterol 81 mg • Dietary Fiber 3 g •
Sodium 183 mg
EXCHANGES 1 vegetable • 1 fruit • 3 very lean meat
CARB CHOICES 1

Super Tip: *Available both fresh and frozen, mahi-mahi is a large fish usually
sold as fillets or steaks. Select mahi-mahi with moist, translucent flesh. To store
properly, remove the fish from its packaging, rinse under cold water and pat dry
with paper towels. Fresh mahi-mahi can be stored in the refrigerator for up to
2 days and up to 2 months in the freezer.*

Orange Roughy Italiano

Easy   • Serves: 4

1 lb. frozen orange roughy fillets
¾ tsp. garlic powder
¾ cup tomato and basil pasta sauce
½ cup canned diced tomatoes with basil, oregano and garlic
¼ cup grated nonfat Parmesan cheese

Preheat oven to 425°F. Spray a baking dish with cooking spray. Arrange fish fillets in dish; sprinkle with garlic powder. Combine pasta sauce and diced tomatoes in a small bowl; pour over fish. Cover dish with foil; bake 25 to 30 minutes. Uncover and sprinkle with Parmesan cheese. Bake 5 to 8 minutes, until cheese is melted and lightly browned.

Shopping List:

DAIRY	CANNED	SEASONINGS
Grated nonfat Parmesan cheese	26-oz. jar tomato and basil pasta sauce	Garlic powder
	14½-oz. can diced	
FISH	tomatoes with basil,	
1 lb. frozen orange roughy fillets	oregano and garlic	

NUTRITION PER SERVING Calories 119 • Fat .8 g (6%) • Carbohydrates 7 g • Protein 19 g • Cholesterol 23 mg • Dietary Fiber • <1 g • Sodium 329 mg
EXCHANGES 2½ very lean meat • 1 vegetable
CARB CHOICES 0

Super Tip: *You can substitute any low-fat or nonfat pasta sauce for the tomato and basil sauce and any chopped tomatoes for the ones specified in the recipe. This recipe can also be prepared with cod or halibut.*

Orange Teriyaki Sauce for Fish

Easy

2 tbsp. chopped green onion
½ tsp. garlic powder
¼ tsp. onion powder
3 tbsp. reduced-sodium teriyaki sauce
⅓ cup orange marmalade
1½ tbsp. water

Combine all ingredients in a small bowl and mix until blended. Use as a marinade for fish or chicken; bake, grill or broil as directed in recipe. It's excellent with salmon, tuna, orange roughly or boneless chicken breasts. If not using immediately, cover and refrigerate for up to 1 week.

Shopping List:

PRODUCE	CONDIMENTS	SEASONINGS
Bunch green onions	Reduced-sodium teriyaki sauce	Garlic powder
	Orange marmalade	Onion powder

FISH & SEAFOOD

NUTRITION PER SERVING Calories 86 • Fat 0 g • Carbohydrates 21 g • Protein 1 g • Cholesterol 0 mg • Dietary Fiber <1 g • Sodium 520 mg
EXCHANGES 1 other carb
CARB CHOICES 1

Super Tip: *Researchers who measured serum vitamin C blood levels concluded that including one extra serving a day of vitamin C–rich foods (oranges, kiwifruit, red bell peppers) could cut the risk of mortality by 20 percent. (Source: Lancet, March 2002.)*

Packet Fish Fillets

Easy   • Serves: 4

1 lb. fish fillets, cut into 4 pieces
2 tsp. Mrs. Dash seasoning
4 lemon slices
1 cup chopped carrots
4 tsp. chopped fresh parsley

Preheat oven to 350°F. Tear 4 heavy-duty aluminum foil sheets and spray each with cooking spray. Place one fillet on each foil sheet; sprinkle Mrs. Dash seasoning on both sides. Top each fillet with 1 lemon slice, ¼ cup carrots and 1 tsp. parsley. Fold foil loosely around fish and fold edges to seal. Place packets on a baking sheet. Bake 18 to 20 minutes, until fish flakes easily with a fork.

Shopping List:

PRODUCE	FISH	SEASONINGS
1 lemon	1 lb. fish fillets (halibut,	Mrs. Dash seasoning
2 large carrots	orange roughy, cod)	
Parsley		

NUTRITION PER SERVING Calories 109 • Fat .8 g(7%) •
Carbohydrates 4 g • Protein 21 g • Cholesterol 49 mg • Dietary Fiber 1 g •
Sodium 84 mg
EXCHANGES 2½ very lean meat • 1 vegetable
CARB CHOICES 0

Super Tip: *Parsley leaves, a strong diuretic, can ease the discomfort of premenstrual bloating and jump-start weight loss. Their high vitamin C content also makes them a valuable ally against colds and flu.*

Poached Halibut with Horseradish Sauce

Easy—Do Ahead

1 cup nonfat sour cream
1 tbsp. prepared horseradish
3 tbsp. plus 2 tsp. lemon juice
1 tbsp. plus ¼ tsp. grated lemon zest
½ tsp. sugar
Pepper to taste
3 cups water
2 slices onion
4 sprigs parsley
1 bay leaf
¾ lb. 1-inch-thick halibut fillets

Combine sour cream, horseradish, 2 teaspoons lemon juice, ¼ teaspoon lemon zest, sugar and pepper in a small bowl; mix until blended smooth. Cover and refrigerate 1 to 2 hours before serving.

Combine water, 3 tablespoons lemon juice, 1 tablespoon lemon zest, onion, parsley and bay leaf in a shallow pan or skillet; bring to a boil over high heat. Reduce heat to low and simmer 5 to 10 minutes. Add halibut and simmer, partially covered, for 10 minutes, until fish flakes easily with a fork. Serve poached fish with horseradish sauce.

Shopping List:

PRODUCE	FISH	PACKAGED
Lemon	¾ lb. 1-inch thick halibut	Sugar
Onion	fillets	
Parsley		SEASONINGS
	CONDIMENTS	Bay leaf
DAIRY	Prepared horseradish	Black pepper
8-oz. container nonfat		
sour cream		

NUTRITION PER SERVING Calories 171 • Fat 1.9g (10%) • Carbohydrates 11 g • Protein 24 g • Cholesterol 27 mg • Dietary Fiber <1 g • Sodium 169 mg
EXCHANGES ½ other carb • 3 very lean meat
CARB CHOICES 1

Super Tip: *Lemon, a highly acidic fruit, is not recommended for rheumatoid arthritis sufferers.*

Poached Salmon with Spinach and Cheese

Easy • Serves: 4

1½ cup water
½ cup white wine
1 bay leaf
2 tbsp. chopped green onions
1 lb. salmon fillet, cut into 4 pieces
10-oz. pkg. frozen chopped spinach, cooked and drained
¼ tsp. ground nutmeg
½ cup shredded nonfat mozzarella cheese

FISH & SEAFOOD

Combine water, wine, bay leaf and green onion in a large skillet; bring to a boil over high heat. Carefully add salmon; return to a boil. Reduce heat to low, cover and simmer 8 to 10 minutes, until fish flakes easily with a fork. Remove fish and pat dry. Preheat broiler on high heat. Line a baking sheet with foil and spray with cooking spray. Sprinkle spinach with nutmeg and mix lightly. Arrange fish on baking sheet; top with spinach and sprinkle with cheese. Broil 1 to 2 minutes, until cheese is melted and lightly browned.

Shopping List:

PRODUCE	FISH	SEASONINGS
Green onions	1 lb. salmon fillet	Bay leaf
		Ground nutmeg
DAIRY	**FROZEN**	
Shredded nonfat	10-oz. pkg. frozen	**OTHER**
mozzarella cheese	chopped spinach	White wine

NUTRITION PER SERVING Calories 188 • Fat 5.2g (25%) •
Carbohydrates 4 g • Protein 25 g • Cholesterol 33 mg • Dietary Fiber 2 g •
Sodium 203 mg
EXCHANGES 3 very lean meat • 1 vegetable
CARB CHOICES 0

Super Tip: *Chicken or vegetable broth can be substituted for wine.*

Poached Salmon with Mustard-Dill Sauce

Easy—Do Ahead
♦ Serves: 4

¾ cup nonfat sour cream
¼ cup Dijon mustard
1 tsp. dried dill
½ tsp. onion powder
½ tsp. sugar
¾ lb. 1-inch-thick salmon fillets

3 cups water
½ cup white wine vinegar
½ cup sliced onion
1 rib celery
1 bay leaf
Pepper to taste

Combine sour cream, mustard, dill, onion powder and sugar in a small bowl; mix until blended creamy and smooth. Cover and refrigerate 30 to 60 minutes.

Wrap salmon in a double thickness of aluminum foil and seal tightly. Combine water, vinegar, onion, celery, bay leaf and pepper in a shallow pan or skillet; bring to a boil over high heat; boil 5 minutes. Reduce heat to low and simmer 5 to 10 minutes. Add wrapped salmon and simmer 10 minutes, until fish flakes easily with a fork. Remove from pan and serve with mustard-dill sauce.

Shopping List:

PRODUCE	CONDIMENTS	SEASONINGS
Onion	Dijon mustard	Dried dill
Celery	White wine vinegar	Onion powder
		Bay leaf
DAIRY	**PACKAGED**	Black pepper
6 oz. nonfat sour cream	Sugar	
FISH		
¾ lb. 1-inch-thick salmon fillets		

NUTRITION PER SERVING Calories 187 • Fat 4.4g (21%) • Carbohydrates 17 g • Protein 20 g • Cholesterol 44 mg • Dietary Fiber <1 g • Sodium 322 mg
EXCHANGES 1 other carb • 3 lean meat
CARB CHOICES 1

Super Tip: *Salmon is higher in fat than other fish, but it's unsaturated fat, which helps lower blood cholesterol. According to a recent Harvard study, men eating 3 to 4 ounces of fish a week had half the risk of heart attack than men who did not eat any fish (Source:* Runner's World, *Sept. 2000).*

Salsa-Style Fish Fillets

Easy ♦ Serves: 4

1 lb. frozen halibut fillets
¾ tsp. Southwest seasoning
1 cup Southwest-style salsa with corn and beans
½ cup shredded nonfat mozzarella cheese

Preheat oven to 425°F. Spray a shallow baking dish with cooking spray; arrange fish fillets in a single layer in dish. Sprinkle fillets with Southwest seasoning; pour salsa over top. Cover dish and bake 25 to 30 minutes. Uncover dish; sprinkle with cheese and bake 5 to 8 minutes, until cheese is melted and lightly browned.

Shopping List:

DAIRY	CONDIMENTS	SEASONINGS
Shredded nonfat mozzarella cheese	8 oz. Southwest-style salsa with corn and beans	Southwest seasoning
FISH		
1 lb. frozen halibut fillets		

NUTRITION PER SERVING Calories 164 • Fat 2.6 g (14%) •
Carbohydrates 3 g • Protein 29 g • Cholesterol 36 mg • Dietary Fiber < 1 g •
Sodium 350 mg
EXCHANGES 4 very lean meat • 1 vegetable
CARB CHOICES 0

Super Tip: *Substitute any Mexican or salt-free spicy seasoning, or a blend of black pepper, red pepper, chili powder, cumin and garlic for Southwest seasoning.*

Shrimp Stir-Fry

Easy   ◆ Serves: 4

¾ cup nonfat vegetable broth
½ cup water
16-oz. pkg. frozen sugar snap pea
    stir-fry mix
¼ cup low-sodium soy sauce
1 tbsp. sugar
2 cups instant rice
1 lb. peeled, cooked baby shrimp

Combine vegetable broth, water, stir-fry mix, soy sauce and sugar in a large saucepot; stir to mix. Bring to a boil over high heat. Stir in rice; cover pot and remove from heat. Let stand 5 minutes, until liquid is absorbed. Add shrimp and toss to combine. Cook 5 minutes over medium heat and serve immediately.

Shopping List:

FISH	PACKAGED	CANNED
1 lb. peeled, cooked baby shrimp	Instant rice Sugar	Nonfat vegetable broth
		CONDIMENTS
FROZEN		Low-sodium soy sauce
16-oz. pkg. frozen sugar snap pea stir-fry mix or favorite stir-fry vegetable mix		

NUTRITION PER SERVING Calories 354 • Fat 2.5 g (6%) • Carbohydrates 49 g • Protein 32 g • Cholesterol 175 mg • Dietary Fiber 1 g • Sodium 926 mg
EXCHANGES 2 starch • ½ other carb • 2 vegetable • 2½ very lean meat
CARB CHOICES 3

Super Tip: *Save money, not time. Select uncooked shrimp and boil as directed on package. Follow recipe as directed.*

Shrimp, Tomato and Feta Cheese Bake

Easy—Do Ahead · Serves: 4

2 (14½-oz.) cans diced tomatoes with garlic, oregano and basil, lightly drained
¼ tsp. garlic powder
½ tsp. Italian seasoning
½ tsp. red pepper flakes
1 lb. peeled, deveined, uncooked shrimp
4 oz. reduced-fat feta cheese crumbles

Combine tomatoes, garlic powder, Italian seasoning and red pepper flakes in a medium saucepan; bring to a boil over high heat. Reduce heat to low and simmer 5 to 10 minutes, until sauce is slightly thickened.

Preheat oven to 350°. Spray a 9 × 13-inch baking dish with cooking spray. Spread half the tomato sauce in bottom of dish; top with shrimp and remaining sauce. Sprinkle feta cheese on top; bake 15 to 20 minutes, until shrimp turn pink and casserole is bubbling hot.

Shopping List:

DAIRY	CANNED	SEASONINGS
4 oz. reduced-fat feta cheese crumbles	2 (14½-oz.) cans diced tomatoes with garlic, oregano and basil	Garlic powder Italian seasoning Red pepper flakes
FISH		
1 lb. peeled, deveined, uncooked shrimp		

NUTRITION PER SERVING Calories 219 · Fat 2.7 g (12%) ·
Carbohydrates 16 g · Protein 32 g · Cholesterol 175 mg · Dietary Fiber <1 g ·
Sodium 1623 mg
EXCHANGES 4 very lean meat · 3 vegetable
CARB CHOICES 1

Super Tip: *Lycopene, a powerful antioxidant, is responsible for giving tomatoes their red color. A study conducted at the University of North Carolina at Chapel Hill demonstrated that men who consumed diets high in lycopene were half as likely to suffer a heart attack as those who ate little or no lycopene. Tomato sauce is an excellent source of lycopene.*

FISH & SEAFOOD

Simple Salmon Steaks

Easy ◆ Serves: 4

1 lb. salmon fillets
¾ tsp. onion powder
½ tsp. garlic powder
¼ tsp. lemon pepper
1 tbsp. lemon juice
¼ tsp. dried basil

Preheat broiler on high heat. Line a baking sheet with foil and spray with cooking spray. Arrange salmon fillets on baking sheet. Combine remaining ingredients. Sprinkle fillets with half of the seasoning mixture and broil 8 minutes. Turn fillets and sprinkle with remaining seasonings. Broil 6 to 8 minutes, until fish flakes easily with a fork.

Shopping List:

PRODUCE	FISH	SEASONINGS
Lemon or lemon juice	1 lb. salmon fillets	Onion powder
		Garlic powder
		Lemon pepper
		Dried basil

NUTRITION PER SERVING Calories 136 • Fat 3.9 g (26%) • Carbohydrates 1 g • Protein 23 g • Cholesterol 59 mg • Dietary Fiber 0 g • Sodium 95 mg
EXCHANGES 4 very lean meat
CARB CHOICES 0

Super Tip: *Research suggests that women with higher tissue levels of omega-3s have lower rates of breast cancer. Two to three servings of omega-3-rich salmon per week help lower blood pressure, reduce the risk of stroke and cancer and diminish symptoms associated with rheumatoid arthritis. (Source: www. healthatoz.com.)*

Spicy Cod with Tomatoes and Green Chiles

Easy ◆ Serves: 4

1 lb. cod fillets, cut into 1-inch chunks
1 tbsp. lime juice
1 tbsp. nonfat vegetable broth
2 cups frozen pepper stir-fry mix
¼ tsp. minced roasted garlic
½ tsp. cayenne pepper
14½-oz. can diced tomatoes with green chiles, drained

Spray a large nonstick skillet with cooking spray. Sprinkle cod chunks with lime juice and set aside. Add vegetable broth to skillet and heat over medium-high heat. Add stir-fry mix and garlic; cook, stirring frequently, until vegetables are softened. Add cayenne and mix. Stir in cod and tomatoes; bring to a boil over high heat. Reduce heat to low, cover and simmer until fish flakes easily, 4 to 5 minutes.

Shopping List:

PRODUCE	FROZEN	SEASONINGS
4-oz. jar roasted minced garlic	16-oz. pkg. frozen pepper stir-fry mix	Cayenne pepper
Lime or lime juice		
	CANNED	
FISH	Nonfat vegetable broth	
1 lb. cod fillets	14½-oz. can diced tomatoes with green chiles	

NUTRITION PER SERVING Calories 124 • Fat .8 g (6%) • Carbohydrates 7 g • Protein 21 g • Cholesterol 49 mg • Dietary Fiber 1 g • Sodium 488 mg
EXCHANGES 2½ very lean meat • 1½ vegetable
CARB CHOICES 0

Super Tip: *Substitute 14½-oz. to 15-oz. can chopped tomatoes plus 2 tablespoons minced green chiles for diced tomatoes with green chiles. Substitute any minced garlic, garlic powder or freshly minced garlic for roasted minced garlic.*

PAMPERED POULTRY
AND MEAT DISHES

❖

❖ ❖ ❖

Salt-Free Ways to Season for Spectacular Flavor:
Variety . . . the Ultimate Spice of Life

Herbs, spices and salt-free seasoning blends bring out the best flavors without adding sugar, salt, fat or calories. Packed with phytochemicals, seasonings, herbs and spices help to protect against chronic diseases, boost the immune system and decrease the risk of cardiovascular disease, high blood pressure and cancer. A single tablespoon of fresh oregano equals the antioxidant protection of a whole apple. Here are some tips for turning lackluster food into mouthwatering meals while boosting your intake of disease-fighting antioxidants.

1. Add dried herbs and spices at the beginning of cooking so the flavor can intensify throughout the cooking process.
2. Add fresh herbs the last few minutes of cooking.
3. To substitute fresh and dried herbs: 1 tablespoon finely cut fresh herbs = 1 teaspoon dried leafy herbs = ¼ to ½ teaspoon ground dried herbs.
4. When you double or triple a recipe, *do not* double or triple the herbs or spices. Add 1½ times as much of the herb or spice; taste and add more as needed.
5. Keep spices away from heat and light.
6. Keeping herbs fresh:

   - Moist herbs spoil quickly; wash just before using.
   - If herbs are wet, wrap in paper towels or pat until leaves are dry.
   - If leaves wilt, put in an ice water bath to revive them.
   - Store unbagged herbs away from naturally ripening fruits and vegetables such as bananas, tomatoes and peppers.
   - Strong leaves (arugula, oregano, rosemary, sage, thyme) keep up to 2 weeks when stored in a self-sealing plastic bag in the refrigerator's vegetable crisper.
   - Delicate leaves (basil, chervil, dill, tarragon) should be stored with stems or roots in a jar of water and leaves covered with a plastic bag.

7. To freeze fresh herbs: Wash and cut herbs into pieces that will fit in ice-cube tray compartments. Fill tray with herbs, add water to cover and freeze. Transfer frozen herb cubes to plastic freezer bags, label and use as needed.

8. Storing dried herbs:

- Use within 6 months to a year.
- Whole spices stay fresh longer than ground.
- Freshly ground spices are stronger than those that are purchased ground.
- Whole spices keep for up to 2 years under ideal conditions.
- Ground spices keep for 6 months to a year under ideal conditions.

SUBSTITUTES FOR SALT AND SUGAR

Instead of	Try
Salt	Black or cayenne pepper · Coriander · Cumin · Curry powder · Garlic · Ginger · Shallots
Sugar	Allspice · Cinnamon · Cloves · Ginger · Nutmeg · Peppermint

SEASONING/SPICE	BEST USED FOR
Allspice	Fish (boiled or steamed) · Soups · Stews · Vegetables (cabbage, carrots, eggplant, squash, sweet potatoes, tomatoes, onions) · Curries · Cakes, breads, pies · Poached fruits
Basil	Italian cuisine · Tomato-based sauces · Soups · Pasta dishes · Chicken · Beef · Fish and shellfish · Salad greens · Eggs (scrambled) · Vegetables (broccoli, Brussels sprouts, cabbage, green beans, onions, peas, squash, tomatoes, mixed green and tomato salads) · Herb vinegars · Basil also has blends nicely with other herbs and spices such as parsley, rosemary, oregano, thyme, sage and saffron.
Bay leaf	Soups and stews · Beef · Poultry · Meats · Marinades · Sauces · Casseroles · Vegetables (carrots, tomatoes, water for cooking potatoes)
Caraway	Cheese · Sausages · Cabbage dishes · Soups · Pork · Breads · Cheese · Rich fruit cakes
Cardamom	Indian and Middle Eastern curries · Pastries, cakes, quick breads · Meat · Poultry · Fish
Cayenne pepper	Egg and cheese dishes · Baked goods
Chili powder	Indian, Mexican, Cajun, Caribbean and Creole cuisine · Chiles · Seafood
Chives	Eggs · Cheese · Salads · Creamy soups · Fish · Potatoes

POULTRY & MEAT DISHES

SEASONING/SPICE	BEST USED FOR
Cilantro Cilantro is sometimes called fresh coriander. The spice coriander is the seeds of the cilantro plant and is often used in baked goods for a unique flavor.	Soups and stews · Chicken · Fish · Meat · Vegetables · Relishes · Tomato-based sauces
Cinnamon	Desserts · Breads · Rice dishes · Coffee · Vegetables (sweet potatoes, pumpkin, winter squash, spinach) · Puddings · Fruit (baked and stewed apples, apricots, peaches, pineapple or cranberries) · Chocolate
Coriander	Indian and Oriental cuisine · Meat dishes · Chicken · Vegetable dishes · Salsa · Baked goods (breads, cakes, pastries, custards)
Cumin	East Indian and Mexican cuisines · Meat dishes · Vegetable dishes · Relishes · Salads · Soups and stews · Chili · Couscous · Curries · Rice pilafs
Curry powder	Dips · Salad dressings · Stir-fries · Poultry
Dill	Fish or seafood · Omelets · Soups · Potato salad · Breads · Cabbage · Meat stews · Rice · Chicken · Salad dressings or dips · Soft cheese
Dry mustard	Fish · Meat · Salads
Fennel seed	Fish · Pork · Vegetables · Breads · Soups · Salads · Cakes
Garlic (minced, crushed or powder)	Almost anything from meat, poultry or fish to vegetables, soups, stews and more
Ginger	Oriental and Indian cuisines · Chicken · Baked goods · Vegetables (pumpkin, carrots, beets, peas, sweet potatoes, winter squash) · Fruits (broiled grapefruit, pears, melon, rhubarb and compotes)
Marjoram	French, Italian and Greek dishes · Fish (baked, broiled) · Meat · Eggs (omelets, scrambled, egg salads) · Vegetables (green beans, lima beans, carrots, eggplant, peas, potatoes, mixed green and vegetable salads, summer squash, onions, zucchini, tomatoes) · Fruit (fruit salad or fruit cup)
Mint	Cucumber · Potatoes · Chilled soups · Yogurt
Mustard seed	Indian cuisine · Mustard blends · Accent sauces, meats, stews and dressings

POULTRY & MEAT DISHES

Seasoning/Spice	Best Used For
Nutmeg	Baked goods (cakes, breads, cookies) · Puddings, custards · Meat dishes · Vegetable dishes (squash, green beans, asparagus, beets, broccoli, Brussels sprouts, cabbage, cauliflower, peas, carrots) · Egg and cheese dishes · Stuffed pastas
Oregano	French and Italian cuisines, especially in tomato-based sauces · Stew · Salad dressings · Pizza · Vegetables (green beans, broccoli, cabbage) · Eggs (boiled, omelets)
Paprika	Eastern European cuisine · Soups and stews · Meat · Chicken · Fish · Vegetables · Eggs
Parsley	Garnish · Tomato-based sauces · Vegetables · Salads · Potatoes · Omelets · Fish · Soups
Pepper (black, crushed red, ground red, white)	Almost anything—add to personal taste!
Rosemary	Meat · Fish (salmon) · Poultry · Stews · Root vegetables · Eggs (scrambled, omelets) · Vegetables (green beans, cauliflower, lima beans, onions, peas, potatoes, summer squash) · Sauces · Bread
Sage	Pork · Stuffing · Sausage · Tomato sauces · Turkey · Risotto · Pasta
Savory	Legumes · Meat · Fish (especially trout) · Sausage · Stuffing · Tomato sauces
Tarragon	French cuisine · Salad dressings and herb vinegars · Baked or poached chicken or fish · Soups and stews · Sauces · Meat · Chicken · Fish (broiled) · Egg dishes · Vegetables (asparagus, green beans, broccoli, cabbage, carrots, mushrooms, peas, mixed green salads, spinach, tomatoes)
Thyme	Poultry · Beef · Fish · Soup · Sauces · Stuffing · Eggs · Casseroles · Roasted potatoes
Turmeric	Curry powders · Rice · Chutneys

POULTRY & MEAT DISHES

Seasoning Blends
- All-purpose
- Italian
- Mexican
- Cajun
- Lemon pepper
- Taco seasoning mix
- Fajita seasoning mix

Make Your Own Seasoning Blends	Combine These Ingredients in Food Processor or Blender and Store in Airtight Containers
All-purpose seasoning blend	2½ tbsp. dried parsley, 1½ tbsp. dried oregano, 1¼ tbsp. dried paprika, 1 tbsp. dried celery seed, 1 tsp. dried chile pepper, 1 tbsp. dried mustard seed, 1½ tsp. dried marjoram, 1½ tsp. garlic powder, ¾ tsp. dried savory, ½ tsp. dried thyme and ½ tsp. chili powder
Allspice substitute	½ tsp. ground cinnamon and ½ tsp. ground cloves = 1 tsp. ground allspice
Apple pie spice	½ tsp. ground cinnamon, ¼ tsp. ground nutmeg and ⅛ tsp. ground cardamom
Cajun	1 tsp. ground thyme, 2 tsp. paprika, 1 tsp. dried oregano, 1 tsp. garlic powder, ¼ tsp. ground cumin, ½ tsp. ground nutmeg, ½ tsp. salt, ¼ tsp. cayenne pepper and ¼ tsp. black pepper
Chili powder	1 cup dried red pepper flakes, ¼ cup ground cumin, 2 tbsp. garlic powder, 1 tbsp. dried oregano and 1 tbsp. cayenne pepper = 1¼ cups
Chili seasoning (use 3 tablespoons mix per pound of ground beef, chicken or turkey)	¼ cup ground cayenne, ¼ cup paprika, 2 tbsp. dried minced onion, 4 tsp. cumin seeds, 2 tsp. dried oregano, 1 tsp. garlic powder, 1 tsp. crushed dried red pepper and 2 tsp. salt
Chinese five-spice powder	3 tbsp. ground cinnamon, 2 tsp. aniseed, 1½ tsp. fennel seed, 1½ tsp. black pepper and ¾ tsp. ground cloves
Creole seasoning	2½ tbsp. paprika, 2 tbsp. garlic powder, 1 tbsp. onion powder, 1 tbsp. dried oregano, 1 tbsp. dried thyme, 1 tbsp. cayenne pepper, 1 tbsp. black pepper and 1 tbsp. salt
Curry spice mix	⅓ cup ground black pepper, ¼ cup ground cumin, 3 tbsp. dry mustard, 3 tbsp. ground turmeric, 3 tbsp. curry powder, 1½ tbsp. ground cardamom, 1½ tbsp. ground coriander, 1 tbsp. ground mace, 1 tsp. ground nutmeg, 1 tbsp. ground cinnamon, 1 tbsp. ground cloves and 1½ tsp. cayenne pepper = 1½ cups
Italian seasoning	1 tbsp. each oregano, basil and thyme
Lemon-pepper seasoning	Grated lemon zest from 1 lemon and 2 tbsp. cracked black peppercorns
Poultry seasoning	2 tbsp. dried marjoram, 2 tbsp. dried savory, 2 tsp. dried parsley, 1 tbsp. dried sage and 1½ tsp. dried thyme

Make Your Own Seasoning Blends	Combine These Ingredients in Food Processor or Blender and Store in Airtight Containers
Pumpkin pie spice	½ tsp. ground cinnamon, ¼ tsp. ground ginger, ⅛ tsp. ground allspice and ⅛ tsp. ground nutmeg = 1 teaspoon
Salt-free herb substitute	2 tbsp. dried basil, 2 tbsp. dried parsley, 2 tbsp. dried marjoram, 2 tbsp. dried savory, 2 tsp. ground rosemary, 2 tsp. sweet paprika, 2 tsp. onion granules (not powder) and 2 tsp. nonfat powdered milk = ⅔ cup
Salt-free seasoning	5 tsp. onion powder, 1 tbsp. garlic powder, 1 tbsp. paprika, 1 tbsp. dry mustard, 1 tsp. dried thyme, ½ tsp. white pepper and ½ tsp. celery seed = ¼ cup • OR • 6 tbsp. dried parsley, ¼ cup dried oregano, ¼ cup onion powder, 2 tbsp. dried basil, 2 tsp. garlic powder, 1 tsp. dried rosemary, 1 tsp. dried thyme, 1 tsp. dried sage and ½ tsp. cayenne pepper = 1⅓ cups
Seasoning salt	1 cup salt, 1 tsp. paprika, 1 tsp. black pepper, 1 tsp. white pepper, ½ tsp. celery salt and ½ tsp. garlic salt
Taco seasoning	2 tbsp. chili powder, 5 tsp. paprika, 4½ tsp. ground cumin, 1 tbsp. onion powder, 1 tbsp. salt, 2½ tsp. garlic powder and ⅛ tsp. cayenne pepper

POULTRY &
MEAT DISHES

Bacon and Egg Tortilla Wraps

Easy—Do Ahead   • Serves: 4

1½ tbsp. nonfat vegetable broth
16-oz. pkg. roasted onion and potato cubes
1 cup Southwest egg substitute
4 slices low-fat turkey bacon, cooked, drained and crumbled
4 (8-inch) low-fat flour tortillas
1 cup shredded nonfat cheddar cheese
½ cup Southwest-style salsa with beans and corn

Spray a large skillet with cooking spray; add vegetable broth and heat over medium-high heat. Add potato cubes and cook until lightly browned. Add egg substitute and crumbled bacon; cook until eggs are set but still moist. Wrap tortillas in paper towel; microwave on High 45 to 60 seconds until warm. Fill each tortilla with potato-egg mixture; top with ¼ cup cheese and 2 tbsp. salsa. Fold tortillas around filling and serve immediately.

Shopping List:

DAIRY
8 oz. Southwest egg
    substitute
4 oz. shredded nonfat
    cheddar cheese

REFRIGERATED
16-oz. pkg. roasted
    onion and potato
    cubes

MEAT
12-oz. pkg. low-fat
    turkey bacon

PACKAGED
17.5-oz. pkg. 8-inch low-
    fat flour tortillas

CANNED
Nonfat vegetable broth

CONDIMENTS
Southwest-style salsa

NUTRITION PER SERVING Calories 327 • Fat 1 g (3%) • Carbohydrates 52 g • Protein 24 g • Cholesterol 15 mg • Dietary Fiber 5 g • Sodium 1326 mg
EXCHANGES 3 starch 3 • 1 vegetable • 2 very lean meat
CARB CHOICES 3

Super Tip: *You can use any egg substitute for Southwest egg substitute; any precooked and cubed potatoes for roasted onion and potato cubes; and any salsa for the Southwest variety.*

Baked Chicken with Cream Sauce

Easy—Do Ahead   • Serves: 6

1 cup nonfat cottage cheese
2 tsp. onion powder
2 tbsp. lemon juice
2 tbsp. Dijon mustard
1 tsp. lemon-pepper seasoning
½ tsp. Italian seasoning
1½ lbs. boneless, skinless chicken breasts
2 tsp. garlic powder
1 cup cornflake crumbs

Combine cottage cheese, onion powder, lemon juice, mustard, lemon-pepper seasoning and Italian seasoning in a food processor or blender; process until smooth and creamy. Spray an 8- or 9-inch baking dish with cooking spray. Arrange chicken breasts in baking dish; sprinkle with garlic powder. Pour sauce over chicken and turn to coat on all sides. Cover and refrigerate at least 4 hours or overnight.

Preheat oven to 400°F. Sprinkle cornflake crumbs over chicken and turn to coat. Bake 25 to 30 minutes, until chicken is golden brown and cooked through.

Shopping List:

PRODUCE	PACKAGED	SEASONINGS
Lemon or lemon juice	Cornflake crumbs	Onion powder
		Lemon-pepper
DAIRY	**CONDIMENTS**	seasoning
8 oz. nonfat cottage	Dijon mustard	Italian seasoning
cheese		Garlic powder
MEAT		
1½ lbs. boneless,		
skinless chicken		
breasts		

NUTRITION PER SERVING Calories 255 • Fat 5 g (18%) •
Carbohydrates 16 g • Protein 33 g • Cholesterol 86 mg • Dietary Fiber 0 g •
Sodium 440 mg
EXCHANGES 1 starch • 4 very lean meat • 1 fat
CARB CHOICES 1

Super Tip: *Cottage cheese is packed with nourishing minerals, vitamins and protein, which may help protect against osteoporosis, insomnia and headaches, and may also boost the immune system.*

POULTRY &
MEAT DISHES

Barbecue Chicken Tortilla Pizza

Easy   ◆ Serves: 4

4 (8-inch) low-fat flour tortillas
1 cup low-fat barbecued shredded chicken
1 cup chopped red onion
1 cup chopped bell pepper
2 cups shredded nonfat mozzarella cheese

Preheat oven to 400°F. Line baking sheet(s) with foil and spray with cooking spray. Arrange tortillas in a single layer on baking sheet; top each tortilla with ¼ cup of the chicken. Sprinkle each tortilla with ¼ cup of the onion, ¼ cup of the bell peppers and ½ cup of the cheese. Bake 10 to 12 minutes, until cheese is melted and lightly browned.

Shopping List:

PRODUCE	DAIRY	PACKAGED
1 red onion or 7-oz. container diced red onion	½ lb. shredded nonfat mozzarella cheese	17.5-oz. pkg. 8-inch low-fat flour tortillas
1 bell pepper or diced tri-pepper mix	**MEAT** 32-oz. pkg. barbecued shredded chicken	

NUTRITION PER SERVING Calories 341 • Fat 5.5 g (15%) • Carbohydrates 38 g • Protein 31 g • Cholesterol 40 mg • Dietary Fiber 3 g • Sodium 927 mg
EXCHANGES 3 lean meat • 2 starch • 1 vegetable
CARB CHOICES 3

Super Tip: Make your own mix of barbecued shredded chicken by baking, broiling or grilling chicken and mixing with your favorite variety of barbecue sauce.

Chicken and Black Bean Tacos

Easy   • Serves: 4

2 cups chunky-style salsa
3 tbsp. canned chopped green chiles
8¾-oz. can low-fat black beans, rinsed and drained
10-oz. can chunk white chicken in water, drained and flaked
8 (6-inch) corn tortillas
1 cup shredded lettuce
½ cup diced tomatoes with green chiles, drained
1 cup shredded nonfat cheddar cheese

Combine 1 cup of the salsa, green chiles and black beans in a medium
saucepan; heat over medium-high heat, stirring frequently, until heated
through. Add chicken and heat 3 to 5 minutes. Heat tortillas in 350°F oven
for 1 to 2 minutes; remove from oven and fold in half. Fill tortillas with
chicken mixture, lettuce, tomatoes, cheese and remaining salsa, as desired.

Shopping List:

PRODUCE	CANNED	CONDIMENTS
6-oz. pkg. shredded iceberg lettuce	4-oz. can chopped green chiles	16-oz. jar chunky-style salsa
DAIRY	8¾-oz. can low-fat black beans	
4 oz. shredded nonfat cheddar cheese	10-oz. can chunk white chicken in water	
PACKAGED	14½-oz. can diced tomatoes with green chiles	
6-inch corn tortillas		

NUTRITION PER SERVING Calories 363 • Fat 2.5 g (6%) •
Carbohydrates 46 g • Protein 37 g • Cholesterol 32 mg • Dietary Fiber 6 g •
Sodium 1678 mg
EXCHANGES 3 vegetable • 2 starch • 3½ very lean meat
CARB CHOICES 3

*Super Tip: Legumes have been eaten around the world for more than 10,000
years—and even today they remain a popular, healthy and versatile food.
Legumes are high in dietary fibers, low in saturated fat and cholesterol free.*

POULTRY &
MEAT DISHES

Chicken and Rice

Easy—Do Ahead

1 lb. boneless, skinless chicken breasts
½ tsp. garlic powder
½ tsp. onion powder
¾ tsp. Mrs. Dash seasoning
10¾-oz. can low-fat cream of chicken, celery or mushroom soup
1⅔ cups water
1½ cups instant rice, uncooked
16-oz. pkg. frozen vegetable mix of choice

Preheat broiler on high heat. Line a baking sheet with foil and spray with cooking spray. Arrange chicken breasts in a single layer on baking sheet; sprinkle with garlic powder, onion powder and Mrs. Dash seasoning. Broil 10 minutes; turn chicken over and broil 8 to 10 minutes, until cooked through. Slice chicken and set aside. Combine soup and water in a medium saucepan; bring to a boil over high heat. Stir in rice and vegetables. Cover and reduce heat to low; cook until rice is done and vegetables are tender-crisp. Add chicken and cook until heated through.

Shopping List:

FROZEN	PACKAGED	SEASONINGS
16-oz. pkg. frozen mixed vegetables of choice (broccoli, cauliflower, carrots)	14-oz. pkg. instant rice	Garlic powder
		Onion powder
	CANNED	Mrs. Dash seasoning
	10¾-oz. can low-fat cream of chicken, celery or mushroom soup	
MEAT		
1 lb. boneless, skinless chicken breasts		

NUTRITION PER SERVING Calories 375 • Fat 6.3 g (17%) •
Carbohydrates 41 g • Protein 36 g • Cholesterol 86 mg • Dietary Fiber 3 g •
Sodium 373 mg
EXCHANGES 3 very lean meat • 2 starch • 2 vegetable • 1 fat
CARB CHOICES 3

Super Tip: *One glass of water will shut down midnight hunger pangs for almost 100 percent of dieters, reported in a University of Washington study.*

Chicken Breasts in Dijon Sauce

Easy   ◆ Serves: 4

1 lb. boneless, skinless chicken breast tenders
¾ tsp. garlic powder
¾ tsp. onion powder
1 cup nonfat mayonnaise
2 tbsp. Dijon mustard
2 tbsp. nonfat chicken broth

Preheat broiler on high heat. Line a baking sheet with foil and spray with cooking spray. Arrange chicken tenders on baking sheet; season with garlic powder and onion powder. Broil 5 to 6 minutes; turn chicken over and broil 5 to 6 minutes, until cooked through. Combine mayonnaise, Dijon mustard and chicken broth in a medium bowl; cover and microwave on High 1 minute. Stir sauce; microwave 1 to 1½ minutes, until heated through. Serve on the side with chicken tenders.

Shopping List:

MEAT	CONDIMENTS	SEASONINGS
1 lb. boneless, skinless chicken breast tenders	8 oz. nonfat mayonnaise Dijon mustard	Garlic powder Onion powder
CANNED 14½-oz. can nonfat chicken broth		

NUTRITION PER SERVING Calories 175 • Fat 1.2 • Carbohydrates 14 • Protein 26 • Cholesterol 57 • Dietary Fiber 0 • Sodium 749
EXCHANGES 1 other carb • 3 very lean meat
CARB CHOICES 1

Super Tip: *Removing the skin from a whole chicken before cooking reduces the fat grams by about half. However, the skin adds moisture and protects lean meat from drying out. You will get the best results by cooking the poultry with the skin on, then removing it before serving.*

Chicken with Mushrooms and Artichokes

Average   ◆ Serves: 6

1 cup uncooked white rice	¼ tsp. pepper
3 tbsp. plus ½ cup nonfat chicken broth	14-oz. can artichoke hearts, well drained
8 oz. sliced fresh mushrooms	½ cup white wine
1½ lb. boneless, skinless chicken breast tenders	1 tsp. curry powder
1½ tsp. garlic powder	1 tbsp. all-purpose flour
	1 cup nonfat sour cream

Cook rice according to package directions; keep warm. Spray a large nonstick skillet with cooking spray. Add 2 tablespoons broth and heat over medium-high heat. Add mushrooms; cook, stirring frequently, until golden brown. Remove mushrooms from skillet and set aside. Spray skillet again; add 1 tablespoon chicken broth and heat over medium-high heat. Add chicken tenders; sprinkle with garlic powder and pepper. Cook chicken, stirring frequently, until browned on all sides. Return mushrooms to skillet; add artichoke hearts, ½ cup broth and wine. Bring to a boil over high heat. Reduce heat to medium-low; stir in curry powder. Combine flour and sour cream and whisk until blended. Add slowly to chicken mixture and cook over low heat, stirring constantly, until heated through. Serve chicken over hot rice.

POULTRY & MEAT DISHES

Shopping List:

PRODUCE	PACKAGED	SEASONINGS
8 oz. sliced mushrooms	All-purpose flour	Garlic powder
	White rice	Black pepper
DAIRY		Curry powder
8 oz. nonfat sour cream	CANNED	
	14½-oz. can nonfat chicken broth	OTHER
MEAT		White wine
1½ lb. boneless, skinless chicken breast tenders	14-oz. can artichoke hearts	

NUTRITION PER SERVING Calories 314 • Fat 1 g (3%) • Carbohydrates 39 g • Protein 34 g • Cholesterol 57 mg • Dietary Fiber 3 g • Sodium 375 mg
EXCHANGES 3 very lean meat • 1 starch • 1 other carb • 2 vegetable
CARB CHOICES 3

Super Tip: *Although considered a vegetable, an artichoke is actually the plant's flower bud. Fat-free and low in sodium, a 12-ounce artichoke has only 25 calories.*

Chicken-Asparagus Casserole

Easy—Do Ahead   • Serves: 6

10¾-oz. can low-fat cream of chicken, mushroom or celery soup
1 cup nonfat sour cream
1 cup grated nonfat Parmesan cheese
8 oz. linguine, cooked and drained
2 (10-oz) pkgs. frozen asparagus cuts, thawed and drained
2 cups cubed, cooked chicken breast

Preheat oven to 350°F. Spray a 2-quart casserole with cooking spray. Combine soup, sour cream, ¾ cup of the Parmesan cheese, linguine, asparagus and chicken in a large bowl; mix lightly. Spoon into casserole and sprinkle with remaining Parmesan cheese. Bake 25 to 30 minutes, until bubbly hot and lightly browned on top.

Shopping List:

DAIRY	FROZEN	CANNED
8 oz. nonfat sour cream	2 (10-oz.) pkgs.	10¾-oz. can low-fat
4 oz. grated nonfat	asparagus cuts	cream of chicken,
Parmesan cheese		mushroom or celery
	PACKAGED	soup
MEAT	8-oz. pkg. linguine	
12 oz. cooked chicken		
breast cuts		

NUTRITION PER SERVING Calories 327 • Fat 3.7 g (10%) •
Carbohydrates 45 g • Protein 27 g • Cholesterol 32 mg • Dietary Fiber 2 g •
Sodium 951 mg
EXCHANGES 3 very lean meat • 2 starch • 1 vegetable • ½ other carb
CARB CHOICES 3

Super Tip: *Noodles were actually the culinary creation of the Chinese, not Italians, dating back to 100 B.C.*

Chicken Paella

Easy

1½ tbsp. plus 3 cups nonfat chicken broth
1 cup frozen pepper stir-fry mix
2 tsp. minced garlic
1 lb. cubed, cooked chicken breast
3 cups instant rice
10-oz. pkg. frozen peas and carrots

Spray a large nonstick skillet with cooking spray; add 1½ tablespoons chicken broth to skillet and heat over medium-high heat. Add pepper stir-fry mix and garlic; cook 2 to 3 minutes, until vegetables are softened. Add the remaining 3 cups broth and bring to a boil over high heat. Stir in chicken, rice and peas and carrots; cover and reduce heat to low. Cook 5 to 8 minutes, until liquid is absorbed and rice is cooked.

Shopping List:

MEAT	FROZEN	PACKAGED
1 lb. cooked chicken breast cuts or 1 lb. boneless, skinless chicken breasts	16-oz. pkg. frozen pepper stir-fry mix (or 10-oz. pkg. frozen bell peppers and 10-oz. pkg. frozen chopped onions)	Instant rice
		CANNED
		2 (14½-oz.) cans nonfat chicken broth
	10-oz. pkg. frozen peas and carrots	SEASONINGS
		Minced garlic

POULTRY & MEAT DISHES

NUTRITION PER SERVING Calories 218 • Fat 1.9 g (8%) • Carbohydrates 30 g • Protein 19 g • Cholesterol 40 mg • Dietary Fiber 2 g • Sodium 923 mg
EXCHANGES 3 vegetable • 1 starch • 2 very lean meat
CARB CHOICES 2

Super Tip: *Ounce for ounce, red bell peppers have three times the Vitamin C of citrus fruit. They are also a great source of beta-carotene, fiber and vitamin B₆.*

Chili-Dog Casserole

Easy

[•] Serves: 6

8 fat-free hot dogs, thinly sliced
15-oz. can low-fat or nonfat chili
¼ cup frozen chopped onion, thawed
1 tbsp. prepared mustard
2 cups shredded nonfat cheddar cheese
3 low-fat hamburger buns or French bread rolls, lightly toasted

Preheat oven to 350°F. Spray a 9 × 13-inch baking dish with cooking spray. Place sliced hot dogs in bottom of dish; top with chili, onion, mustard and cheese. Bake 25 to 30 minutes until bubbly hot. To serve, place half a hamburger bun on each plate and top with chili-dog mixture.

Shopping List:

MEAT	FROZEN	CANNED
14-oz. pkg. fat-free hot dogs	12-oz. pkg. frozen chopped onions	15-oz. can low-fat or nonfat chili
DAIRY	**PACKAGED**	**CONDIMENTS**
½ lb. shredded nonfat cheddar cheese	Low-fat hamburger buns or French bread rolls	Prepared mustard

POULTRY & MEAT DISHES

NUTRITION PER SERVING Calories 239 • Fat 1.3 g (5%) •
Carbohydrates 29 g • Protein 23 g • Cholesterol 20 mg • Dietary Fiber 3 g •
Sodium 1417 mg
EXCHANGES 2 starch • 2½ very lean meat
CARB CHOICES 2

Super Tip: *Research links onions to a reduced risk of cancer. A study measuring the intake of more than 200 foods found that onions were most strongly associated with lower rates of lung cancer (Source:* Journal of National Cancer Institute, *2000).*

Chicken-Cheese Tortilla Soup

Easy

8 cups water
9-oz. pkg. tortilla soup mix
8-oz. chicken breast, cooked and cubed
½ cup canned Mexican-style corn, drained well
1 cup diced tomatoes with green chiles
½ cup frozen chopped onion
1 cup shredded nonfat cheddar cheese
4 oz. baked tortilla chips, broken into small pieces

Bring the water to a boil in a large soup pot. Shake soup mix to separate ingredients; add to boiling water and whisk until blended. Add chicken, corn, tomatoes and onion; cook over low heat 15 to 20 minutes. Add cheese to soup and heat until cheese is melted. Ladle soup into bowls and top with tortilla chips.

Shopping List:

DAIRY	MEAT	CANNED
4 oz. shredded nonfat cheddar cheese	½ lb. boneless, skinless chicken breasts or tenders	14½-oz. can petite-diced tomatoes with green chiles
FROZEN		11-oz. can Mexican-style corn
12-oz. pkg. frozen chopped onions	**PACKAGED**	
	9-oz. pkg. tortilla soup mix	
	Baked tortilla chips	

POULTRY & MEAT DISHES

NUTRITION PER SERVING Calories 311 • Fat 3.2 g (9%) •
Carbohydrates 53 g • Protein 23 g • Cholesterol 26 mg • Dietary Fiber 5 g •
Sodium 1921 mg
EXCHANGES 1 very lean meat • 2 vegetable • 2 starch • 1 other carb
CARB CHOICES 4

Super Tip: *You can use any brand of tortilla soup mix, but use the amount of water specified on the package. Substitute regular or low-sodium corn kernels for the Mexican-style corn and diced tomatoes and chopped green chiles for the tomatoes with green chiles.*

Chili Enchilada Wraps

Easy ◆ Serves: 4

1.5-oz. pkg. dry enchilada sauce mix
8-oz. can tomato sauce
1½ cups water
4 (8-inch) low-fat flour tortillas
15-oz. can low-fat or nonfat chili with or without beans
1½ cups shredded nonfat cheddar cheese
4 tsp. canned chopped green chiles

Preheat oven to 350°F. Line a baking pan with foil and spray with cooking spray. Combine enchilada sauce mix, tomato sauce and water in a small saucepan; bring to a boil over high heat. Reduce heat to low and simmer while preparing chili wraps. Spoon 2 to 3 tablespoons chili down center of each tortilla. Sprinkle with ¼ cup cheese and 1 teaspoon green chiles. Fold tortilla around filling and place, seam side down, in baking pan. Pour enchilada sauce over tortillas; sprinkle with remaining cheese. Bake 15 to 20 minutes, until bubbly hot and lightly browned.

Shopping List:

DAIRY	PACKAGED	CANNED
6 oz. shredded nonfat cheddar cheese	17.5-oz. pkg. low-fat flour tortillas 1.5-oz. pkg. dry enchilada sauce mix	15-oz. can low-fat or nonfat chili with or without beans 4-oz. can chopped green chiles 8-oz. can tomato sauce

NUTRITION PER SERVING Calories 307 • Fat .5 g (1%) •
Carbohydrates 49 g • Protein 22 g • Cholesterol 0 mg • Dietary Fiber 5 g •
Sodium 1947 mg
EXCHANGES 1 vegetable • 3 starch • 1½ very lean meat
CARB CHOICES 3

Super Tip: *Find dry enchilada sauce mix with all the packaged seasonings in your supermarket or substitute low-fat canned enchilada sauce for seasoning packet, water and tomato sauce.*

Chinese Chicken Stir-Fry

Average   ◆ Serves: 4

1 lb. boneless, skinless chicken breast tenders
½ cup bottled stir-fry sauce
2 tbsp. nonfat chicken or vegetable broth
16-oz. pkg. frozen vegetable stir-fry mix
1 cup frozen pepper strips
10-oz. pkg. shredded Chinese cabbage
¼ cup water

Combine chicken and stir-fry sauce in a medium bowl; toss until coated. Spray a large nonstick skillet or wok with cooking spray; add 1 tablespoon of the broth and heat over medium-high heat until hot. Add frozen vegetable mix and peppers to skillet; cook, stirring frequently, until tender-crisp, 5 to 6 minutes. Remove from skillet and set aside. Add remaining broth to skillet and heat over medium-high heat; add cabbage. Cook, stirring constantly, until cabbage softens. Add cabbage to vegetable mixture. Re-spray skillet with cooking spray; add chicken and cook, stirring frequently, until no longer pink, 4 to 5 minutes. Return vegetables to skillet; pour in water and cook 1 to 3 minutes, until heated through. Serve immediately.

POULTRY & MEAT DISHES

Shopping List:

PRODUCE	FROZEN	CANNED
10-oz. pkg. shredded Chinese cabbage	16-oz. pkg. frozen vegetable stir-fry mix (select vegetables of choice)	Nonfat chicken or vegetable broth
MEAT	16-oz. pkg. frozen pepper strips	**CONDIMENTS**
1 lb. boneless, skinless chicken breast tenders		Bottled stir-fry sauce

NUTRITION PER SERVING Calories 257 · Fat .5 g (2%) ·
Carbohydrates 33 g · Protein 30 g · Cholesterol 57 mg · Dietary Fiber 3 g ·
Sodium 1157 mg
EXCHANGES 3 very lean meat · 3 vegetable · 1 other carb
CARB CHOICES 2

Super Tip: *Cooking your veggies increases iron absorption. A Rutgers University study found that the absorption from broccoli with 1.3 milligrams of iron per cup, jumped from 6 percent in the raw state to 30 percent when cooked.*

Cooktop Turkey and Rice

Easy—Do Ahead   • Serves: 6

1½ cups long-grain rice
2 tbsp. nonfat chicken broth
1 cup frozen chopped bell peppers
¾ cup frozen chopped onion
1 tbsp. celery flakes
1½ lbs. turkey breast tenderloin, cut into 1-inch cubes
14½-oz. can Mexican-style stewed tomatoes, drained

Cook rice according to package directions; keep warm. Spray a large skillet with cooking spray; add chicken broth and heat over medium-high heat. Add bell peppers, onion and celery flakes and cook until softened, 3 to 4 minutes. Add turkey and cook, stirring frequently, until turkey is lightly browned. Add tomatoes. Cover, reduce heat to low and simmer 20 to 25 minutes, until turkey is completely cooked through. Serve over hot cooked rice.

Shopping List:

MEAT	PACKAGED	SEASONINGS
1½ lbs. turkey breast tenderloin	Long-grain rice	Celery flakes
FROZEN	**CANNED**	
10-oz. pkg. frozen diced peppers	14½-oz. can Mexican-style stewed tomatoes	
12-oz. pkg. frozen chopped onions		

NUTRITION PER SERVING Calories 318 • Fat .8 g (2%) •
Carbohydrates 44 g • Protein 32 g • Cholesterol 68 mg • Dietary Fiber 1 g •
Sodium 248 mg
EXCHANGES 2 vegetable • 2 starch • 3 very lean meat
CARB CHOICES 3

Super Tip: *Substitute any low-fat chicken breast tenders for the turkey breast tenderloin.*

Easy Cheesy Barbecue Beef Fries

Easy

4 medium baking potatoes, each cut into 8 wedges
4 tsp. salt-free spicy seasoning
1 lb. extra-lean ground beef
½ cup barbecue sauce
1 cup shredded nonfat cheddar cheese

Preheat oven to 400°F. Line baking sheet(s) with foil and spray with cooking spray; arrange potato wedges on baking sheet(s). Sprinkle potatoes with spicy seasoning; bake 20 to 25 minutes, until cooked through. Spray non-stick skillet with cooking spray; add ground beef and cook, stirring frequently, until browned and cooked through. Add barbecue sauce; cook until hot and bubbly, 3 to 4 minutes, Pour meat sauce over potato wedges; top with cheese and bake 5 to 6 minutes, until cheese is melted.

Shopping List:

PRODUCE	MEAT	SEASONINGS
4 medium baking potatoes	1 lb. extra-lean ground beef (4% fat)	Salt-free spicy seasoning
DAIRY	**CONDIMENTS**	
4 oz. shredded nonfat cheddar cheese	Barbecue sauce	

POULTRY & MEAT DISHES

NUTRITION PER SERVING Calories 372 • Fat 4.7 g (11%) •
Carbohydrates 46 g • Protein 32 g • Cholesterol 61 mg • Dietary Fiber 4 g •
Sodium 549 mg
EXCHANGES 2½ starch • ½ other carb • 3 lean meat
CARB CHOICES 3

Super Tip: *Substitute extra-lean ground turkey or textured soy protein for ground beef.*

Garlic Chicken Rolls

Easy—Do Ahead   • Serves: 4

4 boneless, skinless chicken breast fillets
¾ to 1 lb. fresh thin asparagus spears, trimmed and cleaned
¾ tsp. Mrs. Dash seasoning
Pepper to taste
2 tbsp. minced roasted garlic
8 oz. sliced fresh mushrooms
2 tbsp. nonfat chicken broth

Preheat oven to 375°F. Line a baking sheet with foil and spray with cooking spray. Roll each chicken fillet around 2 to 3 asparagus spears; insert toothpick to hold chicken together and place, seam side down, on baking sheet. Sprinkle chicken with Mrs. Dash seasoning and pepper. Top chicken with garlic and mushrooms; drizzle with chicken broth. Bake 25 to 30 minutes, until chicken is cooked through.

Shopping List:

PRODUCE	MEAT	SEASONINGS
¾ to 1 lb. thin asparagus spears	1 lb. boneless, skinless chicken breasts	Mrs. Dash seasoning Black pepper
4 oz. roasted minced garlic		
	CANNED	
8 oz. sliced mushrooms	Nonfat chicken broth	

NUTRITION PER SERVING Calories 218 • Fat 3.9 g • Carbohydrates 8 • Protein 35 • Cholesterol 85 • Dietary Fiber 2 • Sodium 89
EXCHANGES 2 vegetable • 5 very lean meat
CARB CHOICES 1

Super Tip: *Garlic belongs to the onion family and is one of the oldest cultivated plants in the world. For optimum health, consume 1 to 2 cloves per day, or choose an odorless garlic supplement.*

Hamburger Potato Hash

Easy   • Serves: 4

1 lb. extra-lean ground beef
1 cup frozen chopped onion, thawed
1 lb. 4-oz. pkg. diced potatoes with onion
2 tbsp. beef bouillon granules
Water

Spray a large saucepan with cooking spray. Add beef and onion; cook over medium heat, stirring frequently, until meat is no longer pink. Add potatoes, bouillon granules and enough water to cover. Cover saucepan and cook over low heat 25 to 30 minutes, until water has evaporated.

Shopping List:

PRODUCE	FROZEN	SEASONINGS
1 lb 4-oz. pkg. diced potatoes with onion	12-oz. pkg. frozen chopped onions	Beef bouillon granules
MEAT		
1 lb. extra-lean ground beef (4% fat)		

NUTRITION PER SERVING Calories 291 • Fat 4.6 g (14%) • Carbohydrates 33 g • Protein 25 g • Cholesterol 61 mg • Dietary Fiber 3 g • Sodium 733 mg
EXCHANGES 1½ starch • 2 vegetable • 2½ meat • 1 fat
CARB CHOICES 2

Super Tip: *Cooked potato cubes, shreds and slices can be found in the produce or refrigerated section of the supermarket.*

Honey Mustard Sauce

Easy—Do Ahead   • Serves: 8

¼ cup prepared mustard
1 cup honey
1 tbsp. barbecue sauce

Combine all ingredients in a small bowl; blend well. Cover and refrigerate until ready to serve with sandwiches, chicken tenders or burgers.

Shopping List:

CONDIMENTS
Mustard
Honey
Barbecue sauce

NUTRITION PER SERVING Calories 139 • Fat .2 g (1%) •
Carbohydrates 34 g • Protein <1 g • Cholesterol 0 mg • Dietary Fiber <1 g •
Sodium 115 mg
EXCHANGES 2 other carb
CARB CHOICES 2

Super Tip: *Gram for gram, honey is as rich in antioxidants as some fruits and veggies.*

Lemon Chicken and Rice

Easy • Serves: 4

1 lb. chicken breast tenders, cut into 1-inch pieces
1 tsp. garlic powder
¾ tsp. onion powder
14½-oz. can nonfat chicken broth
2 cups instant rice
¾ cup shredded carrots
2 tsp. grated lemon peel

Spray a large nonstick skillet with cooking spray. Add chicken tenders; sprinkle with garlic powder and onion powder. Cook chicken over medium-high heat, stirring frequently, until browned and cooked through, 7 to 8 minutes. Add broth, rice, carrots and lemon peel; bring to a boil over high heat. Reduce heat to low, cover and let stand 5 minutes, until rice is tender. Serve immediately.

Shopping List:

PRODUCE	PACKAGED	SEASONINGS
8-oz. pkg. shredded carrots or 1 to 2 whole carrots	Instant rice	Garlic powder
		Onion powder
Lemon	CANNED	
	14½-oz. can nonfat chicken broth	
MEAT		
1 lb. chicken breast tenders		

POULTRY & MEAT DISHES

NUTRITION PER SERVING Calories 291 • Fat .7 g (2%) • Carbohydrates 39 g • Protein 30 g • Cholesterol 57 mg • Dietary Fiber 2 g • Sodium 539 mg
EXCHANGES 2 starch • 1 vegetable • 3 very lean meat
CARB CHOICES 3

Super Tip: One cooked carrot has approximately 150 percent of the recommended daily amount of beta-carotene, which is converted into vitamin A. Vitamin A helps to prevent night blindness, dry skin, poor bone growth, weak tooth enamel, diarrhea and slow growth.

Old-New Country Casserole

Average—Do Ahead

• Serves: 6

1 lb. extra-lean ground beef
1½ tsp. onion powder
½ tsp. garlic powder
¾ tsp. Mrs. Dash seasoning
6-oz. can Italian tomato paste with roasted garlic
1 cup seasoned tomato sauce for meat loaf

8-oz. can corn kernels, drained
14½-oz. can diced tomatoes with garlic and onion
1½ cups yolk-free egg noodles, cooked and drained
1½ cups shredded nonfat mozzarella cheese

Spray a large nonstick skillet with cooking spray and heat over medium-high heat. Add beef, onion powder, garlic powder and Mrs. Dash seasoning. Cook, stirring frequently, until meat is browned. Add tomato paste, tomato sauce, corn and tomatoes with liquid; mix well.

Preheat oven to 350°F. Spray a 2-quart casserole with cooking spray. Spoon beef mixture into dish; add noodles and toss until mixed. Bake 15 minutes; remove from oven and top with cheese. Bake 15 to 20 minutes, until cheese is melted and lightly browned.

Shopping List:

DAIRY
6 oz. shredded nonfat mozzarella cheese

MEAT
1 lb. extra-lean ground beef

PACKAGED
8-oz. pkg. yolk-free noodles

CANNED
6-oz. can Italian tomato paste with roasted garlic

14½-oz. can seasoned tomato sauce for meat loaf
8-oz. can corn kernels
14½-oz. can diced tomatoes with garlic and onion

NUTRITION PER SERVING Calories 366 • Fat 3.9 g (10%) • Carbohydrates 48 g • Protein 32 g • Cholesterol 41 mg • Dietary Fiber 6 g • Sodium 1319 mg
EXCHANGES 2 vegetable • 2½ starch • 3 very lean meat • ½ fat
CARB CHOICES 3

Super Tip: *Substitute a 6-ounce can tomato paste and ½ teaspoon garlic powder for Italian tomato paste and/or any tomato or pasta sauce for that specified in recipe.*

Pineapple Chicken Tenders

Easy—Do Ahead   • Serves: 4

1 lb. boneless, skinless chicken tenders
1½ tsp. garlic powder
8-oz. can pineapple chunks in juice
¼ cup low-sodium soy sauce
1 cup cornflake crumb

Preheat oven to 350°F. Line a baking sheet with cooking spray. Arrange chicken tenders in a single layer on baking sheet; sprinkle with garlic powder. Drain pineapple juice into a medium bowl; add soy sauce and mix until blended. Brush chicken tenders on both sides with soy mixture. Generously sprinkle both sides of chicken with cornflake crumbs. Lightly spray with cooking spray. Place pineapple chunks on and around chicken. Bake 20 to 25 minutes, until chicken is tender and cooked through.

Shopping List:

MEAT	PACKAGED	CONDIMENTS
1 lb. boneless, skinless chicken tenders or chicken breasts cut into slices	Cornflake crumbs	Low-sodium soy sauce
	CANNED	**SEASONINGS**
	8-oz. can pineapple chunks in juice	Garlic powder

POULTRY & MEAT DISHES

NUTRITION PER SERVING Calories 300 • Fat 4.9 (15%) •
Carbohydrates 27 g • Protein 34 g • Cholesterol 85 mg • Dietary Fiber <1 g •
Sodium 899 mg
EXCHANGES 3 lean meat • 1 starch • 1 fruit
CARB CHOICES 2

Super Tip: Pineapples are jam-packed with potassium, sodium, phosphorus, magnesium, sulfur, calcium, iron, iodine and choline. They have loads of vitamins including vitamin C and are an excellent source of bromelain, an enzyme that helps digestion and has been associated with curing laryngitis or soothing a sore throat.

Southwestern Turkey Casserole

Average—Do Ahead ♦ Serves: 8

1½ lbs. extra-lean ground turkey
2 tbsp. instant minced onion
2 (11-oz.) cans Mexican-style corn
28-oz. can tomato sauce
8 cups nonfat plain croutons

1½ cups Southwest egg substitute
2 cups skim milk
1 tbsp. Italian seasoning
2 cups shredded nonfat mozzarella cheese

Spray a large nonstick skillet with cooking spray; add turkey and onion. Cook over medium-high heat, stirring frequently, until turkey is browned and cooked through. Remove skillet from heat. Stir in corn and tomato sauce and mix well. Preheat oven to 350°F. Spray a 9 × 13-inch baking dish with cooking spray. Place half of the croutons in the bottom of the dish. Top with turkey-corn mixture. In a medium bowl, combine egg substitute, milk and Italian seasoning; beat until blended. Pour over meat mixture and top with remaining croutons. Cover top of casserole with cheese. Spray a large sheet of foil with cooking spray; place, sprayed side down, on casserole to cover. Bake for 45 minutes. Remove cover and bake 15 minutes, until cheese is lightly browned.

Shopping List:

DAIRY	PACKAGED	SEASONINGS
1 pint skim milk	15 oz. nonfat croutons	Instant minced onion
12 oz. Southwest egg substitute, or plain egg substitute		Italian seasoning
8 oz. shredded nonfat mozzarella cheese	CANNED	
	2 (11-oz). cans Mexican-style corn or regular corn kernels	
MEAT	28-oz. can tomato sauce	
1½ lbs. extra-lean ground turkey	or 2 (15-oz.) cans tomato sauce with seasoning	

NUTRITION PER SERVING Calories 386 · Fat 1.9 g (5%) ·
Carbohydrates 54 g · Protein 43 g · Cholesterol 35 mg · Dietary Fiber 3 g · Sodium 1546 mg
EXCHANGES 4 very lean meat · ¼ milk · 2½ starch · 1 vegetable
CARB CHOICES 4

Super Tip: *Make your own Italian seasoning. Use ½ teaspoon each oregano, marjoram, thyme, basil, rosemary and sage to make 1 tablespoon.*

POULTRY & MEAT DISHES

Spanish Rice Soup

Easy—Do Ahead

1 lb. extra-lean ground beef
1½ tsp. onion powder
¼ tsp. garlic powder
6.8-oz. pkg. Spanish-style rice mix
14.5-oz. can Mexican-style stewed tomatoes
2 (8-oz.) cans tomato sauce
4½ cups water

Spray a Dutch oven with cooking spray. Add ground beef; sprinkle with onion powder and garlic powder and cook over medium heat, stirring frequently, until beef is browned. Add rice mix, tomatoes, tomato sauce and water. Bring to a boil; reduce heat to low and simmer for 20 to 30 minutes, until rice is cooked.

Shopping List:

MEAT	CANNED	SEASONINGS
1 lb. extra-lean ground beef	14½-oz. can Mexican-style stewed tomatoes	Onion powder
		Garlic powder
PACKAGED	2 (8-oz.) cans tomato sauce	
6.8-oz. pkg. Spanish-style rice mix		

POULTRY & MEAT DISHES

NUTRITION PER SERVING Calories 369 • Fat 5.7 g (14%) •
Carbohydrates 51 g • Protein 28 g • Cholesterol 61 mg • Dietary Fiber 4 g •
Sodium 1801 mg
EXCHANGES 2 starch • 4 vegetable • 2 very lean meat • 1 fat
CARB CHOICES 3

Super Tip: *This recipe was tested with Rice-A-Roni Spanish rice mix, but you can substitute other varieties with equivalent servings and weight. You can also substitute plain stewed tomatoes and ¾ teaspoon Mexican seasoning for Mexican-style stewed tomatoes.*

10-Minute Chicken Chili

Easy   • Serves: 6

2 (15-oz.) cans nonfat chili beans
2 (14½-oz.) cans petite diced tomatoes with green chiles, undrained
2 (6-oz.) pkgs. cooked chicken breast cuts
Optional garnishes: chopped onions, shredded nonfat cheddar cheese, nonfat
   sour cream

Combine beans, tomatoes and chicken in a microwave-safe dish and mix
well; cover with plastic wrap and microwave on High 5 to 6 minutes, until
bubbly hot. Serve with onions, cheese and nonfat sour cream, if desired.

Shopping List:

MEAT	CANNED	OPTIONAL INGREDIENTS
2 (6-oz.) pkg. cooked chicken breast cuts	2 (15-oz.) cans nonfat chili beans 2 (14½-oz.) cans diced tomatoes with green chiles	Onion Shredded nonfat cheddar cheese Nonfat sour cream

NUTRITION PER SERVING Calories 209 • Fat 2 g (10%) •
Carbohydrates 26 g • Protein 21 g • Cholesterol 40 mg • Dietary Fiber 5 g •
Sodium 1572 mg
EXCHANGES 1 starch • 2 vegetable • 2 very lean meat
CARB CHOICES 5

Super Tip: *Substitute any canned diced tomatoes and 2 tablespoons diced
green chiles for diced tomatoes with green chiles.*

Three-Ingredient Meat Loaf

Easy—Do Ahead—Freeze
• Serves: 6

1 cup seasoned bread crumbs
2 cups roasted tomato and garlic pasta sauce
1½ lbs. extra-lean ground beef

Preheat oven to 350°F. Spray a 9 × 5-inch loaf pan with cooking spray. Combine bread crumbs and 1½ cups of the pasta sauce in a large bowl. Add beef and mix until ingredients are well combined. Press mixture into loaf pan; bake uncovered 1 hour. Spread remaining pasta sauce over top and cook 30 minutes, until meat loaf is completely cooked through.

Shopping List:

MEAT	PACKAGED	CANNED/JAR
1½ lbs. extra-lean ground beef	Seasoned bread crumbs	26-oz. jar roasted tomato and garlic pasta sauce of choice

NUTRITION PER SERVING Calories 247 • Fat 6 g (22%) • Carbohydrates 19 g • Protein 25 g • Cholesterol 61 mg • Dietary Fiber 2 g • Sodium 384 mg
EXCHANGES 1 starch • 1 vegetable • 2½ lean meat
CARB CHOICES 1

Super Tip: *Substitute extra-lean ground turkey for beef, crushed croutons for bread crumbs, and/or your favorite pasta sauce for the roasted tomato and garlic variety.*

POULTRY & MEAT DISHES

Turkey Tenderloins with Orange-Mustard Sauce

Easy—Do Ahead

◆ Serves: 6

1 cup tomato-vegetable juice cocktail
½ cup orange marmalade
1 tbsp. Dijon mustard
1½ lbs. boneless, skinless turkey breast tenderloins
2 tsp. garlic powder
1½ tsp. onion powder

Combine juice cocktail, orange marmalade and mustard in a small saucepan; bring to a boil over medium-high heat. Reduce heat to low and simmer, stirring frequently, until thickened, 10 minutes. Preheat broiler on high heat. Line a baking sheet with foil and spray with cooking spray. Arrange turkey tenderloins on baking sheet; sprinkle with 1 teaspoon of the garlic powder and ¾ teaspoon of the onion powder. Broil 10 minutes; turn turkey over, season with remaining garlic and onion powder. Broil 5 minutes. Generously brush turkey with orange-mustard sauce and broil 5 to 8 minutes, until cooked through and lightly browned. Serve leftover sauce on the side or drizzle over cooked rice.

Shopping List:

MEAT	CONDIMENTS	SEASONINGS
1½ lbs. boneless, skinless turkey breast tenderloins	Orange marmalade Dijon mustard	Garlic powder Onion powder
CANNED 8 oz. tomato-vegetable juice cocktail		

NUTRITION PER SERVING Calories 213 • Fat .6 g (3%) •
Carbohydrates 23 g • Protein 28 g • Cholesterol 68 mg • Dietary Fiber 1 g •
Sodium 240 mg
EXCHANGES 1½ other carb • 3 very lean meat
CARB CHOICES 2

Super Tip: *You can substitute boneless, skinless chicken breasts for turkey tenderloins and prepare as directed. You can also use chicken tenders but reduce the cooking time to 12 to 14 minutes.*

Yakisoba Noodles with Chicken and Pineapple

Easy   • Serves: 6

1 tbsp. nonfat chicken broth
1 cup frozen broccoli florets
1½ cups frozen pepper stir-fry mix
2 (7-oz.) pkgs. yakisoba noodles
1 cup water
8-oz. chicken breast, cooked and cubed
1 cup pineapple chunks
½ cup original gourmet or teriyaki sauce

Spray a large nonstick skillet with cooking spray. Add chicken broth and heat over medium-high heat. Add broccoli and stir-fry mix to skillet; cook, stirring frequently, until vegetables are tender, 2 to 3 minutes. Add noodles and ½ cup of the water; cook 1 to 2 minutes, breaking noodles apart. Add contents of seasoning packets from noodles and remaining ½ cup water. Stir in chicken and pineapple; pour sauce over top, mix well and cook, until heated through, 3 to 4 minutes. Serve immediately.

Shopping List:

PRODUCE		CANNED
2 (7-oz.) pkgs. yakisoba noodles with sweet and sour sauce	16-oz. pkg. frozen pepper stir-fry mix	Nonfat chicken broth 8-oz. can pineapple chunks in juice
	MEAT	
FROZEN	8-oz. boneless, skinless chicken breasts or tenders	**CONDIMENTS**
10-oz. pkg. frozen broccoli florets		4 oz. original gourmet or teriyaki sauce

NUTRITION PER SERVING Calories 285 • Fat 2.5 g (8%) •
Carbohydrates 50 g • Protein 16 g • Cholesterol 26 mg • Dietary Fiber 2 g •
Sodium 1,128 mg
EXCHANGES 1 vegetable • 2 starch • 1 other carb • 1 very lean meat
CARB CHOICES 3

Super Tip: *March marks the start of pineapple's peak season. Fresh pineapple is a great source of vitamin C, which helps fight off heart disease and cancer; and manganese, which keeps bones strong. One cup of pineapple contains 76 calories.*

BOIL OR BAKE PASTA AND RICE DISHES

❖

❖ ❖ ❖

Noodle Know-How for Passionate Pasta Lovers

An excellent source of complex carbohydrates for sustained energy; pasta is one of America's favorite foods. Inexpensive, filling and nutritious, the average American consumes 19 pounds of pasta each year.

- Store uncooked pasta in its original package or a tightly sealed container in a cool, dry place for up to 2 years. Egg noodles are best used within 1 year.
- Store cooked pasta in a sealed container in the refrigerator for 3 to 4 days.

Pasta	Includes	Best Sauce	Best Uses	Uncooked vs. Cooked
Fresh pasta	Any variety	Rich sauces made with cream, cheese, or sour cream		
Dried pasta	Any variety	Heartier, tomato-based sauces		
Long, thin pasta	Angel hair pasta, spaghettini	Thin, smooth sauce (tomato- or broth-based) that coats pasta evenly	Light entrée side dishes or broken into soup	
Long, thick pasta	Fettuccine	Dense, strongly flavored sauce; chicken-, seafood-, cream- or tomato-based sauce	Entrée or side dishes	Spaghetti: 8 oz. pkg. uncooked = 1½-inch diameter bundle = 4 cups cooked
	Linguine	Hearty tomato, cream or vegetable sauce	Entrée or side dishes	Egg noodles: 8 oz. uncooked = 2 cups dry = 2½ cups cooked

167

Pasta	Includes	Best Sauce	Best Uses	Uncooked vs. Cooked
	Spaghetti	Tomato-, cream-, broth-based, or meat sauce	Entrée, side dishes, cold salads or broken into soup	
	Lasagna	Tomato, cream, meat or vegetable sauce	Oven-baked entrée	
	Fusilli	Thick, heavy sauce; cream or tomato sauce with or without vegetables	Entrée; cut fusilli can be used in side dishes and salads	
Short, thick pasta	Gemelli Rotini		Salads	
Cut pasta including tubular, ridged, twisted or holey pasta	Macaroni	Heavier, chunkier sauces where bits of meat or vegetables can get caught in pasta shapes	Baked dishes, salads, soups, or entrée	8 oz. uncooked = 2 cups dry = 4 cups cooked
	Penne	Light tomato and vegetable sauces	Entrée, side dishes, soup, oven-baked casseroles, or cold salads	
	Mostaccioli or Ziti	Tomato-based sauce and mozzarella cheese	Entrée, oven-baked dishes, side dishes or cold salads	
	Rigatoni	Hearty, rich sauces; creamy, tomato-based, chunky vegetable or meat sauce	Oven-baked dishes, entrée or salads	
	Cavatappi	Chunky vegetable sauce	Good substitute for rigatoni in oven baked dishes or salads	

Pasta	Includes	Best Sauce	Best Uses	Uncooked vs. Cooked
Small pasta	Cavatelli		Entrée, side dishes, cold salads, baked dishes or soup	
	Farfalle (bow-ties)			
	Radiatore	Light to medium-thick sauce	Entrée, side dish, oven-baked dish or cold salad	
	Ruote (wagon wheels)		Salad, soup, stew, pilafs or casseroles (great substitute for rice)	
	Orzo			

Cooking Noodle Know-How:

- General guideline: Use 7 quarts of water per pound of pasta. Stir with a pasta fork or wooden fork to separate strands or pieces.
- Salt or salt-free? Adding salt to the water before cooking pasta is a matter of personal taste for flavor but will not affect the texture. Unsalted water comes to a boil faster than salted water, so only add salt once the water is boiling.
- Timing is everything. Once the water comes to a rapid boil, add pasta, cover pan and return the water to a boil as quickly as possible. Remove the lid and cook pasta according to package directions (times vary depending on pasta shapes).
- Out of the pot and into the colander! Drain pasta quickly to prevent too much drying and sticking. Overdraining or overrinsing creates a sticky mess and removes the slippery, starchy surface that helps sauce cling to pasta. Do not rinse pasta unless you plan to use it in a pasta salad or casserole. Return drained pasta to its cooking pan, a heated dish or another pan with sauce and toss until coated and serve immediately.
- To reheat pasta: Place individual portions of unsauced, cooked pasta in a colander and immerse in boiling water for 1 minute. Drain, top with sauce and serve. Or combine cooked pasta with sauce and place in microwave-safe bowl. Cover with plastic wrap and microwave on High 30 to 60 seconds per serving.

Angel Hair Pasta with Clam Sauce

Easy • Serves: 4

2 tsp. nonfat chicken or vegetable broth
⅓ cup frozen chopped onion
¼ cup frozen diced bell pepper
2 tsp. minced garlic
2 (14½-oz.) cans diced tomatoes with roasted garlic and onions
8-oz. can tomato sauce
½ tsp. red pepper flakes
10¾-oz. can minced clams
8 oz. angel hair pasta

Spray a large nonstick skillet with cooking spray; add broth and heat over medium-high heat. Add onion, bell pepper and garlic; cook, stirring frequently, until vegetables are tender. Add tomatoes with juice, tomato sauce and red pepper flakes; reduce heat to medium-low, cover and simmer 20 minutes. Drain clams, reserving the juice. Add clam juice to sauce and cook 5 to 10 minutes. Stir in clams and cook until heated through; keep warm. Cook pasta according to package directions; drain and place in a large bowl. Pour sauce over pasta; toss and serve immediately.

Shopping List:

FROZEN	CANNED	SEASONINGS
12-oz. pkg. frozen chopped onions	Nonfat vegetable broth	Minced garlic
12-oz. pkg. frozen bell peppers	2 (14½-oz.) cans diced tomatoes with roasted garlic and onions	Red pepper flakes
	8-oz. can tomato sauce	
PACKAGED	10¾-oz. can minced	
8 oz. angel hair pasta	clams	

NUTRITION PER SERVING Calories 388 • Fat 2.8 g (7%) •
Carbohydrates 63 g • Protein 18 g • Cholesterol 47 mg • Dietary Fiber 3 g •
Sodium 1391 mg
EXCHANGES 4 vegetable • 3 starch
CARB CHOICES 4

Super Tip: Clams are an excellent source of iron, which can help prevent anemia.

PASTA &
RICE DISHES

Angel Hair Pasta with Sun-Dried Tomato Sauce

Easy—Do Ahead ◆ Serves: 6

3 tbsp. nonfat vegetable broth
1½ cups frozen chopped onions
½ cup minced celery
½ cup minced carrot
28-oz. can crushed tomatoes, lightly drained
3-oz. pkg. dry-pack sun-dried tomatoes
1½ tsp. minced garlic
1 tsp. Italian seasoning
12-oz. pkg. angel hair pasta, cooked and drained

Spray a large nonstick skillet or saucepan with cooking spray; add broth and heat over medium-high heat. Add onions, celery and carrot; cook, stirring frequently, until vegetables are softened. Add canned tomatoes, sun-dried tomatoes, garlic and Italian seasoning; bring to a boil over high heat. Reduce heat to low and simmer 30 to 45 minutes. Cool slightly; puree sauce in a food processor or blender until smooth. Return to skillet and heat over medium heat just until warmed. Serve over hot pasta.

Shopping List:

PRODUCE	PACKAGED	SEASONINGS
Celery	12-oz. pkg. angel hair	Minced garlic
Carrot	pasta	Italian seasoning
3-oz. pkg. dry-pack sun-dried tomatoes		
	CANNED	
FROZEN	Nonfat vegetable broth	
12-oz. pkg. frozen chopped onions	28-oz. can crushed tomatoes	

PASTA & RICE DISHES

NUTRITION PER SERVING Calories 299 • Fat 1.4 g (4%) •
Carbohydrates 63 g • Protein 11 g • Cholesterol 0 mg • Dietary Fiber 4 g •
Sodium 275 mg
EXCHANGES 3 vegetable • 3 starch
CARB CHOICES 4

Super Tip: Use 2 cups frozen or fresh packaged chopped onion and celery mix.

Cinnamon-Raisin Couscous

Average • Serves: 8

1¾ cups plus 1 tbsp. nonfat vegetable broth
8-oz. pkg. sliced fresh mushrooms
1 tsp. onion powder
15-oz. can low-sodium garbanzo beans
¾ cup golden raisins
¼ cup apple juice
¾ tsp. ground cinnamon
¼ cup water
10-oz. pkg. quick-cooking plain couscous

Spray a large nonstick skillet with cooking spray; add 1 tablespoon vegetable broth and heat over medium-high heat. Add mushrooms; sprinkle with onion powder and cook, stirring frequently, until mushrooms are softened, 3 to 5 minutes. Add beans, raisins, apple juice and cinnamon to mushrooms. Toss mixture lightly and remove skillet from heat. Pour remaining broth and water into a small saucepan; bring to a boil over high heat. Add couscous to mushroom mixture in skillet; pour boiling broth over top. Cover and let mixture stand 5 minutes, until liquid is absorbed. Fluff with a fork and serve immediately.

Shopping List:

PRODUCE	CANNED	SEASONINGS
8-oz. pkg. sliced mushrooms	14¾-oz. can nonfat vegetable broth	Onion powder
		Ground cinnamon
	15-oz. can low-sodium	
PACKAGED	garbanzo beans	
10-oz. pkg. plain couscous	Apple juice	
Golden raisins		

NUTRITION PER SERVING Calories 248 • Fat 1.4 g (5%) •
Carbohydrates 51 g • Protein 9 g • Cholesterol 0 mg • Dietary Fiber 9 g •
Sodium 396 mg
EXCHANGES 1½ vegetable • 1½ starch • 1½ fruit
CARB CHOICES 3½

Super Tip: *In a study, Japanese men, who ate about 4 ounces of fresh shiitake mushrooms or 2 ounces of dried, experienced a substantial reduction in cholesterol within 1 week. A similar study among health women demonstrated a significant drop in cholesterol after a week of eating about 3 ounces of fresh shiitakes daily.*

Creamy Basil Rotini Pasta

Easy   ◆ Serves: 4

8-oz. pkg. rotini pasta
1 cup nonfat cottage cheese
1 cup nonfat ricotta cheese
14½-oz. can diced tomatoes with garlic, oregano and basil
¼ cup chopped fresh basil
Grated nonfat Parmesan cheese, to serve

Cook pasta according to package directions; drain. Stir in remaining ingredients except Parmesan cheese; toss, heat through. Serve with Parmesan cheese.

Shopping List:

PRODUCE	PACKAGED	OPTIONAL
Fresh basil	8-oz. pkg. rotini pasta	Grated Parmesan cheese
DAIRY	**CANNED**	
8-oz. nonfat cottage cheese	14½-oz. can diced tomatoes with garlic, oregano and basil or any canned chopped or diced tomatoes	
8-oz. nonfat ricotta cheese		

NUTRITION PER SERVING Calories 286 • Fat .8 g (3%) •
Carbohydrates 49 g • Protein 19 g • Cholesterol 11 mg • Dietary Fiber 1 g •
Sodium 332 mg
EXCHANGES 2 starch • 1 vegetable • 1 very lean meat • 1 milk
CARB CHOICES 3

Super Tip: *Try this recipe with mostaccioli, rotelle or bow-tie pasta.*

Fajita Pasta

Easy   • Serves: 6

1 tbsp. nonfat chicken broth
3 cups frozen pepper stir-fry mix
4-oz. can chopped green chiles
½ cup taco sauce
½ cup water
1¼-oz. pkg. taco seasoning mix
3 (6-oz.) pkgs. cooked chicken breast cuts
8-oz. spaghetti or linguine, cooked and drained

Spray a large nonstick skillet with cooking spray; add chicken broth and heat over medium-high heat. Add stir-fry mix and green chiles; cook, stirring frequently, 2 to 3 minutes, until vegetables are softened. Add taco sauce, water and seasoning mix; bring to a boil over high heat. Reduce heat to low; cook, stirring frequently, 2 to 3 minutes, until mixture thickens. Add chicken and heat through. Serve over cooked pasta.

Shopping List:

FROZEN	PACKAGED	CONDIMENTS
2 (16-oz.) pkgs. frozen pepper stir-fry mix	8-oz. pkg. spaghetti or linguine	4 oz. taco sauce
		SEASONINGS
MEAT	**CANNED**	1¼-oz. pkg. taco seasoning mix
3 (6-oz.) pkg. cooked chicken breast cuts	4-oz. can chopped green chiles	
	Nonfat chicken broth	

NUTRITION PER SERVING Calories 298 • Fat 3.6 g (11%) •
Carbohydrates 37 g • Protein 27 g • Cholesterol 60 mg • Dietary Fiber 1 g •
Sodium 1634 mg
EXCHANGES 2 vegetable • 3 very lean meat • 2 starch
CARB CHOICES 2

Super Tip: *There are more than 200 varieties of chiles; they vary in color from green and red to yellow, purple or black and range from ¼ inch to nearly 12 inches long.*

Farfalle with Creamy Dijon Sauce

Easy   ♦ Serves: 5

10-oz. pkg. farfalle (bow-tie pasta)
1 cup nonfat half-and-half
2 tbsp. Dijon mustard
¼ tsp. pepper
¾ cup grated nonfat Parmesan cheese

Cook farfalle according to package directions; drain well. Spray a small saucepan with cooking spray; add half-and-half, mustard and pepper. Cook over low heat, stirring constantly, until mixture is smooth and creamy; do not boil. Combine pasta, sauce and Parmesan cheese in a large serving bowl; toss carefully to mix. Serve immediately.

Shopping List:

DAIRY	PACKAGED	CONDIMENTS
8 oz. nonfat half-and-half	10-oz. pkg. farfalle (bow-tie pasta)	Dijon mustard
Grated nonfat Parmesan cheese		SEASONINGS
		Black pepper

NUTRITION PER SERVING Calories 296 • Fat 1.5 g (5%) •
Carbohydrates 57 g • Protein 12 g • Cholesterol 0 mg • Dietary Fiber <1 g •
Sodium 202 mg
EXCHANGES 3 starch • 1 other carb
CARB CHOICES 4

Super Tip: *Dijon mustard, which originated in Dijon, France, is made from brown mustard seeds, spices and white wine, making it more flavorful than ordinary yellow mustard.*

PASTA &
RICE DISHES

Fettuccine Primavera with Cream Sauce

Easy   • Serves: 4

¾ lb. boneless, skinless chicken tenders, cut into ½-inch strips
¾ tsp. garlic powder
1 tsp. onion powder
8-oz. pkg. fettuccine
16-oz. pkg. frozen broccoli, cauliflower and carrot mix
⅔ cup nonfat ranch salad dressing
¼ cup grated nonfat Parmesan cheese

Preheat broiler on high heat. Line a baking sheet with foil and spray with cooking spray. Arrange chicken tenders in a single layer on baking sheet; sprinkle with garlic powder and onion powder. Broil 4 to 5 minutes; turn chicken tenders over and broil 4 to 5 minutes, until cooked through. While chicken is broiling, cook fettuccine according to package directions; add frozen vegetables to pasta for the last 5 minutes of cooking time. Drain pasta and vegetables. Spray pot used to cook pasta with cooking spray; return pasta and vegetables to pot. Add chicken, salad dressing and cheese; mix lightly and heat, stirring constantly, over low heat until heated through. Serve immediately.

Shopping List:

DAIRY	MEAT	CONDIMENTS
Grated nonfat Parmesan cheese	¾ lb boneless, skinless chicken tenders	Nonfat ranch salad dressing
FROZEN	**PACKAGED**	**SEASONINGS**
16-oz. pkg. frozen broccoli, cauliflower and carrot mix	8-oz. pkg. fettuccine	Garlic powder Onion powder

NUTRITION PER SERVING Calories 346 • Fat 2.7 g (7%) •
Carbohydrates 50 g • Protein 31 g • Cholesterol 105 mg • Dietary Fiber 3 g •
Sodium 604 mg
EXCHANGES 2 starch • 2 very lean meat • 2 vegetable • ½ other carb
CARB CHOICES 3

Super Tip: *Save preparation and cook time by substituting 2 (6-oz.) packages cooked chicken breast cuts for chicken tenders.*

Fettuccine with Artichokes, Tomatoes and Peppers

Easy   ◆ Serves: 4

12-oz. pkg. fettuccine
2 tsp. nonfat vegetable broth
½ tsp. minced garlic
½ cup frozen pepper stir-fry mix
14½-oz. can diced tomatoes with roasted garlic and onions, drained
1 tbsp. Italian seasoning
9-oz. pkg. frozen artichoke hearts, thawed and drained
½ cup grated nonfat Parmesan cheese

Cook fettuccine according to package directions; drain. Spray a large non-stick skillet with cooking spray; add vegetable broth and heat over medium-high heat. Add garlic and stir-fry mix; cook, stirring frequently, until vegetables are softened and lightly browned. Add tomatoes and Italian seasoning; cook over low heat 8 to 10 minutes, stirring occasionally. Add artichoke hearts and cook 2 to 3 minutes, until heated through. Add fettuccine and toss until mixed. Sprinkle Parmesan cheese over top and serve.

Shopping List:

DAIRY	FROZEN	CANNED
Grated nonfat Parmesan cheese	16-oz. pkg. frozen pepper stir-fry mix	14½-oz. can diced tomatoes with roasted garlic and onions
	9-oz. pkg. frozen artichoke hearts	Nonfat vegetable broth
	PACKAGED	**SEASONING**
	12-oz. pkg. fettuccini	Minced garlic
		Italian seasoning

NUTRITION PER SERVING Calories 417 • Fat 2 g (4%) •
Carbohydrates 83 g • Protein 19 g • Cholesterol 0 mg • Dietary Fiber <1 g •
Sodium 644 mg
EXCHANGES 4 starch • 4 vegetable
CARB CHOICES 6

Super Tip: *Substitute any canned diced tomatoes for tomatoes with roasted garlic and onions; substitute 13¾-oz. can chopped or quartered artichokes for the frozen variety. You can also use fresh sliced bell peppers and onions instead of frozen stir-fry mix.*

PASTA & RICE DISHES

Garlic-Parmesan Linguine

Easy ◆ Serves: 6

12-oz. pkg. linguine
½ cup nonfat chicken or vegetable broth
½ cup grated nonfat Parmesan cheese, plus extra for serving (optional)
3 tbsp. roasted minced garlic
2 tsp. onion powder
Pepper to taste

Cook linguine according to package directions; drain and keep warm. Combine remaining ingredients in a food processor or blender and process until smooth. Pour into a microwave-safe bowl and heat on High 1 to 2 minutes, until warm. Pour sauce over linguine and serve with additional Parmesan cheese, if desired.

Shopping List:

DAIRY	CANNED	SEASONINGS
Grated nonfat Parmesan cheese	Nonfat chicken or vegetable broth	Roasted minced garlic
		Onion powder
		Black pepper
PACKAGED		
12-oz. pkg. linguine		

NUTRITION PER SERVING Calories 235 • Fat .8 g (3%) •
Carbohydrates 46 g • Protein 10 g • Cholesterol 0 mg • Dietary Fiber 0 g •
Sodium 130 mg
EXCHANGES 3 starch
CARB CHOICES 3

Super Tip: Can different noodles or pasta shapes be used without changing the recipe? In most cases . . . yes. For best results, mix and match, thin, delicate noodles with light, thin sauces; thick, heavier noodles with heavier sauces; and shells, ridged, or tubular noodles with chunkier sauces.

Ginger Couscous

Easy

2 (14½-oz.) cans nonfat vegetable broth
¼ cup shredded carrot
½ tsp. ground ginger
1 tsp. minced garlic
2 cups quick-cooking couscous

Combine all ingredients except couscous in a large saucepan; bring to a boil over medium-high heat. Reduce heat to low and simmer until carrot is tender, 2 to 3 minutes. Add couscous; stir to mix, cover saucepan and remove from heat. Let couscous stand, covered, 5 to 8 minutes, until liquid is absorbed. Fluff with a fork and serve.

Shopping List:

PRODUCE	CANNED	SEASONINGS
8-oz. pkg. shredded carrots	2 (14½-oz.) cans nonfat vegetable broth	Ground ginger Minced garlic
PACKAGED 2 (10-oz.) pkgs. quick-cooking couscous		

NUTRITION PER SERVING Calories 365 • Fat .5 g (1%) •
Carbohydrates 72 g • Protein 14 g • Cholesterol 0 mg • Dietary Fiber 14 g •
Sodium 681 mg
EXCHANGES 4 Starch • 2 vegetable
CARB CHOICES 5

Super Tip: *You can substitute nonfat chicken broth for vegetable broth and ½ teaspoon garlic powder for the minced garlic.*

PASTA & RICE DISHES

179

Italian Chicken Pasta

Easy   • Serves: 6

1 lb. boneless, skinless chicken breast tenders
2 tsp. garlic powder
1 tsp. Italian seasoning
2 cups nonfat pasta sauce
12-oz. pkg. fettuccine or other pasta of choice, cooked

Preheat broiler on high heat. Line a baking sheet with foil and spray with
cooking spray. Arrange chicken tenders on baking sheet; sprinkle with garlic
powder and Italian seasoning. Broil 10 to 15 minutes, until chicken is
cooked through. Pour pasta sauce into a medium saucepan; add chicken
and heat until warmed through. Serve over hot fettuccine.

Shopping List:

MEAT	CANNED	SEASONINGS
1 lb. boneless, skinless chicken breast tenders	16-oz. can or jar nonfat pasta sauce	Garlic powder Italian seasoning
PACKAGED 12-oz. pkg. fettuccine or other pasta of choice		

NUTRITION PER SERVING Calories 356 • Fat 4 g (10%) •
Carbohydrates 49 g • Protein 29 g • Cholesterol 57 mg • Dietary Fiber 0 g •
Sodium 275 mg
EXCHANGES 2 starch • 4 vegetable • 2 very lean meat • ½ fat
CARB CHOICES 3

Super Tip: *Save time by substituting cooked chicken breast cuts; add seasonings to pasta sauce and prepare as directed.*

Lemon Noodle Kugel

Easy—Do Ahead   ◆ Serves: 10

16-oz. pkg. yolk-free egg noodles
2 cups nonfat cottage cheese
1 cup nonfat sour cream
1 cup egg substitute
1 cup sugar
2 tsp. lemon juice
1 cup golden raisins

Preheat oven to 350°F. Spray a 9 × 13-inch baking dish with cooking spray. Cook noodles according to package directions; drain and place noodles in baking dish. Combine cottage cheese, sour cream, egg substitute, sugar and lemon juice in a food processor, blender or bowl with an electric mixer; blend until smooth. Pour mixture over noodles; add raisins and toss until well mixed. Bake 45 to 50 minutes, until lightly browned. Remove from oven and let stand 5 to 8 minutes to set before serving.

Shopping List:

PRODUCE	DAIRY	PACKAGED
Lemon or lemon juice	16-oz. carton nonfat cottage cheese	16-oz. pkg. yolk-free egg noodles
	8-oz. carton nonfat sour cream	Sugar
	8 oz. egg substitute	Golden raisins

PASTA & RICE DISHES

NUTRITION PER SERVING Calories 326 • Fat .5 g (1%) •
Carbohydrates 68 g • Protein 13 g • Cholesterol <1 mg • Dietary Fiber 2 g •
Sodium 111 mg
EXCHANGES 1 fruit • 2½ starch • 1 very lean meat • 1 other carb
CARB CHOICES 6

Super Tip: *Save 54 milligrams of cholesterol and 2 grams of saturated fat per 2-ounce serving when you use yolk-free egg noodles rather than whole egg noodles.*

Linguine with White Clam Sauce

Easy
• Serves: 4

2 tbsp. nonfat vegetable broth
2 tbsp. roasted minced garlic
⅛ tsp. red pepper flakes
1 cup bottled clam juice
¾ cup dry white wine
½ cup minced fresh Italian parsley

2 (6½-oz.) cans chopped clams,
 drained and rinsed
8 oz. linguine
Grated nonfat Parmesan cheese
 (optional)

Spray a medium saucepan with cooking spray; add broth and heat over medium-high heat. Add garlic and red pepper flakes; cook over medium heat until garlic is golden, 2 to 3 minutes. Combine clam juice, wine and parsley; pour mixture into saucepan. Cook 5 minutes. Add clams and heat 5 to 6 minutes. Cover pan and remove from heat. Cook linguine according to package directions; drain and toss with clam sauce. Sprinkle with Parmesan cheese if desired.

Shopping List:

PRODUCE	CANNED	SEASONINGS
Italian parsley	14½-oz. can nonfat vegetable broth	Roasted minced garlic
		Red pepper flakes
DAIRY	2 (6½-oz.) cans	
Grated nonfat	chopped clams (not	OTHER
Parmesan cheese	minced)	Dry white wine
		8 oz. bottled clam juice
PACKAGED		
8 oz. linguine		

NUTRITION PER SERVING Calories 382 • Fat 2.7 g (6%) •
Carbohydrates 48 g • Protein 31 g • Cholesterol 62 mg • Dietary Fiber <1 g •
Sodium 267 mg
EXCHANGES 1 other carb • 2 starch • 3 very lean meat
CARB CHOICES 3

Super Tip: *Peel garlic and let it sit for 15 minutes before cooking to boost cancer-fighting and health benefits. According to Dr. John Milner, professor of nutrition at Penn State University, peeling garlic releases allinase, an important enzyme that starts a series of chemical reactions to help protect against cancer.*

PASTA & RICE DISHES

Long Grain and Wild Rice Pilaf

Easy   • Serves: 4

2 (4.3-oz.) pkgs. long-grain and wild rice
3 tbsp. nonfat Promise margarine
½ onion, sliced into thin wedges
2 tsp. light brown sugar
⅓ cup dried cranberries
⅓ cup golden raisins
⅓ cup orange juice
⅛ tsp. pepper

Prepare rice according to package directions, using 2 tablespoons of the
nonfat margarine. While rice is cooking, spray a medium skillet with cooking spray; add the remaining 1 tbsp. nonfat margarine and cook over low
heat until melted. Add onion; sprinkle with brown sugar and cook, stirring
frequently, until onion is tender and lightly browned. Add onion, cranberries, raisins, orange juice and pepper to cooked rice; mix well. Cook over
medium-low heat until heated through. Serve immediately.

Shopping List:

PRODUCE	PACKAGED	SEASONINGS
Small onion	2 (4.3-oz.) pkgs. long-grain and wild rice	Black pepper
DAIRY	Light brown sugar	
Orange juice	Dried cranberries	
Nonfat Promise margarine	Golden raisins	

PASTA & RICE DISHES

NUTRITION PER SERVING Calories 310 • Fat .6 g (2%) •
Carbohydrates 71 g • Protein 6 g • Cholesterol 0 mg • Dietary Fiber 3 g •
Sodium 1007 mg
EXCHANGES 2 starch • 2½ fruit
CARB CHOICES 5

Super Tip: *Substitute your favorite dried fruit such as apricots or cherries for
dried cranberries or raisins. You can use low-fat or regular margarine but the
nutritional information provided is based on nonfat margarine.*

Mac 'n' Cheese in Minutes

Easy

• Serves: 6

12-oz. pkg. elbow macaroni
12 oz. nonfat American, Cheddar or Swiss cheese slices
½ cup nonfat half-and-half
Pepper to taste

Cook macaroni according to package directions; drain well. Spray pot with cooking spray; return macaroni to pot. Add cheese, half-and-half and pepper; cook over low heat, stirring constantly, until cheese is melted.

Shopping List:

DAIRY	PACKAGED	SEASONINGS
12 oz. nonfat American, Cheddar or Swiss cheese slices	12-oz. pkg. elbow macaroni	Black pepper
4 oz. nonfat half-and-half		

NUTRITION PER SERVING Calories 289 • Fat .8 g (2%) •
Carbohydrates 42 g • Protein 23 g • Cholesterol 0 mg • Dietary Fiber 1 g •
Sodium 450 mg
EXCHANGES 2 very lean meat • 2 starch • ½ other carb
CARB CHOICES 3

Super Tip: *You can substitute rotelle or rotini pasta for macaroni and skim milk for half-and-half (the mixture will not be as thick and creamy with skim milk). For a twist in flavor, use a combination of cheeses.*

Moroccan Couscous

Easy

• Serves: 5

2 cups water
⅓ cup golden raisins
½ tsp. ground cinnamon
½ tsp. ground turmeric
¼ tsp. ground cumin
10-oz. pkg. quick-cooking plain couscous

Pour water into a medium saucepan; add raisins, cinnamon, turmeric and cumin. Bring to a boil over high heat. Stir in couscous; cover and remove from heat. Let stand, covered, 5 minutes. Fluff with a fork and serve.

Shopping List:

PACKAGED	SEASONINGS

10-oz. pkg. quick-
    cooking plain
    couscous
Golden raisins
	Ground cinnamon
	Ground turmeric
	Ground cumin

NUTRITION PER SERVING Calories 248 • Fat .4 g (1%) •
Carbohydrates 53 g • Protein 8 g • Cholesterol 0 mg • Dietary Fiber 9 g •
Sodium 7 mg
EXCHANGES 2 starch • 1½ fruit
CARB CHOICES 4

Super Tip: *Couscous is small yellow granules of semolina made from durum wheat, which are precooked and then dried. Couscous is a pasta, not a grain as is often believed; it is versatile and can be prepared and served as a salad base, soup addition, simple side dish or even the basis for a dessert.*

**PASTA &
RICE DISHES**

Pasta with Chicken, Peppers and Tomatoes

Easy

• Serves: 6

12-oz. pkg. elbow macaroni
2 cups frozen pepper stir-fry mix
1 lb. boneless, skinless chicken tenders, cut into cubes
2 (14½-oz.) cans diced tomatoes with garlic, basil and oregano, undrained

Cook macaroni according to package directions; drain. While pasta is cooking, spray a large nonstick skillet with cooking spray and heat over medium-high heat. Add stir-fry mix; cook, stirring frequently, until tender, 3 to 4 minutes. Add chicken cubes and cook 3 to 4 minutes, until lightly browned. Add ¾ cup diced tomatoes and cook, stirring frequently, until chicken is cooked through. Add remaining tomatoes; cook over medium heat until heated through, 4 to 5 minutes. Pour over macaroni, toss and serve.

Shopping List:

FROZEN	PACKAGED	CANNED
16-oz. pkg. frozen pepper stir-fry mix	12-oz. pkg. elbow macaroni	2 (14½-oz.) cans diced tomatoes with garlic, basil and oregano
MEAT 1 lb. boneless, skinless chicken tenders		

NUTRITION PER SERVING Calories 324 • Fat 1.2 g (3%) •
Carbohydrates 51 g • Protein 26 g • Cholesterol 38 mg • Dietary Fiber 2 g •
Sodium 348 mg
EXCHANGES 4 vegetable • 2 starch • 2 very lean meat
CARB CHOICES 3

Super Tip: *Substitute 2 (14½-oz.) cans diced tomatoes plus 2 teaspoons Italian seasoning for diced tomatoes with garlic, basil and oregano, if desired.*

Pasta with Sun-Dried Tomatoes

Easy   • Serves: 6

½ cup dry-pack sun-dried tomatoes chopped
1 cup warm water
1¼ cups nonfat chicken broth
¾ cup nonfat cream cheese
4½ tbsp. chopped fresh basil
¾ tsp. pepper
6 cups cooked rotini pasta

Place tomatoes in a small bowl; pour warm water over top and let stand until softened, 10 to 15 minutes. Strain; set tomatoes aside. Pour broth into a saucepan; heat over medium-high heat until hot, but do not boil. Remove pan from heat; stir in cream cheese and mix until completely blended and smooth. Add tomatoes, basil and pepper; fold in pasta and toss to coat. Serve immediately.

Shopping List:

PRODUCE	PACKAGED	CANNED
Fresh basil	3-oz. pkg. dry-pack sun-dried tomatoes	14½-oz. can nonfat chicken broth
DAIRY	12-oz. pkg. rotini pasta	
6-oz. nonfat cream cheese		**SEASONINGS**
		Black pepper

NUTRITION PER SERVING Calories 227 • Fat 1.5 g (6%) •
Carbohydrates 40 g • Protein 12 g • Cholesterol 47 mg • Dietary Fiber 2 g •
Sodium 378 mg
EXCHANGES 1 vegetable • 2 starch • ½ other carb
CARB CHOICES 3

Super Tip: *Substitute gemelli ("twins" or double-twisted pasta) for rotini, if desired.*

PASTA &
RICE DISHES

Penne Pasta with Beans

Easy

• Serves: 4

2 tbsp. nonfat vegetable broth
¾ cup frozen chopped onion
14½ oz. diced tomatoes with garlic, oregano and basil, drained
15-oz. can cannellini beans
8 oz. penne pasta, cooked and drained

Spray a large saucepan or skillet with cooking spray; add vegetable broth and heat over medium-high heat. Add onion to skillet and cook, stirring frequently, until softened. Stir in tomatoes and beans; bring to a boil over high heat. Immediately reduce heat to low and simmer 10 minutes. Add cooked pasta; toss and serve.

Shopping List:

FROZEN	CANNED
12-oz. pkg. frozen chopped onions	14½-oz. can nonfat vegetable broth
	14½-oz. can diced tomatoes with garlic, oregano and basil
PACKAGED	15-oz. can cannellini beans (white kidney beans)
8 oz. penne pasta	

NUTRITION PER SERVING Calories 364 • Fat 1.6 g (4%) • Carbohydrates 72 g • Protein 16 g • Cholesterol 0 mg • Dietary Fiber 1 g • Sodium 205 mg
EXCHANGES 2 vegetable • 4 starch
CARB CHOICES 5

Super Tip: *Substitute fava or other canned beans for the cannellini, as well as any variety of diced tomatoes for the diced tomatoes with garlic, oregano and basil.*

PASTA &
RICE DISHES

Perfect Parmesan Pasta

Easy

• Serves: 4

8-oz. pkg. penne or mostaccioli
16-oz. pkg. frozen broccoli, cauliflower and carrot mix
6 oz. cooked chicken breast cuts
¼ tsp. garlic powder
¼ cup nonfat chicken broth
1 cup grated nonfat Parmesan cheese

Prepare pasta as directed on package; add frozen vegetables during last 5 minutes of cooking time. Drain well. Spray pot with cooking spray; add chicken and sprinkle with garlic powder. Cook until heated through, 2 to 3 minutes. Add pasta and vegetables, broth and cheese; toss until ingredients are coated and heated through. Serve immediately.

Shopping List:

DAIRY	MEAT	CANNED
4 oz. grated nonfat Parmesan cheese	6 oz. cooked chicken breast cuts	Nonfat chicken broth
		SEASONINGS
FROZEN	**PACKAGED**	Garlic powder
16-oz. pkg. frozen broccoli, cauliflower and carrot mix	8-oz. pkg. penne or mostaccioli pasta	

NUTRITION PER SERVING Calories 360 • Fat 2.1 g (5%) • Carbohydrates 57 g • Protein 28 g • Cholesterol 30 mg • Dietary Fiber 1 g • Sodium 633 mg
EXCHANGE 3 starch • 2 vegetable • 2 very lean meat
CARB CHOICES 4

Super Tip: Substitute any cooked chicken for packaged chicken breast cuts, as well as your favorite vegetable mix for the frozen broccoli, cauliflower and carrot mix.

PASTA & RICE DISHES

189

Radiatore Pasta with Chiles and Cheese

Easy   ◆ Serves: 8

12-oz. pkg. radiatore pasta
1 cup shredded nonfat cheddar cheese
1 cup skim milk
½ cup pimentos, drained well
2 (4-oz.) cans chopped green chiles, drained well

Cook pasta according to package directions; drain and return to pot. Add remaining ingredients. Cook over medium-low heat, stirring constantly, until cheese is melted and sauce is hot.

Shopping List:

DAIRY	PACKAGED	CANNED
Skim milk	12-oz. pkg. radiatore	2 (4-oz.) cans chopped
4 oz. shredded nonfat	pasta	green chiles
cheddar cheese		4-oz. jar pimentos

NUTRITION PER SERVING Calories 195 • Fat .7 g (3%) • Carbohydrates 36 g • Protein 10 g • Cholesterol <1 mg • Dietary Fiber <1 mg • Sodium 484 mg
EXCHANGES 1 very lean meat • 2 vegetable • 1½ starch
CARB CHOICES 2

Super Tip: *Substitute farfalle or wagon-wheel pasta for radiatore, if desired.*

Rigatoni Primavera with Cheese

Easy   • Serves: 8

2 (14½-oz.) cans tomatoes with basil, garlic and oregano, undrained
2 (14½-oz.) cans nonfat beef broth
2 cups water
½ cup Italian tomato paste with roasted garlic
1 cup frozen chopped onion
2 cups frozen sliced carrots
2 cups frozen sliced yellow squash or zucchini
8 oz. rigatoni
1½ cups shredded nonfat mozzarella cheese

Spray a large pot or Dutch oven with cooking spray. Combine tomatoes, broth, water, tomato paste, onion, carrots and squash in pot; bring to a boil over high heat. Reduce heat to medium-low; cook 10 to 12 minutes, until vegetables are tender. Cook pasta according to package directions; drain. Add pasta to vegetable-tomato sauce and toss to mix.

Preheat oven to 375°F. Spray a 9 × 13-inch baking dish with cooking spray; spoon pasta mixture into baking dish. Top with mozzarella cheese. Bake 10 to 15 minutes, until cheese is melted and lightly browned. Serve immediately.

Shopping List:

DAIRY
6 oz. shredded nonfat mozzarella cheese

FROZEN
12-oz. pkg. frozen chopped onions
16-oz. pkg. frozen sliced carrots

16-oz. pkg. frozen sliced yellow squash or zucchini (or combination)

PACKAGED
8 oz. rigatoni

CANNED
2 (14½-oz.) cans tomatoes with basil, garlic and oregano
2 (14½-oz.) cans nonfat beef broth
6-oz. can Italian tomato paste with roasted garlic

PASTA & RICE DISHES

NUTRITION PER SERVING Calories 226 • Fat .7 g (3%) • Carbohydrates 39 g • Protein 14 g • Cholesterol 0 mg • Dietary Fiber 4 g • Sodium 950 mg
EXCHANGE 1 very lean meat • 5 vegetable • 1 starch
CARB CHOICES 3

Super Tip: Substitute mostaccioli, ziti or penne pasta for rigatoni, if desired.

Shrimp Pasta Toss

Easy • Serves: 6

12-oz. pkg. spaghettini
1 tbsp. nonfat vegetable broth
¾ cup frozen chopped onion
1 tsp. minced garlic
¼ tsp. red pepper flakes
2 (14½-oz.) cans diced tomatoes with garlic and onions, undrained
1 lb. deveined, shelled large shrimp, thawed if frozen

Cook pasta according to package directions. Prepare shrimp sauce while pasta is cooking. Spray a large nonstick skillet with cooking spray; add vegetable broth and heat over medium-high heat. Add onion; cook, stirring frequently, 4 to 5 minutes, until onion is softened and golden. Add garlic and red pepper; cook, stirring constantly, 1 minute. Add tomatoes; bring to a boil over high heat. Reduce heat to medium-low, cover and cook 5 minutes. Add shrimp; cover and cook 5 to 6 minutes until shrimp turn opaque and curl. Drain pasta and return to pot. Add shrimp sauce and toss until coated. Serve immediately.

Shopping List:

FISH	PACKAGED	SEASONINGS
1 lb. deveined, shelled large shrimp	12-oz. pkg. spaghettini (thin spaghetti)	Minced garlic Red pepper flakes
FROZEN 12-oz. pkg. frozen chopped onions	**CANNED** Nonfat vegetable broth 2 (14½-oz.) cans diced tomatoes with garlic and onions	

PASTA & RICE DISHES

NUTRITION PER SERVING Calories 342 • Fat 2.7 g (7%) • Carbohydrates 54 g • Protein 25 g • Cholesterol 117 mg • Dietary Fiber <1 g • Sodium 792 mg
EXCHANGES 2 very lean meat • 2 vegetable • 3 starch
CARB CHOICES 4

Super Tip: Purchasing deveined, peeled shrimp saves time, but you can save dollars by peeling and deveining the shrimp yourself.

Southwest Spaghetti

Easy

• Serves: 4

¾ lb. extra-lean ground turkey
1 tbsp. onion powder
16-oz. jar Southwest chunky-style salsa
11-oz. can Mexican-style corn kernels, drained
¾ cup water
1.25-oz. pkg. taco seasoning mix
8 oz. spaghetti
½ cup shredded nonfat cheddar cheese (optional)

Spray a large nonstick skillet with cooking spray; add turkey and sprinkle with onion powder. Cook over medium-high heat, stirring frequently, until turkey is browned. Add salsa, corn, water and seasoning mix to skillet; bring to a boil over medium-high heat. Reduce heat to medium and cook until thickened. Cook pasta according to package directions, drain and toss with sauce. Sprinkle cheese over top if desired and toss lightly. Serve immediately.

Shopping List:

DAIRY	PACKAGED	CONDIMENTS
Shredded nonfat cheese	8 oz. spaghetti	16-oz. jar Southwest-style salsa
MEAT	**CANNED**	
¾ lb. extra-lean ground turkey	11-oz. can Mexican-style corn or regular corn	**SEASONINGS**
		1.25-oz. pkg. taco seasoning mix
		Onion powder

NUTRITION PER SERVING Calories 450 • Fat 2.4 g (5%) •
Carbohydrates 69 g • Protein 34 g • Cholesterol 34 mg • Dietary Fiber 3 g •
Sodium 1864 mg
EXCHANGES 2 vegetable • 3½ starch • 4 very lean meat
CARB CHOICES 5

Super Tip: Turkey is an excellent source of protein with sufficient amounts of essential amino acids to promote growth and development, as well as niacin and phosphorus promoting the normal development of bones and teeth.

PASTA & RICE DISHES

Speedy Pasta Bake

Easy—Do Ahead   ◆ Serves: 6

16-oz. pkg. ziti, rotini or rotelle pasta
1 lb. extra-lean ground beef
¾ tsp. garlic powder
¾ tsp. onion powder
2 (15-oz.) cans tomato sauce for lasagna
8 oz. sliced fresh mushrooms
15-oz. can Italian-style stewed tomatoes, undrained
1½ cups shredded nonfat mozzarella cheese
2 tbsp. grated nonfat Parmesan cheese (optional)

Cook pasta according to package directions; drain well. Preheat oven to 350°F. Spray a 9 × 13-inch baking dish with cooking spray and set aside.

Spray a large nonstick skillet with cooking spray; add beef, garlic powder and onion powder. Cook, stirring frequently, until beef is browned and crumbled. Drain well. Add tomato sauce, mushrooms and stewed tomatoes with juice; bring to a boil over medium-high heat. Reduce heat to low and simmer 10 minutes. Combine pasta and meat sauce in baking dish; toss lightly until mixed. Sprinkle with mozzarella cheese and bake 20 to 25 minutes, until bubbly hot and lightly browned. Sprinkle with Parmesan cheese just before serving, if desired.

Shopping List:

PRODUCE	MEAT	CANNED
8 oz. sliced mushrooms	1 lb. extra-lean ground beef	2 (15-oz.) cans tomato sauce for lasagna
DAIRY		15-oz. can Italian-style stewed tomatoes
6 oz. shredded nonfat mozzarella cheese	**PACKAGED**	
Grated nonfat Parmesan cheese (optional)	16-oz. pkg, ziti, rotini or rotelle pasta	**SEASONINGS**
		Garlic powder
		Onion powder

NUTRITION PER SERVING Calories 505 • Fat 4.4 g (9%) •
Carbohydrates 75g • Protein 37 g • Cholesterol 41 mg • Dietary Fiber 3 g •
Sodium 1049 mg
EXCHANGES 3 starch • 3 very lean meat • 6 vegetable
CARB CHOICES 5

Super Tip: *Substitute any canned tomato sauce for tomato sauce for lasagna and/or low-fat ground turkey for beef.*

Split-Second Rice with Broccoli and Cheese

Easy   • Serves: 4

1 cup water
1 cup instant rice
10-oz. pkg. frozen cut broccoli
1 cup shredded nonfat cheddar cheese

Combine water, rice and broccoli in a medium saucepan; bring to a boil over high heat, stirring occasionally. Cover saucepan, remove from heat and let stand 5 minutes. Add cheese and stir until cheese is melted (if cheese does not melt, place over very low heat).

Shopping List:

DAIRY	FROZEN	PACKAGED
4 oz. shredded nonfat cheddar cheese	10-oz. pkg. frozen cut broccoli	Instant rice

NUTRITION PER SERVING Calories 146 • Fat .3 g (2%) • Carbohydrates 23 g • Protein 12 g • Cholesterol 0 mg • Dietary Fiber 3 g • Sodium 302 mg
EXCHANGES 1 very lean meat • 1 vegetable • 1 starch
CARB CHOICES 2

Super Tip: *You can substitute frozen chopped spinach and shredded nonfat Swiss cheese for the broccoli and cheddar cheese.*

PASTA & RICE DISHES

Vegetable Barley Casserole

Easy—Do Ahead   • Serves: 4

3 tbsp. plus 2½ cups nonfat chicken or vegetable broth
⅔ cup barley
1 cup frozen chopped onion, thawed and patted dry
1 cup frozen chopped broccoli, thawed and patted dry
1 cup shredded carrots
4-oz. can mushroom stems and pieces, drained well and chopped
½ tsp. garlic powder

Preheat oven to 350°F. Spray a baking dish with cooking spray and set aside.

Spray a nonstick skillet with cooking spray; add the 3 tablespoons broth and heat over medium-high heat. Add barley and cook, stirring frequently, just until lightly browned, 2 to 3 minutes. Transfer barley to baking dish. Add onion, broccoli and carrots to skillet and cook, stirring frequently, just until softened, 2 to 3 minutes. Spoon vegetables and mushrooms into casserole. Add garlic powder to the 2½ cups broth and mix well. Pour broth over vegetables; mix ingredients until moistened. Cover and bake 1 to 1¼ hours, until liquid has been absorbed and barley is tender, stirring every 20 minutes while casserole is baking. Remove from oven and let stand 5 minutes before serving.

Shopping List:

PRODUCE	PACKAGED	SEASONINGS
16-oz. pkg. shredded carrots	Barley	Garlic powder
	CANNED	
FROZEN	4-oz. can mushroom stems and pieces	
12-oz. pkg. frozen chopped onions	2 (14½-oz.) cans nonfat chicken or vegetable broth	
10-oz. pkg. frozen chopped broccoli		

NUTRITION PER SERVING Calories 167 • Fat 1.1 g (6%) •
Carbohydrates 33 g • Protein 8 g • Cholesterol 0 mg • Dietary Fiber 8 g •
Sodium 677 mg
EXCHANGES 1 starch • 4 vegetable
CARB CHOICES 2

Super Tip: *Broccoli florets have 8 times as much beta-carotene as the stalks.*

1-2-3 SIMPLE
SIDE DISHES

❖

❖ ❖ ❖

Salubrious Side Dishes with Star Power

Watch out, entrées! Side dishes are no longer second-rate—their supporting role at mealtime has been elevated to celebrity status. Visually appealing with an array of colors, textures and flavors, these dishes satisfy the senses in all respects. Why get stuck in a side-dish rut with baked potatoes, boiled pasta or frozen peas and carrots when you can present heart-healthy, palate-pleasing dishes with star quality? These trouble-free side dishes take you from simple to sensational without sacrificing flavor. Whether you focus on a single product or a combination of ingredients, side dishes no longer play second fiddle to starring entrées. They sizzle with star power, providing multiple health benefits and great taste. Go from ordinary to extraordinary with a combination of garden-fresh, canned or frozen fruits and vegetables, whole grains and zesty herbs and spices. Often providing the same satisfaction and health-boosting benefits of a full-course meal, side dishes please diners from grazers to voracious eaters alike.

5 A Day Really Can Keep the Doctor Away

Recommended and supported by the American Institute for Cancer Research, including at least 5 servings of fruits and vegetables in your daily diet will provide:

1. Powerful antioxidants and phytochemicals, which may help prevent up to 20 percent of all cancers.
2. Low-calorie and high-fiber foods, which may contribute to weight loss or weight maintenance.
3. Phytochemicals, soluble fiber and folate, which may help reduce the risk of heart disease.
4. Potassium and magnesium, which may lower blood pressure.
5. Phytochemicals and potassium, which may cut stroke risk by up to 25 percent.
6. Vitamin C and carotenoids to protect eyes against disease.
7. High fiber to help prevent diverticulosis (an intestinal disorder) and reduce blood sugar levels to help dodge diabetes.
8. Sweet flavors to satisfy your sweet tooth.

Asparagus with Cream Sauce

Easy   ◆ Serves: 4

10-oz. pkg. frozen asparagus spears
2 tbsp. nonfat sour cream
2 tbsp. nonfat mayonnaise
½ tsp. orange extract
Dash crushed red pepper

Cook asparagus according to package directions until crisp-tender. Drain
and keep warm. Combine remaining ingredients in a small bowl and mix
until blended. Drizzle sauce over hot asparagus and serve immediately.

Shopping List:

DAIRY	CONDIMENTS	SEASONINGS
Nonfat sour cream	Nonfat mayonnaise	Orange extract
		Crushed red pepper
FROZEN		
10-oz. pkg. frozen asparagus spears		

NUTRITION PER SERVING Calories 32 · Fat .2 g (6%) · Carbohydrates 5 g ·
Protein 3 g · Cholesterol 0 mg · Dietary Fiber 1 g · Sodium 60 mg
EXCHANGES 1 vegetable
CARB CHOICES 0

*Super Tip: Substitute fresh asparagus for frozen; cook in boiling water for 4 to
6 minutes or microwave on High until crisp-tender.*

SIDE DISHES

Asparagus with Fresh Herbs

Easy ◆ Serves: 4

¾ lb. fresh asparagus spears, cleaned and trimmed
2 tsp. nonfat chicken or vegetable broth
1 tbsp. chopped green onion
¾ tsp. snipped fresh tarragon
1½ tsp. chopped fresh parsley
¾ tsp. lemon juice

Place asparagus spears in microwave-safe baking dish; sprinkle with water and microwave on High 4 to 5 minutes, just until crisp-tender. While asparagus is cooking, combine remaining ingredients in a small saucepan. Cook, stirring constantly, over medium-high heat. When asparagus is done, spoon sauce over top and serve immediately.

Shopping List:

PRODUCE	CANNED
¾ lb. asparagus spears	Nonfat chicken or
Bunch green onions	vegetable broth
Fresh tarragon	
Fresh parsley	
Lemon or lemon juice	

NUTRITION PER SERVING Calories 10 · Fat .1 g (9%) · Carbohydrates 2 g · Protein 1 g · Cholesterol 0 mg · Dietary Fiber <1 g · Sodium 10 mg
EXCHANGES 0
CARB CHOICES 0

Super Tip: *Substitute frozen asparagus spears; cook as directed on package and top with herb sauce.*

SIDE DISHES

Basil and Garlic Potato Fries

Easy

• Serves: 4

1 lb. 4-oz. pkg. sliced potato home fries
1 tsp. garlic powder
1 tsp. crushed dried basil leaves
⅔ cup nonfat vegetable broth

Preheat oven to 350°F. Spray a shallow baking dish with cooking spray. Layer half the potato slices in baking dish and sprinkle with ½ teaspoon of the garlic powder and ½ teaspoon of the basil. Repeat layers; pour vegetable broth over top. Bake 45 to 55 minutes, until potatoes are crisp.

Shopping List:

REFRIGERATED OR PRODUCE	CANNED	SEASONINGS
1 lb. 4 oz.-pkg. sliced potato home fries	14½-oz. can nonfat vegetable broth	Garlic powder Dried basil leaves

NUTRITION PER SERVING Calories 137 • Fat 0 g (0%) •
Carbohydrates 30 g • Protein 4 g • Cholesterol 0 mg • Dietary Fiber 1 g •
Sodium 241 mg
EXCHANGES 2 starch
CARB CHOICES 2

Super Tip: *Substitute 3 to 4 fresh potatoes, thinly sliced, for packaged potatoes.*

SIDE DISHES

202

Brown Rice Pilaf

Easy ♦ Serves: 6

4 cups nonfat vegetable broth
1½ cups frozen chopped celery and onions
1½ cups long-grain brown rice

Spray a large saucepan with cooking spray; pour ¼ cup of the vegetable broth into saucepan. Add celery and onions and cook over medium-high heat until tender, 3 to 4 minutes. Add rice; cook, stirring frequently, until lightly browned. Add remaining vegetable broth; bring to a boil over high heat. Reduce heat and simmer, covered, until rice is tender and liquid is absorbed, about 20 minutes.

Shopping List:

FROZEN	PACKAGED	CANNED
12-oz. pkg. frozen chopped celery and onions	Long-grain brown rice	2 (14½-oz.) cans nonfat vegetable broth

NUTRITION PER SERVING Calories 192 • Fat 1.7 g (8%) •
Carbohydrates 38 g • Protein 6 g • Cholesterol 0 mg • Dietary Fiber 3 g •
Sodium 538 mg
EXCHANGES 2 starch • 1 vegetable
CARB CHOICES 3

Super Tip: *Substitute fresh celery and onions for frozen; chop and cook 6 to 7 minutes, until tender.*

SIDE DISHES

Carrots with Fruit Sauce

Easy

4 cups shredded carrots
3 tbsp. apricot preserves or orange marmalade

Spray a microwave-safe bowl with cooking spray; place carrots in bowl and drizzle with water. Cover and microwave on High 5 to 6 minutes. Spread apricot preserves over top; microwave 45 to 60 seconds, until slightly melted. Stir and serve immediately.

Shopping List:

PRODUCE	CONDIMENTS
16-oz. pkg. shredded carrots	Apricot preserves or orange marmalade

NUTRITION PER SERVING Calories 89 • Fat .2 g (2%) • Carbohydrates 22 g • Protein 1 g • Cholesterol 0 mg • Dietary Fiber 4 g • Sodium 40 mg
EXCHANGES 3 vegetable • ½ other carb
CARB CHOICES 1

Super Tip: *Carrots contain so much beta-carotene that a single carrot provides enough for your body to convert it into an entire day's requirement of vitamin A.*

SIDE DISHES

Cheesy Potato Home Fries

Easy   • Serves: 6

1 lb. 4-oz. pkg. sliced potato home fries
1½ cups shredded nonfat cheddar cheese
1 cup cornflake crumbs

Preheat oven to 400°F. Line baking sheet(s) with foil and spray with cooking spray. Arrange potato slices on baking sheet(s); sprinkle with cheese and top with crumbs. Bake 25 to 30 minutes, until potatoes are crisp and cheese is lightly browned.

Shopping List:

DAIRY	REFRIGERATED OR PRODUCE	PACKAGED
6 oz. shredded nonfat cheddar cheese	1 lb. 4-oz. pkg. sliced potato home fries	Cornflake crumbs

NUTRITION PER SERVING Calories 185 • Fat 0 g • Carbohydrates 32 g • Protein 11 g • Cholesterol 0 mg • Dietary Fiber 1 g • Sodium 503 mg
EXCHANGES 2 starch • 1 very lean meat
CARB CHOICES 2

Super Tip: *Substitute thinly sliced fresh potatoes for packaged; increase baking time to 35 to 40 minutes.*

SIDE DISHES

Creamed Corn with Chiles

Easy   ◆ Serves: 4

¼ cup nonfat cream cheese
1 tbsp. skim milk
10-oz. pkg. frozen corn kernels, thawed and drained
2 tbsp. chopped green chiles, drained

Spray a medium saucepan with cooking spray. Combine cream cheese and milk in saucepan; cook over medium heat, stirring constantly, until cheese is melted and mixture is smooth. Fold in corn kernels and green chiles; cook, stirring constantly, until heated through.

Shopping List:

DAIRY	FROZEN	CANNED
3 oz. nonfat cream cheese	10-oz. pkg. frozen corn kernels	4-oz. can chopped green chiles
Skim milk		

NUTRITION PER SERVING Calories 72 • Fat 0 g • Carbohydrates 16 g •
Protein 4 g • Cholesterol 0 mg • Dietary Fiber 2 g • Sodium 155 mg
EXCHANGES 1 starch
CARB CHOICES 1

Super Tip: *Substitute an 11-ounce can corn kernels for frozen; drain well before adding to cream sauce.*

SIDE DISHES

Green Chile Corn Cakes with Salsa

Easy—Do Ahead   ◆ Serves: 4

2 tbsp. all-purpose flour
¼ tsp. chili powder
¼ tsp. salt-free spicy seasoning
⅛ tsp. baking powder
2 tbsp. Southwestern-style egg substitute
¼ cup skim milk
11-oz. can Mexican-style corn, drained
1 tbsp. chopped green chiles, drained
Salsa

Combine flour, chili powder, spicy seasoning and baking powder in a medium bowl; add egg substitute and milk; mix until blended. Fold in corn and green chiles. Spray a large nonstick skillet with cooking spray and heat over medium heat. For each corn cake, spoon 2 to 3 tablespoons of the corn mixture into skillet; press lightly to flatten. Cook 2 to 3 minutes; turn corn cakes over and cook 2 to 3 minutes, until browned on both sides. Wrap corn cakes in foil and keep warm in 200°F oven. Spray skillet and cook remaining batter. Serve cakes with salsa. If prepared ahead and refrigerated, bake in 350°F oven for 5 to 8 minutes, until hot.

Shopping List:

DAIRY
Skim milk
Southwestern-style egg
  substitute

PACKAGED
All-purpose flour
Baking powder

CANNED
11-oz. Mexican-style
  corn or regular corn
  kernels
4-oz. can chopped
  green chiles

CONDIMENTS
Salsa

SEASONINGS
Chili powder
Salt-free spicy
  seasoning or Mexican
  seasoning

SIDE DISHES

NUTRITION PER SERVING Calories 82 • Fat .5 g (5%) • Carbohydrates 18 g • Protein 3 g • Cholesterol <1 g • Dietary Fiber 2 g • Sodium 325 mg
EXCHANGES ½ starch • ½ other carb
CARB CHOICES 1

Super Tip: *You can substitute regular egg substitute plus 2 tablespoons chopped bell pepper for the Southwestern-style egg substitute.*

Grilled Peppers and Onions

Easy

• Serves: 4

1-lb. pkg. frozen pepper stir-fry mix
¼ cup red wine vinegar
1 tbsp. Dijon mustard
2 tsp. roasted minced garlic
¼ tsp. black pepper

Preheat broiler on high heat. Line a baking sheet with foil and spray with cooking spray. Spread pepper stir-fry mix on baking sheet. Combine remaining ingredients in a small bowl and mix well. Brush peppers with vinegar-mustard mixture; broil 3 minutes. Turn peppers over, brush with sauce and broil 2 to 3 minutes, until browned.

Shopping List:

FROZEN	CONDIMENTS	SEASONINGS
1-lb. pkg. frozen pepper stir-fry mix	Red wine vinegar Dijon mustard	Roasted minced garlic or regular minced garlic Black pepper

NUTRITION PER SERVING Calories 43 • Fat .5 g (10%) •
Carbohydrates 11 g • Protein 1 g • Cholesterol 0 mg • Dietary Fiber 2 g •
Sodium 59 mg
EXCHANGES 1 vegetable • ½ other carb
CARB CHOICES 1

Super Tip: *You can substitute 3 fresh bell peppers and 1 onion for frozen stir-fry mix; cut peppers and onion into thick strips or chunks and prepare as directed.*

SIDE DISHES

Hash Brown Potatoes

Easy—Do Ahead ◆ Serves: 4

1 lb. 4-oz. pkg. diced cubed potatoes with onion
½ cup frozen diced bell peppers
1½ tsp. salt-free spicy seasoning

Preheat oven to 450°F. Line a baking sheet with foil and spray with cooking spray. Spray a large nonstick skillet with cooking spray. Add potato mixture and bell peppers; sprinkle with seasoning. Cook, stirring frequently, until potatoes are lightly browned, 5 to 8 minutes. Spread potatoes on baking sheet in a single layer; bake 10 to 15 minutes, until golden brown and crisp.

Shopping List:

REFRIGERATED OR PRODUCE	FROZEN	SEASONINGS
1 lb. 4-oz. pkg. diced cubed potatoes with onion	10-oz. pkg. frozen diced peppers	Salt-free spicy seasoning

NUTRITION PER SERVING Calories 133 · Fat 0 g · Carbohydrates 30 g · Protein 3 g · Cholesterol 0 mg · Dietary Fiber 3 g · Sodium 277 mg
EXCHANGES 1½ starch · 1 vegetable
CARB CHOICES 2

Super Tip: *Substitute 4 cups cubed potatoes and ½ cup chopped onion for packaged cubed potatoes with onion. Adjust cooking times as needed for fresh potatoes.*

SIDE DISHES

Lemon-Garlic Steamed Spinach

Easy

• Serves: 4

16-oz. pkg. fresh spinach leaves
1 tsp. roasted minced garlic
3 tbsp. lemon juice

Place spinach leaves in a microwave-safe baking dish; sprinkle with roasted garlic. Cover with plastic wrap and microwave on High for 6 to 7 minutes. Remove plastic wrap, drizzle with lemon juice and serve immediately.

Shopping List:

PRODUCE	SEASONINGS
16-oz. pkg. fresh spinach leaves	Roasted minced garlic or regular minced garlic
Lemon or lemon juice	

NUTRITION PER SERVING Calories 41 • Fat .5 g (11%) • Carbohydrates 7 g • Protein 5 g • Cholesterol 0 mg • Dietary Fiber 4 g • Sodium 134 mg
EXCHANGES 2 vegetable
CARB CHOICES 0

Super Tip: Experts say that the amino acids in garlic actually encourage nail growth. Slice 1 garlic clove and massage into nail bed and cuticle. Slip on cotton gloves for 10 minutes and rinse well. Rubbing wet hands with salt will wash away the garlic odor.

SIDE DISHES

More than Mom's Mashed Potatoes

Easy—Do Ahead

• Serves: 4

16-oz. pkg. precooked cubed potatoes
½ cup nonfat sour cream
½ cup skim milk
1½ tsp. prepared horseradish
Pepper to taste

Cook potatoes according to package directions; drain well and mash. Add remaining ingredients and beat to desired consistency. If potatoes are too dry, add additional milk and sour cream until desired consistency is reached.

Shopping List:

REFRIGERATED OR PRODUCE	DAIRY	CONDIMENTS
16-oz. pkg. precooked cubed potatoes	4 oz. nonfat sour cream 4 oz. skim milk	Prepared horseradish
		SEASONINGS Black pepper

NUTRITION PER SERVING Calories 123 • Fat .1 g (0%) •
Carbohydrates 24 g • Protein 5 g • Cholesterol <1 g • Dietary Fiber 2 g •
Sodium 93 mg
EXCHANGES 1 starch • ½ other carb
CARB CHOICES 2

Super Tip: *Horseradish has a million recipe possibilities, lots of flavor and no fat. One tablespoon of prepared horseradish contains a mere 6 calories along with 1.4 grams of carbohydrates, 14 milligrams of sodium, 44 milligrams of potassium, 9 milligrams of calcium, 5 milligrams of phosphorous and 0 grams of fat.*

SIDE DISHES

Orange Potato Puffs

Easy—Do Ahead ◆ Serves: 8

3 (29-oz.) cans cut sweet potatoes in light syrup, drained well
⅓ cup orange juice
¼ cup egg substitute
1 tbsp. grated orange peel
¾ tsp. ground cinnamon
½ tsp. ground nutmeg
¼ cup honey wheat germ

Preheat oven to 375°F. Line a baking sheet with foil and spray with cooking spray. Place potatoes in large bowl; mash until smooth. Add orange juice, egg substitute, orange peel, cinnamon and nutmeg; mix until blended. Spoon potato mixture into mounds on baking sheet; sprinkle with wheat germ. Bake 25 to 30 minutes, until lightly browned.

Shopping List:

PRODUCE	PACKAGED	SEASONINGS
Orange (for orange peel and juice)	Honey wheat germ	Ground cinnamon
		Ground nutmeg
	CANNED	
DAIRY	3 (29-oz) cans cut sweet	
Egg substitute	potatoes in light syrup	

NUTRITION PER SERVING Calories 303 • Fat 1 g (3%) •
Carbohydrates 69 g • Protein 7 g • Cholesterol 0 mg • Dietary Fiber 8 g •
Sodium 174 mg
EXCHANGES 5 vegetable • 1 fruit • 2 other carb
CARB CHOICES 5

Super Tip: Some migraine sufferers are sensitive to orange zest; simply inhaling the oily zest can trigger a migraine attack.

SIDE DISHES

Pepperoni Pizza Potatoes

Easy—Do Ahead   • Serves: 4

4 large baking potatoes
1 cup nonfat pasta or pizza sauce
2 cups shredded nonfat mozzarella cheese
3 slices reduced-fat pepperoni slices, chopped

Prick potatoes with a knife or fork. Microwave on High for 9 minutes per potato. Preheat oven to 450°F. Place potatoes in oven and bake 20 to 25 minutes. Remove from oven and cool 5 minutes. Line a baking sheet with foil and spray with cooking spray. Cut each potato in half lengthwise; scoop out potato flesh and fluff with a fork. Place potato flesh back in shell; top each potato half with 2 tablespoons of the sauce; sprinkle with ¼ of the mozzarella cheese and 1 tablespoon chopped pepperoni. Bake 10 to 15 minutes, until cheese is melted and lightly browned. Serve immediately.

Shopping List:

PRODUCE	MEAT	CANNED

4 large baking potatoes	3-oz. pkg. reduced-fat
	   pepperoni slices
		14½-oz. can nonfat
		   pasta or pizza sauce

DAIRY		
8 oz. shredded nonfat mozzarella cheese		

NUTRITION PER SERVING Calories 341 • Fat 1 g (3%) •
Carbohydrates 55 g • Protein 25 g • Cholesterol 5 mg • Dietary Fiber 6 g •
Sodium 707 mg
EXCHANGES 3 starch • 2 vegetable • 2 very lean meat
CARB CHOICES 4

Super Tip: *Nutritionists recommend that the bread, cereals and potatoes group make up 47 to 50 percent of your daily diet, including 18 grams of fiber each day.*

Portobellos Parmesan

Easy—Do Ahead ◆ Serves: 4

1 cup seasoned bread crumbs
¼ cup grated nonfat Parmesan cheese
4 portobello mushrooms
½ cup nonfat pasta sauce
1 cup canned diced tomatoes, drained
1 cup shredded nonfat mozzarella cheese

Preheat oven to 450°F. Line a baking sheet with foil and spray with cooking spray. Combine bread crumbs and Parmesan cheese in a self-sealing plastic bag and shake until well mixed. Add mushrooms, one at a time, and shake until coated. Arrange mushrooms on baking sheet, stem ends up. Spread each mushroom with 2 tablespoons of the pasta sauce and top with ¼ cup tomatoes. Sprinkle cheese over top. Bake 15 to 18 minutes, until cheese is melted and lightly browned. Serve with additional pasta sauce, if desired.

Shopping List:

PRODUCE	PACKAGED
4 portobello mushrooms	Seasoned bread crumbs
DAIRY	**CANNED**
4 oz. shredded nonfat mozzarella cheese	14½-oz. can diced tomatoes (any variety)
Grated nonfat Parmesan cheese	Nonfat pasta sauce

NUTRITION PER SERVING Calories 184 • Fat 1.3 g (6%) • Carbohydrates 26 g • Protein 16 g • Cholesterol 0 mg • Dietary Fiber 2 g • Sodium 618 mg
EXCHANGES 1½ very lean meat • 2 vegetable • 1 starch
CARB CHOICES 2

Super Tip: *Serve Portobellos Parmesan with a salad and pasta for a complete meal.*

SIDE DISHES

Potato-Carrot Pancakes

Easy—Do Ahead—Freeze   ◆ Serves: 8; 16 pancakes

1 lb. 4-oz. pkg. shredded potatoes
1½ cups shredded carrots
½ cup egg substitute with vegetables
2 tbsp. all-purpose flour
1 tsp. dried thyme
1 tsp. dried basil
½ tsp. pepper
2 cups applesauce

Spray a large nonstick skillet with cooking spray. Combine all ingredients except applesauce in a large bowl and mix well. Heat a large skillet over medium-high heat. For each pancake, ladle ¼ cup batter into skillet; flatten slightly if needed. Cook pancakes 3 minutes; turn pancakes over and cook 3 to 4 minutes, until golden brown on both sides. Remove pancakes from skillet and keep warm while cooking remaining batter. Serve pancakes with applesauce.

Shopping List:

RODUCE	REFRIGERATED	CANNED
8-oz. pkg. shredded carrots	1 lb. 4-oz. shredded potatoes	16 oz. applesauce (flavor of choice)
DAIRY	**PACKAGED**	**SEASONINGS**
4 oz. egg substitute with vegetables or plain egg substitute	All-purpose flour	Dried thyme Dried basil Black pepper

NUTRITION PER SERVING Calories 108 • Fat .2 g (2%) •
Carbohydrates 25 g • Protein 3 g • Cholesterol 0 mg • Dietary Fiber 2 g •
Sodium 29 mg
EXCHANGES ½ starch • ½ fruit • 1 vegetable
CARB CHOICES 2

Super Tip: *You can substitute frozen shredded potatoes for the refrigerated shredded potatoes; thaw and drain well before combining with other ingredients.*

SIDE DISHES

Ranch Fries

Easy

• Serves: 6

1 lb. 4-oz pkg. sliced potato home fries
2-oz. pkg. nonfat ranch salad dressing mix

Preheat oven to 400°F. Line baking sheet(s) with cooking spray. Combine potatoes and dressing mix in a large bowl; toss carefully to coat. Arrange potato slices in a single layer on baking sheet(s); spray lightly with cooking spray. Bake 10 to 15 minutes. Turn potatoes over, spray with cooking spray and bake 10 to 15 minutes, until golden brown and crisp.

Shopping List:

REFRIGERATED OR PRODUCE	CONDIMENTS
1 lb. 4-oz. pkg. sliced potato home fries	2-oz. pkg. nonfat ranch salad dressing mix

NUTRITION PER SERVING Calories 112 • Fat 0 g (0%) •
Carbohydrates 24 g • Protein 2 g • Cholesterol 0 mg • Dietary Fiber 1 g •
Sodium 1138 mg
EXCHANGES 1 starch • ½ other carb
CARB CHOICES 2

Super Tip: *Dispel the myths about carbs! Your body needs complex carbohydrates for fuel, and their fiber reduces the risk of heart disease, diverticulitosis and certain cancers.*

SIDE DISHES

216

Shortcut Stuffing

Easy—Do Ahead ◆ Serves: 10

3½ cups nonfat chicken or vegetable broth
1½ cups frozen chopped onion and celery
4-oz. can mushroom stems and pieces, drained (optional)
3 (5-oz.) boxes fat-free herb-seasoned croutons

Spray a Dutch oven or large saucepan with cooking spray. Combine broth, onion and celery and mushrooms, if using, in pan and bring to a boil over high heat. Reduce heat to low, cover and simmer 3 to 5 minutes, until vegetables are softened. Remove pan from heat; stir in croutons and mix until blended and moistened. (If mixture is too dry, add additional broth.) Serve immediately or bake in 350°F oven for 35 to 45 minutes, until lightly browned.

Shopping List:

CANNED	FROZEN	PACKAGED
2 (14½-oz.) cans nonfat chicken or vegetable broth	12-oz. pkg. frozen chopped onion and celery or 7-oz. container diced onion and celery, found in produce section	3 (5-oz.) boxes fat-free herb-seasoned croutons
4-oz. can mushroom stems and pieces (optional)		

NUTRITION PER SERVING Calories 106 • Fat .1 g (0%) •
Carbohydrates 25 g • Protein 4 g • Cholesterol 0 mg • Dietary Fiber 1 g •
Sodium 526 mg
EXCHANGES ½ starch • 3 vegetable
CARB CHOICES 2

Super Tip: *Another reason to cut the fat, migraine sufferers who cut their fat intake by more than half (from 66 to 28 grams a day) had fewer, shorter and less painful attacks (Source: University of California-Irvine study led by Zuzana Bic).*

SIDE DISHES

Spanish Rice

Easy

• Serves: 4

2 tbsp. plus 1¾ cups nonfat chicken or vegetable broth
1 cup uncooked long-grain white rice
¼ cup tomato sauce
¼ cup water

Spray a medium saucepan with cooking spray; add the 2 tablespoons broth and heat over medium-high heat. Add rice; cook 3 to 5 minutes, until lightly browned. Add remaining ingredients. Bring to a boil over high heat; reduce heat to low, cover and simmer 18 to 20 minutes, until rice is tender.

Shopping List:

PACKAGED	CANNED
Long-grain white rice	14½-oz. can nonfat chicken or vegetable broth
	Tomato sauce

NUTRITION PER SERVING Calories 174 • Fat .3 g (2%) •
Carbohydrates 38 g • Protein 4 g • Cholesterol 0 mg • Dietary Fiber 1 g •
Sodium 144 mg
EXCHANGES 2 starch • 1 vegetable
CARB CHOICES 2

Super Tip: *In terms of cooking texture, rice is classified into three different categories: short, medium and long-grain. Basmati and jasmine rice are two types of long-grain rice with an aromatic, nutlike flavor.*

SIDE DISHES

218

Spinach-Artichoke Pie

Easy   ♦ Serves: 6

2 (10-oz.) pkgs. frozen chopped spinach, thawed, drained and pressed dry
9-oz. pkg. frozen artichoke hearts, thawed, drained and diced
4 cups fat-free herb-seasoned croutons
2 cups shredded nonfat mozzarella cheese
1 cup egg substitute with vegetables
2 cups skim milk
½ cup grated nonfat Parmesan cheese
¼ tsp. ground pepper

Preheat oven to 350°F. Spray a 9 × 13-inch baking dish with cooking spray. Combine spinach, artichokes, croutons and 1 cup of the mozzarella cheese in a large bowl; mix well and spread mixture in baking dish. Sprinkle remaining mozzarella cheese over top. Combine egg substitute, milk, Parmesan cheese and pepper in bowl; mix until ingredients are completely blended. Pour mixture over cheese layer, pressing croutons into liquid to keep moistened. Bake 20 minutes. Increase temperature to 400°F; bake 15 to 20 minutes, until casserole is lightly browned.

Shopping List:

DAIRY	FROZEN	PACKAGED
8 oz. egg substitute with vegetables	2 (10-oz.) pkgs. frozen chopped spinach	2 (5-oz.) boxes fat-free herb-seasoned croutons
1 pint skim milk	9-oz. pkg. frozen artichoke hearts	
Grated nonfat Parmesan cheese		**SEASONINGS**
8 oz. shredded nonfat mozzarella cheese		Black pepper

NUTRITION PER SERVING Calories 279 • Fat .4 g (1%) • Carbohydrates 42 g • Protein 29 g • Cholesterol 1 mg • Dietary Fiber 2 g • Sodium 831 mg
EXCHANGES 4 vegetable • 1 starch • 2 very lean meat • ½ milk
CARB CHOICES 3

Super Tip: *Substitute 1 cup plain egg substitute or 8 egg whites for egg substitute with vegetables. Use any variety of fat-free croutons or stuffing mix for herb-seasoned croutons.*

SIDE DISHES

219

Spinach-Cheese Potatoes

Easy—Do Ahead

4 medium baking potatoes
10¾-oz. can low-fat cream of celery soup
¾ cup shredded nonfat cheddar cheese
1 tsp. Dijon mustard
10-oz. pkg. frozen chopped spinach, thawed and drained

Pierce potatoes in several places with a fork. Microwave on High for 7 minutes per potato. Preheat oven or toaster oven to 450°F. Place potatoes in oven and bake about 20 minutes. Meanwhile, combine soup, cheese, mustard and spinach in a medium saucepan; bring to a boil over medium-high heat. Reduce heat to low; simmer 5 minutes. Cut potatoes in half lengthwise; spoon spinach-cheese sauce over tops and serve.

Shopping List:

PRODUCE	FROZEN	CONDIMENTS
4 medium baking potatoes	10-oz. pkg. frozen chopped spinach	Dijon mustard
DAIRY	**CANNED**	
3 oz. shredded nonfat cheddar cheese	10¾-oz. can low-fat cream of celery soup	

NUTRITION PER SERVING Calories 253 • Fat 2.6 g (10%) •
Carbohydrates 45 g • Protein 13 g • Cholesterol 3 mg • Dietary Fiber 6 g •
Sodium 869 mg
EXCHANGES 2 vegetable • 2 starch • ½ very lean meat • ½ fat
CARB CHOICES 3

Super Tip: *Scientists at the National Institute of Environmental Health Sciences discovered that eating 2 or more servings of spinach a week might lower women's breast cancer risk.*

SIDE DISHES

Sweet Potatoes with Apricot-Pineapple Sauce

Easy—Do Ahead

• Serves: 4

17-oz. can whole sweet potatoes, drained well
½ cup apricot fruit spread
8-oz. can pineapple chunks in juice, drained well

Preheat oven to 375°F. Spray an 8- or 9-inch baking dish with cooking spray. Cut sweet potatoes into 1-inch slices and arrange in dish. Spoon apricot spread over potatoes; add pineapple chunks and toss lightly. Cover dish with foil and bake 12 to 15 minutes, until heated through.

Shopping List:

CANNED	CONDIMENTS
17-oz. can whole sweet potatoes	Apricot fruit spread
8-oz. can pineapple chunks in juice	

NUTRITION PER SERVING Calories 254 • Fat .3 g (1%) •
Carbohydrates 62 g • Protein 2 g • Cholesterol 0 mg • Dietary Fiber 4 g •
Sodium 69 mg
EXCHANGES 3 fruit • 1 starch
CARB CHOICES 4

Super Tip: Substitute fresh sweet potatoes for canned; cook in boiling water for 25 minutes. Peel, slice and prepare according to recipe directions.

SIDE DISHES

Veggie-Cheese Bake

Easy—Do Ahead • Serves: 8

2 (8-oz.) pkg. yolk-free egg noodles, cooked and drained
16-oz. pkg. frozen broccoli and cauliflower florets, thawed
2 cups nonfat cottage cheese
2 cups shredded nonfat cheddar cheese

Preheat oven to 350°F. Spray a 2-quart baking dish with cooking spray. Combine noodles, broccoli and cauliflower, cottage cheese and ½ cup of the cheddar cheese in baking dish; toss until well mixed. Sprinkle remaining cheese on top; bake 15 to 20 minutes, until bubbly hot and lightly browned.

Shopping List:

DAIRY	FROZEN	PACKAGED
16-oz. carton nonfat cottage cheese	16-oz. pkg. frozen broccoli and cauliflower florets	2 (8-oz.) pkgs. yolk-free egg noodles
8 oz. shredded nonfat cheddar cheese		

NUTRITION PER SERVING Calories 281 • Fat .6 g (2%) •
Carbohydrates 47 g • Protein 20 g • Cholesterol 1 mg • Dietary Fiber 5 g •
Sodium 369 mg
EXCHANGES 2 starch • 3 vegetable • 1½ very lean meat
CARB CHOICES 3 •

Super Tip: *Use fresh broccoli and cauliflower florets, if desired.*

SIDE DISHES

Wild Rice and Apricot Stuffing

Average   ◆ Serves: 6

2 (14½-oz.) cans nonfat vegetable broth
1 cup frozen chopped onion
1½ tsp. dried thyme
8 oz. sliced fresh mushrooms
½ tsp. dried sage
¾ tsp. poultry seasoning
⅔ cup wild rice
½ cup long-grain white rice
½ cup diced dried apricots
Pepper to taste

Combine ½ cup of broth, onion and thyme in a large pot; cook on medium heat for 15 minutes. Add mushrooms and cook until vegetables are softened, 10 to 15 minutes. Pour mixture into a bowl and set aside. Pour remaining broth into pot; add sage and poultry seasoning and bring to a boil over high heat. Add wild rice; reduce heat to low, cover and simmer 30 minutes. Stir in white rice; cover and simmer until rice is tender and most of the liquid is absorbed, 15 to 20 minutes. Stir in reserved mushroom mixture and apricots. Cover pot and simmer until heated through, 10 to 15 minutes. Season with pepper and serve.

Shopping List:

PRODUCE	PACKAGED	SEASONINGS
8 oz. sliced mushrooms	Wild rice	Dried thyme
	Long-grain white rice	Dried sage
FROZEN	Dried apricots	Poultry seasoning
12-oz. pkg. frozen		Black pepper
chopped onions	**CANNED**	
	2 (14½-oz.) cans nonfat	
	vegetable or chicken	
	broth	

SIDE DISHES

NUTRITION PER SERVING Calories 176 • Fat .4 g (2%) • Carbohydrates 37 g • Protein 7 g • Cholesterol 0 mg • Dietary Fiber 2 g • Sodium 452 mg
EXCHANGES 1 vegetable • 1 starch • 1 fruit
CARB CHOICES 2

Super Tip: *You can substitute dried cranberries for the apricots and diced fresh onion for frozen.*

FEARLESS AND
FLAWLESS DESSERTS

❖

❖ ❖ ❖

Smarten up about Snacking: Save Room for Scrumptious Desserts

The bottom line: With healthy choices, snacking can enhance, rather than hurt, your diet.

Snack Foods under 100 Calories

1. ½ whole wheat pita filled with broccoli slaw mix and 1 to 2 tablespoons nonfat ranch salad dressing.
2. ½ cantaloupe.
3. 8 oz. skim milk with 2 tbsp. nonfat chocolate syrup.
4. ½ cup unsweetened applesauce sprinkled with cinnamon.
5. 2 low-fat graham crackers.
6. ½ cup Kashi cereal with ¼ cup nonfat vanilla yogurt.
7. 1 cup nonfat broth with 5 nonfat saltine crackers.
8. 6 large boiled shrimp with cocktail sauce.
9. 1-oz. box of raisins.
10. 8 to 10 celery stalks with ½ cup chunky salsa.
11. 2 cups air-popped popcorn sprinkled with grated nonfat Parmesan cheese.
12. 20 thin salted pretzel sticks with 2 tablespoons spicy brown mustard.
13. 2- to 3-inch slice angel food cake topped with ½ cup sliced strawberries and 1 tablespoon nonfat frozen whipped topping.
14. 20 baby carrots with 2 tablespoons nonfat ranch salad dressing.
15. 8 animal crackers.
16. ½ baked potato topped with 2 tablespoons salsa.
17. 1 slice raisin bread with 1 tablespoon nonfat cream cheese.
18. Frozen banana dipped in 2 tablespoons nonfat chocolate syrup.
19. 1 apple sliced and dipped in 2 tablespoons nonfat caramel dip and 1 tablespoon wheat germ.
20. ½ English muffin with 1 teaspoon apple butter or low-sugar preserves and a cup of herbal tea.
21. ½ cup sugar-free gelatin, any flavor, and two tablespoons nonfat whipped topping.
22. 15 chocolate-covered raisins.
23. 6 fat-free saltine crackers with 2 teaspoons peanut butter.
24. Pudding parfait: ½ cup fat-free pudding layered with 2 vanilla wafers and a dollop of nonfat whipped topping.

25. S'more: Microwave one marshmallow on top of a low-fat graham cracker until gooey. Drizzle with 1 teaspoon nonfat chocolate syrup.
26. ½ apple sliced and dipped into 2 teaspoons peanut butter.
27. Freeze ½ cup orange juice and eat with a spoon.
28. ½ baked sweet potato drizzled with sugar-free syrup.
29. 2 sliced canned pears drizzled with 1 tablespoon nonfat chocolate syrup.
30. 5 medium apricots.
31. 15 pieces candy corn.
32. 3 fortune cookies.
33. 1 frozen fruit bar.
34. 2 fat-free fig bars.
35. 15 gummy bears.
36. 1½ cups frozen grapes.
37. 8 large jelly beans.
38. 2 kiwifruit.
39. 6 bite-size pieces of red licorice.
40. 10 oyster crackers with 1 cup nonfat broth.

Brownie Sundae Treat

Easy • Serves: 8

¾ cup all-fruit strawberry spread
8 (2-inch) brownie squares
4 cups nonfat frozen yogurt (flavor of choice)
3 bananas, peeled and sliced
4 maraschino cherries, cut in half

Place strawberry spread in a microwave-safe cup and heat on High 45 to 60 seconds, until warmed through. To assemble dessert: Place one brownie on each dessert plate; top with ½ cup of the frozen yogurt and one-eighth of the bananas. Drizzle with strawberry spread and top with maraschino cherry halves.

Shopping List:

PRODUCE	PACKAGED	OTHER
3 bananas	Fat-free brownies or brownie mix	Maraschino cherries
FROZEN		
1 quart nonfat frozen yogurt (flavor of choice)	**CONDIMENTS** 10-oz. jar Smucker's Simply Fruit strawberry fruit spread	

NUTRITION PER SERVING Calories 376 • Fat .2 g (0%) • Carbohydrates 87 g • Protein 6 g • Cholesterol 0 mg • Dietary Fiber 1 g • Sodium 308 mg
EXCHANGES 6 other carbs
CARB CHOICES 6

Super Tip: *Purchase fat-free prepared brownies such as Entenmann's Light Fudge, or prepare 1 package Krusteaz fat-free brownie mix as directed on package. Simple substitutions: any low-fat or fat-free chocolate cake or brownie.*

DESSERTS

Caramel-Banana Sundae

Easy
• Serves: 4

2 bananas, sliced lengthwise
2 cups vanilla or praline nonfat frozen yogurt
¼ cup caramel fat-free ice cream topping
1 cup frozen nonfat whipped topping
1 tbsp. chopped nuts

Place one banana slice in each of four dessert dishes. Top each banana with
½ cup of the frozen yogurt and drizzle with 1 tablespoon of the caramel topping. Spoon ¼ cup of the whipped topping on top and sprinkle with nuts.
Serve immediately.

Shopping List:

PRODUCE	FROZEN	PACKAGED
2 bananas	16-oz. carton nonfat frozen yogurt (vanilla, praline or other flavor of choice)	Chopped nuts
	8-oz. container frozen nonfat whipped topping	**OTHER** 12.25-oz. jar caramel fat-free ice cream topping

NUTRITION PER SERVING Calories 249 • Fat 1.3 g (5%) •
Carbohydrates 53 g • Protein 5 g • Cholesterol 0 mg • Dietary Fiber 1 g •
Sodium 100 mg
EXCHANGES 3½ other carb
CARB CHOICES 4

Super Tip: *In a recent study of 10,000 people at Tulane University, researchers
discovered that people with low potassium levels have a higher risk of stroke.
The good news: one banana a day is all most people need to boost their intake
to the recommended 2,300 mg a day and reduce their stroke risk by 28 percent.*

DESSERTS

Caramel-Pineapple Loaf Cake

Easy—Do Ahead

♦ Serves: 8

13.6-oz. fat-free loaf cake
½ cup caramel fat-free ice cream topping
3 canned pineapple slices, drained well
3 maraschino cherries

Preheat oven to 350°F. Spray a large baking dish with cooking spray. Place loaf cake upside down in dish; brush cake with caramel topping. Place pineapple slices on top and place a maraschino cherry in the center of each pineapple slice. Bake 30 minutes and serve while hot.

Shopping List:

PACKAGED	CANNED	OTHER
13.6-oz. Entenmann's fat-free loaf cake	8-oz. can pineapple slices in juice	12.25-oz. jar caramel fat-free ice cream topping Maraschino cherries

NUTRITION PER SERVING Calories 187 • Fat 0 g • Carbohydrates 44 g • Protein 2 g • Cholesterol 0 mg • Dietary Fiber 1 g • Sodium 212 mg
EXCHANGES 3 other carb
CARB CHOICES 3

Super Tip: *Royal Anne cherries are the ones specially processed, dyed red and sold as maraschino cherries.*

DESSERTS

Carrot Cake with Cream Cheese Frosting

Easy—Do Ahead

♦ Serves: 12

18-oz. pkg. carrot cake mix
1 cup crushed pineapple, lightly drained
¾ cup egg substitute
8-oz. pkg. soft-style nonfat cream cheese
1 cup marshmallow creme
1 tsp. lemon juice
1 tsp. vanilla extract
1 cup powdered sugar

Preheat oven to 350°F. Spray a 9 × 13-inch baking dish with cooking spray. Combine cake mix, pineapple and egg substitute in a mixing bowl; beat with electric mixer until creamy and smooth. Pour batter into pan. Bake 27 to 33 minutes, until toothpick inserted in center comes out clean. Cool completely in pan on a wire rack.

Combine cream cheese, marshmallow creme, lemon juice, vanilla and powdered sugar in a medium bowl. Carefully beat ingredients until mixture is creamy and smooth. When cake is completely cooled, spread frosting on top. Refrigerate cake if not serving immediately.

Shopping List:

DAIRY	BAKING	OTHER
6 oz. egg substitute	18-oz. pkg. super moist	Lemon juice
8-oz. pkg. soft-style	carrot cake mix	
nonfat cream cheese	7-oz. jar marshmallow	
	creme	
CANNED	Powdered sugar	
8-oz. can crushed	Vanilla extract	
pineapple in juice		

NUTRITION PER SERVING Calories 263 • Fat 3 g (11%) •
Carbohydrates 55 g • Protein 5 g • Cholesterol 0 mg • Dietary Fiber<1 g •
Sodium 415 mg
EXCHANGES 3½ other carb • ½ fat
CARB CHOICES 4

Super Tip: *Read labels carefully. For healthier choices, select a cake mix with 2.5 to 3 grams of fat per serving.*

Carrot-Raisin Cake with Orange Glaze

Easy—Do Ahead
• Serves: 12

18-oz. pkg. carrot cake mix
¾ cup egg substitute
1¼ cups orange juice
⅔ cup crushed pineapple in juice, drained lightly
¾ cup raisins
2 cups powdered sugar
1 tsp. lemon juice
1 tsp. grated orange zest

Preheat oven to 350°F. Spray a 9 × 13-inch baking dish with cooking spray. Combine cake mix, egg substitute, 1 cup of the orange juice and pineapple in a large bowl; beat with an electric mixer until creamy and smooth. Fold in raisins. Pour batter into pan. Bake 27 to 33 minutes, until toothpick inserted in center comes out clean. Cool completely in pan on a wire rack.

Combine powdered sugar, remaining ¼ cup orange juice, lemon juice and orange zest in a medium bowl; mix until creamy and smooth. Spoon glaze over cooled cake.

Shopping List:

PRODUCE	REFRIGERATED	PACKAGED
Lemon or lemon juice	Orange juice	18-oz. pkg. super moist
Orange		carrot cake mix
		Raisins
DAIRY		Powdered sugar
Egg substitute		

NUTRITION PER SERVING Calories 288 • Fat 3.1 g (10%) •
Carbohydrates 64 g • Protein 3 g • Cholesterol 0 mg • Dietary Fiber 1 g •
Sodium 292 mg
EXCHANGES 4 other carb
CARB CHOICES 4

Super Tip: *Raisins, naturally cholesterol free, low in sodium and totally fat-free, are one of the most nutritious dried fruits. They are a good source of vitamins and minerals, including iron, potassium, calcium and certain B vitamins, as well as fiber and antioxidants.*

DESSERTS

Carrot-Raisin Cookies

Easy—Do Ahead   ◆ Serves: 36

18-oz. pkg. carrot cake mix
½ cup egg substitute
⅓ cup cinnamon applesauce
1 cup raisins
2 tsp. cinnamon-sugar mixture

Preheat oven to 350°F. Line baking sheet(s) with foil and spray with cooking spray. Combine cake mix, egg substitute and applesauce in a medium bowl; mix by hand until blended. Add raisins into batter; sprinkle with cinnamon-sugar mixture; fold into batter. Drop batter by tablespoons onto baking sheet(s); bake 8 to 10 minutes. Cool cookies 5 minutes before removing from baking sheets.

Shopping List:

DAIRY	PACKAGED	SEASONINGS
Egg substitute	18-oz. pkg. super moist carrot cake mix Cinnamon applesauce Raisins	Cinnamon-sugar mixture

NUTRITION PER SERVING Calories 73 • Fat 1 g (12%) •
Carbohydrates 16 g • Protein 1 g • Cholesterol 0 mg •
Dietary Fiber <1 g • Sodium 95 mg
EXCHANGES 1 other carb
CARB CHOICES 1

Super Tip: *Raisins have been a favorite fruit for centuries. Phoenicians and Armenians traded raisins with Greeks and Romans; they were often used to decorate places of worship, and sporting contests awarded raisins to the winners. Raisins were even used for trading slaves in ancient Rome.*

DESSERTS

234

Chocolate Chip Cookies

Easy—Do Ahead

• Serves: 36

18.25-oz. pkg. French vanilla cake mix
¼ cup egg substitute
¼ cup packed light brown sugar
¾ cup unsweetened applesauce
¾ cup miniature chocolate chips

Preheat oven to 350°F. Line baking sheet(s) with foil and spray with cooking spray. Combine cake mix, egg substitute, brown sugar and applesauce in a medium bowl; mix by hand until blended. Fold in chocolate chips. Drop dough by tablespoons onto baking sheet(s); bake 5 to 7 minutes. Cool on baking sheets 10 to 15 minutes before carefully removing.

Shopping List:

DAIRY	PACKAGED	
Egg substitute	18.25-oz. pkg. super moist French vanilla cake mix	Unsweetened applesauce
	Light brown sugar	Miniature chocolate chips

NUTRITION PER SERVING Calories 84 • Fat 1.7 g (18%) • Carbohydrates 17 g • Protein 1 g • Cholesterol 0 mg • Dietary Fiber <1 g • Sodium 95 mg
EXCHANGES 1 other carb
CARB CHOICES 2

Super Tip: *Chocolate contains more antioxidants (cancer-preventing enzymes) than red wine. In order to be significantly beneficial, the chocolate must contain at least 70 percent cocoa solids.*

DESSERTS

Chocolate-Cinnamon Dip

Easy—Do Ahead   ◆ Serves: 16

1 cup skim milk
3¾-oz. pkg. devil's food instant pudding mix
2 cups frozen nonfat whipped topping
½ tsp. ground cinnamon
Apple slices, strawberries or fat-free loaf cake cubes, to serve

Pour milk into a blender; add pudding mix and blend until smooth. Spoon mixture into a large bowl; fold in whipped topping until completely blended. Sprinkle with cinnamon. Cover and refrigerate 1 hour before serving with apple slices.

Shopping List:

DAIRY	FROZEN	SEASONINGS
8 oz. skim milk	8-oz. container frozen nonfat whipped topping	Ground cinnamon
PACKAGED		
3¾ oz. pkg. devil's food instant pudding mix		

NUTRITION PER SERVING Calories 44 • Fat 0 g • Carbohydrates 10 g • Protein 1 g • Cholesterol <1 mg • Dietary Fiber <1 g • Sodium 114 mg
EXCHANGES ½ other carb
CARB CHOICES 1

Super Tip: *University of Pennsylvania researchers found that the mere scent of chocolate makes us happier. Buy why stop at simply sniffing? Consuming the phenylethylamine (PEA) in a morsel of chocolate stimulates the nervous system, increases alertness and produces those head-over-heels happy feelings we get when we fall in love.*

DESSERTS

Chocolate Waffle Sundae Treat

Easy—Do Ahead   • Serves: 6

6 frozen nonfat waffles
3 cups chocolate nonfat frozen yogurt, sorbet or ice cream
¾ cup nonfat chocolate syrup or ice cream topping
3 tsp. chopped nuts

Bake or toast waffles according to package directions. Place a waffle on each dessert plate; top each waffle with ½ cup of the frozen yogurt, 2 tablespoons of the chocolate syrup and ½ teaspoon of the chopped nuts. Serve immediately.

Shopping List:

FROZEN	PACKAGED	OTHER
24 oz. chocolate nonfat frozen yogurt, sorbet or ice cream 6 frozen nonfat waffles	Chopped nuts	Chocolate nonfat syrup or ice cream topping

NUTRITION PER SERVING Calories 239 • Fat 1 g (4%) •
Carbohydrates 53 g • Protein 8 g • Cholesterol 0 mg • Dietary Fiber 1 g •
Sodium 236 mg
EXCHANGES 1½ starch • 2 other carb
CARB CHOICES 4

Super Tip: *Researchers at Brigham and Women's Hospital in Boston recently reported that eating a handful of nuts two or more times a week may drop a person's risk of sudden cardiac death by 47 percent. Nuts also lowered the risk of dying from heart disease by as much as 30 percent.*

DESSERTS

237

Dessert Dip

Easy—Do Ahead   ◆ Serves: 4

8-oz. pkg. nonfat cream cheese, softened
7-oz. jar marshmallow creme
1 tbsp. light brown sugar
½ tsp. ground cinnamon
Apple wedges, pineapple chunks, strawberries or cubes of Entenmann's fat-free
    golden or chocolate loaf cake

Combine all ingredients, except apple wedges, in a medium bowl; beat with
an electric mixer until creamy and smooth. Cover and refrigerate 45 to 60
minutes. Serve dip with fresh fruit.

Shopping List:

DAIRY	BAKING	SEASONINGS
8-oz. pkg. nonfat cream cheese	7-oz. jar marshmallow creme	Ground cinnamon
	Light brown sugar	

NUTRITION PER SERVING Calories 221 • Fat 0 g (0%) •
Carbohydrates 48 g • Protein 7 g • Cholesterol 0 mg • Dietary Fiber 0 g •
Sodium 397 mg
EXCHANGES 3 other carb
CARB CHOICES 3

Super Tip: *On average Americans eat more than 150 pounds of sugar a year.*
That's twice the recommended amount.

German Chocolate Cake
with Whipped Topping

Easy—Do Ahead   ◆ Serves: 12

18.25-oz. pkg. German chocolate cake mix
1⅓ cups water
½ cup unsweetened applesauce
¾ cup egg substitute
14-oz. can nonfat sweetened condensed milk
12.25-oz. jar caramel fat-free ice cream topping
8-oz. container frozen nonfat whipped topping, thawed

Preheat oven to 350°F. Spray a 9 × 13-inch baking dish with cooking spray and set aside. Combine cake mix, water, applesauce and egg substitute in a large mixing bowl; beat with an electric mixer until creamy and smooth. Pour batter into baking dish; bake 30 to 35 minutes, until toothpick inserted in center comes out clean. Cool cake in pan 15 minutes. Poke top of warm cake with skewer or wooden spoon handle. Drizzle milk over cake and let stand until absorbed into cake. Drizzle with caramel topping. Cover and refrigerate 2 to 4 hours, until chilled. Just before serving, spread cake with whipped topping.

Shopping List:

DAIRY	PACKAGED	OTHER
6 oz. egg substitute	18.25-oz. pkg. super moist German chocolate cake mix	12.25-oz. jar caramel nonfat ice cream topping
FROZEN	Unsweetened applesauce	
8-oz. container frozen nonfat whipped topping		
	CANNED	
	14-oz. can nonfat sweetened condensed milk	

NUTRITION PER SERVING Calories 400 • Fat 3 g (7%) •
Carbohydrates 85 g • Protein 6 g • Cholesterol 0 mg • Dietary Fiber <1 g •
Sodium 379 mg
EXCHANGES 5½ other carb
CARB CHOICES 6

Super Tip: *One piece of regular German chocolate cake contains more than 400 calories and 20 grams of fat.*

DESSERTS

German Chocolate Cupcakes with Caramel Topping

Easy—Do Ahead
◆ Serves: 24

18.25-oz.pkg. German chocolate cake mix
1 cup vanilla nonfat yogurt
¼ cup unsweetened applesauce
½ cup water
¾ cup egg substitute
12.25-oz. jar caramel nonfat ice cream topping

Preheat oven to 350°F. Spray 24 muffin cups with cooking spray. Combine cake mix, yogurt, applesauce, water and egg substitute in a large mixing bowl; beat with an electric mixer until creamy and smooth. Fill each muffin cup two-thirds full; bake 18 to 23 minutes, until toothpick inserted in center comes out clean. Cool cupcakes in pan 5 minutes. Carefully remove from pan; when cupcakes are completely cooled, drizzle with caramel topping.

Shopping List:

DAIRY	PACKAGED	OTHER
6 oz. egg substitute	18.25-oz. pkg. super	12.25-oz. jar caramel
8-oz. carton vanilla	moist German	nonfat ice cream
nonfat yogurt	chocolate cake mix	topping
	Unsweetened	
	applesauce	

NUTRITION PER SERVING Calories 141 • Fat 1.5 g (10%) •
Carbohydrates 30 g • Protein 2 g • Cholesterol <1 mg • Dietary Fiber 0 g •
Sodium 176 mg
EXCHANGES 2 other carb
CARB CHOICES 2

Super Tip: *Solid chocolate as we know it was not around until the nineteenth century. Prior to 1830, chocolate was only consumed as a hot or cold beverage.*

DESSERTS

Kahlua Cake Parfait

Easy—Do Ahead   • Serves: 8

8- or 10-inch angel food cake
1 cup Kahlua
2 cups frozen nonfat whipped topping, thawed
¼ cup miniature chocolate chips

Cut angel food cake into bite-size pieces. Place half the cake cubes in 8 parfait glasses. Drizzle each serving with about 1 tablespoon Kahlua. Spoon 2 tablespoons whipped topping on cake; sprinkle with half the chocolate chips. Repeat layers with cake, Kahlua, whipped topping and chocolate chips. Cover and refrigerate at least 4 hours or overnight.

Shopping List:

FROZEN	PACKAGED	OTHER
8-oz. container frozen nonfat whipped topping	Miniature chocolate chips	8 oz. Kahlua
	BAKERY	
	8- or 10-inch angel food cake	

NUTRITION PER SERVING Calories 314 • Fat 1.3 g (4%) •
Carbohydrates 58 g • Protein 4 g • Cholesterol 0 mg • Dietary Fiber 0 g •
Sodium 153 mg
EXCHANGES 4 other carb
CARB CHOICES 4

Super Tip: Prepare your own angel food cake from scratch or a mix and use as directed in recipe. You can substitute brewed coffee for Kahlua, if desired.

DESSERTS

241

Lemon Sugar Cookies

Easy

♦ Yields: 48 cookies

1 cup egg substitute
1 cup granulated sugar, plus extra for coating
1 cup powdered sugar
½ tsp. lemon extract
3 cups all-purpose flour
2 tsp. baking powder

Combine egg substitute, sugars and lemon extract in a medium bowl; mix with an electric mixer until creamy and smooth. Add 1½ cups of the flour and baking powder to bowl; beat with mixer until ingredients are blended. Add remaining flour and carefully beat in until dough is blended. Add additional flour 1 tablespoon at a time if dough is too sticky. Wrap dough in plastic wrap and refrigerate 30 minutes.

Preheat oven to 350°F. Line baking sheets with foil and spray with cooking spray. Roll dough into 1-inch balls; roll in granulated sugar to coat. Place cookies on prepared baking sheets and flatten with hand or back of a glass. Bake 12 to 15 minutes, until lightly browned.

Shopping List:

DAIRY	BAKING
8-oz. egg substitute	All-purpose flour
	Granulated sugar
	Powdered sugar
	Lemon extract
	Baking powder

NUTRITION PER SERVING Calories 53 • Fat 0 g • Carbohydrates 12 g • Protein 1 g • Cholesterol 0 mg • Dietary Fiber <1 g • Sodium 21 mg
EXCHANGES ½ other carb
CARB CHOICES 1

Super Tip: *Lemons contain terpenes, a phytochemical that helps induce protective enzymes, interferes with the action of carcinogens and prevents dental decay.*

Mixed Fruit Rice Pudding

Easy

• Serves: 4

4.1-oz. pkg. French vanilla rice pudding mix
14-oz. can fruit cocktail, drained well

Prepare rice pudding according to package directions. Remove from heat; add fruit and let stand 10 to 15 minutes before serving.

Shopping List:

PACKAGED	CANNED
4.1-oz. pkg. French vanilla rice pudding mix	14-oz. can fruit cocktail

NUTRITION PER SERVING Calories 151 • Fat 0 g • Carbohydrates 36 g • Protein 2 g • Cholesterol 0 mg • Dietary Fiber 1 g • Sodium 83 mg
EXCHANGES 2 other carb
CARB CHOICES 2

Super Tip: *Due to the health hazards associated with trans fat, the FDA has finalized a rule that would require trans-fat labeling on packaged foods. Labeling not only will help consumers cut back on trans fat, but would hopefully dissuade manufacturers from using partially hydrogenated oils, the source of trans fats, in their products.*

Peach-Melba Dessert Shake

Easy   ◆ Serves: 6

2 (16-oz.) cans raspberry-flavored peach slices
2 tbsp. lemon juice
1 cup raspberry nonfat sorbet
1 cup vanilla nonfat frozen yogurt or ice cream

Drain peach slices and reserve 1 cup juice. Combine peaches, reserved juice, and lemon juice in a blender or food processor; puree until smooth. Add sorbet and frozen yogurt and process until smooth. Serve immediately.

Shopping List:

PRODUCE	FROZEN	CANNED
1 lemon	8 oz. raspberry nonfat sorbet	2 (16-oz.) cans raspberry flavored peach slices or regular peach slices packed in juice
	8 oz. vanilla nonfat frozen yogurt or ice cream	

NUTRITION PER SERVING Calories 158 • Fat .6 g (3%) •
Carbohydrates 38 g • Protein 2 g • Cholesterol 2 mg • Dietary Fiber 0 g •
Sodium 43 mg
EXCHANGES 2½ other carb
CARB CHOICES 3

Super Tip: *When selecting fresh peaches, look for those that are slightly firm with a sweet fragrance and no tan spots. Ripen peaches in a brown paper bag and store at room temperature. Select canned peaches labeled "packed in their own juice" and "no sugar added."*

DESSERTS

Peach Nectar Sauce with Fresh Fruit

Easy—Do Ahead   • Serves: 4

1 cup vanilla nonfat yogurt
2 tbsp. light brown sugar
¼ tsp. ground cinnamon
⅔ cup peach nectar
4 cups cut-up fruit (fresh peaches, strawberries, pineapple, melon or apples)

Combine all ingredients except fruit in a food processor or blender; process until smooth. Cover and refrigerate up to 4 days. Arrange fruit on plates or in bowls; pour peach sauce over top and serve.

Shopping List:

PRODUCE	DAIRY	CANNED
4 cups cut-up fruit (combination of choice)	8-oz. carton vanilla nonfat yogurt	6 oz. peach nectar
	PACKAGED	SEASONINGS
	Light brown sugar	Ground cinnamon

NUTRITION PER SERVING Calories 181 • Fat .3 g (1%) •
Carbohydrates 45 g • Protein 3 g • Cholesterol 1 mg • Dietary Fiber 7 g •
Sodium 46 mg
EXCHANGES 2 fruit • 1 other carb
CARB CHOICES 3

Super Tip: Peach nectar is peach concentrate mixed with water and sugar.

DESSERTS

Crisp Pecan Cookies

Easy—Do Ahead ◆ Serves: 36

4 large egg whites
1 cup sugar
1 teaspoon vanilla extract
4 cups cornflake crumbs
¾ cup chopped pecans

Preheat oven to 200°F. Line a baking sheet with foil. Place egg whites in a medium bowl; beat with an electric mixer until stiff. Gradually add sugar, beat until stiff peaks form. Fold in vanilla, cornflake crumbs and pecans. Drop batter by tablespoons onto baking sheet. Bake 1 hour, until crisp. Remove from oven and cool on baking sheet 10 minutes. Cool completely before storing.

Shopping List:

DAIRY	PACKAGED	BAKING
4 eggs	Sugar	Vanilla extract
	21-oz. box cornflake crumbs	
	Chopped pecans	

NUTRITION PER SERVING Calories 73 • Fat 1.5 g (18%) • Carbohydrates 13 g • Protein 1 g • Cholesterol 0 mg • Dietary Fiber <1 g • Sodium 113 mg
EXCHANGES 1 other carb
CARB CHOICES 1

Super Tip: *Pecans are a good source of vitamin E and fiber; they contain more than 19 vitamins and minerals.*

DESSERTS

Praline Pound Cake

Easy   ♦ Serves: 8

13.6-oz. fat-free Entenmann's loaf cake, cut into 8 slices
½ cup fat-free caramel ice cream topping
1½ tbsp. toffee crunch chips
2 cups nonfat pecan praline frozen yogurt or ice cream

Preheat broiler on high heat. Line a baking sheet with foil and spray with cooking spray; arrange cake slices in a single layer on baking sheet. Broil 30 to 45 seconds until lightly browned. Cool slightly. Spread each slice with 1 tablespoon caramel topping; sprinkle with toffee crunch chips and top with ½ cup nonfat frozen yogurt or ice cream.

Shopping List:

FROZEN	PACKAGED	OTHER
1 pint nonfat pecan praline frozen yogurt or ice cream	13.6-oz. Entenmann's fat-free loaf cake Toffee crunch chips	12.25-oz. jar caramel fat-free ice cream topping

NUTRITION PER SERVING Calories 308 • Fat .4 g (1%) •
Carbohydrates 68 g • Protein 7 g • Cholesterol 2 mg • Dietary Fiber 1 g •
Sodium 308 mg
EXCHANGES 4½ other carb
CARB CHOICES 5

Super Tip: *You can substitute chopped nuts or miniature chocolate chips for toffee crunch chips.*

Pumpkin Parfait with Honey Wheat Germ

Easy—Do Ahead   • Serves: 6

16-oz. can pumpkin
⅓ cup packed light brown sugar
⅓ cup apple juice concentrate, thawed
2 tsp. pumpkin pie spice
1 cup frozen nonfat whipped topping, thawed
1½ cups vanilla nonfat yogurt
¼ cup honey wheat germ

Combine pumpkin, brown sugar, apple juice concentrate, pumpkin pie spice and ½ cup of the whipped topping in a large bowl; mix until ingredients are blended smooth. Using a glass round casserole, alternate layers of pumpkin mixture and yogurt. Top with remaining whipped topping and sprinkle with wheat germ. Cover and refrigerate several hours before serving.

Shopping List:

DAIRY	PACKAGED	SEASONINGS
12 oz. vanilla nonfat yogurt	Light brown sugar Honey wheat germ	Pumpkin pie spice
FROZEN Apple juice concentrate 8-oz. container frozen nonfat whipped topping	**CANNED** 16-oz. can pumpkin	

NUTRITION PER SERVING Calories 159 • Fat .8 g (5%) •
Carbohydrates 35 g • Protein 4 g • Cholesterol 1 mg • Dietary Fiber 2 g •
Sodium 50 mg
EXCHANGES 2 other carb
CARB CHOICES 2

Super Tip: *Substitute 1 teaspoon cinnamon, ¼ teaspoon ginger, ¼ teaspoon nutmeg, ¼ teaspoon mace and ¼ teaspoon ground cloves for 2 teaspoons pumpkin pie spice. You can use nonfat granola or Grape Nuts cereal instead of wheat germ if desired.*

Raspberry Shortcake

Easy—Do Ahead ◆ Serves: 8

8- to 10-inch angel food cake
.6-oz. pkg. sugar-free raspberry-flavored gelatin
4 cups raspberries, plus extra for garnish
8-oz. container frozen nonfat whipped topping

Tear angel food cake into small pieces and place in a 9 × 13-inch baking dish. Prepare gelatin as directed on package and pour over cake pieces. Top with raspberries; cover and refrigerate until gelatin is set. Just before serving, top with whipped topping and garnish with berries, if desired.

Shopping List:

PRODUCE	PACKAGED	BAKED GOODS
2 pints raspberries	.6-oz. pkg. sugar-free raspberry-flavored gelatin	Angel food cake (or purchase angel food cake mix and prepare as directed)
FROZEN		
8-oz. container frozen nonfat whipped topping		

NUTRITION PER SERVING Calories 219 • Fat .4 g (1%) • Carbohydrates 47 g • Protein 5 g • Cholesterol 0 mg • Dietary Fiber 3 g • Sodium 178 mg
EXCHANGES 3 other carb
CARB CHOICES 3

Super Tip: *The tannins in raspberries stop the build-up of bacteria that produces tooth-decaying plaque, helping keep teeth and gums healthy.*

DESSERTS

S'more Chocolate Cake

Easy

• Serves: 8

13.6-oz. fat-free chocolate loaf cake
4 cups nonfat frozen yogurt (flavor of choice)
½ cup marshmallow creme
½ cup butterscotch, caramel, pineapple or strawberry fat-free ice cream topping

Slice cake into 8 pieces. Place one piece of cake on each dessert plate. Top each slice with ½ cup of the frozen yogurt, 1 tablespoon of the marshmallow creme and 1 tablespoon of the ice cream topping.

Shopping List:

FROZEN	BAKING	OTHER
1 qt. nonfat frozen yogurt (flavor of choice)	7-oz. jar marshmallow creme	12.25-oz. jar ice cream topping
PACKAGED		
13.6-oz. Entenmann's fat-free chocolate loaf cake		

NUTRITION PER SERVING Calories 227 • Fat 0 g (0%) •
Carbohydrates 51 g • Protein 7 g • Cholesterol 0 mg • Dietary Fiber 2 g •
Sodium 339 mg
EXCHANGES 3½ other carb
CARB CHOICES 3

Super Tip: *As a nation, we consume 2,478,000 pounds of chocolate each year or 11.7 pounds per person; 7.6 billion dollars worth of chocolate is manufactured each year and retail sales have skyrocketed to 11.7 billion dollars annually.*

DESSERTS

Strawberry Fluff

Easy—Do Ahead   • Serves: 6

3-oz. pkg. strawberry-flavored gelatin
1 cup boiling water
⅔ cup cold water
8-oz. carton strawberry nonfat yogurt
2 cups fresh sliced strawberries
6 tbsp. frozen nonfat whipped topping, thawed (optional)

In a medium bowl, dissolve gelatin in boiling water. Stir in cold water, cover
and refrigerate 45 to 50 minutes, until partially set. Add yogurt; beat with
electric mixer until light and fluffy. Place ¼ cup strawberries in each of 6
dessert dishes. Divide gelatin mixture and spoon over strawberries. Top
with remaining strawberries. Cover and chill 2 hours or overnight before
serving. Top each dessert with 1 tablespoon whipped topping and remaining strawberries before serving if desired.

Shopping List:

PRODUCE	FROZEN	PACKAGED
1 pint fresh strawberries	8-oz. container nonfat whipped topping (optional)	3-oz. pkg. strawberry-flavored gelatin
DAIRY		
8-oz. carton strawberry or vanilla nonfat yogurt		

NUTRITION PER SERVING Calories 79 • Fat .2 g (2%) • Carbohydrates 17 g •
Protein 4 g • Cholesterol 1 mg • Dietary Fiber 1 g • Sodium 29 mg
EXCHANGES 1 other carb
CARB CHOICES 1

Super Tip: *You can substitute a 16-oz. package frozen sliced strawberries for
fresh; thaw and drain before assembling dessert.*

DESSERTS

Strawberry Waffle Sundae

Easy   • Serves: 6

6 frozen nonfat waffles
3 cups strawberry nonfat frozen yogurt or sorbet
¾ cup strawberry ice cream topping
1½ cups frozen sweetened strawberry slices, thawed
⅓ cup nonfat whipped topping, thawed (optional)

Cook waffles according to package directions. Top each waffle with ½ cup of the frozen yogurt, 2 tablespoons of the ice cream topping and ¼ cup strawberry slices. Top with a dollop of whipped topping, if desired, and serve immediately.

Shopping List:

FROZEN	10-oz. pkg. frozen	OTHER
6 nonfat frozen waffles	sweetened strawberry slices	12.25-oz. jar strawberry ice cream topping
24 oz. strawberry nonfat frozen yogurt or sorbet	8-oz. container nonfat whipped topping (optional)	

NUTRITION PER SERVING Calories 255 • Fat 0 g (0%) •
Carbohydrates 57 g • Protein 7 g • Cholesterol 0 mg • Dietary Fiber 6 g •
Sodium 212 mg
EXCHANGES 1½ starch • 2 other carb
CARB CHOICES 4

Super Tip: Watch out for trans-fat rich waffles. Skip the trans fat and save your health. Researchers found that when women replaced 2 percent of the trans fats they ate with polyunsaturated fat, they dropped their risk of diabetes by 40 percent.

DESSERTS

TEST FOODS

❖ ❖ ❖

The principle of *Supermarket Gourmet* was to develop quick, easy and healthy meals from easy-to-find foods at the local supermarket. Below is a list of the products used for testing recipes, as well as packaged foods that work well as simple side dishes or snacks. You can usually substitute similar varieties without affecting composition or flavor, but, again, this takes practice, trial and error. This list is simply a guideline and you may refer to it when comparison shopping. It is important to follow the specific serving sizes in the ingredient list. For example, do not substitute a 28-ounce can of whole tomatoes for a 14½-ounce can of diced tomatoes and expect the same results.

PRODUCT	NAME BRAND	PACKAGE SIZE/ SERVINGS
PRODUCE		
Salad Packages	Ready Pac	(7 to 10 oz.)
	Fresh Express	6 oz. = 2 servings 10 oz. = 3 servings 16 oz. = 5 servings
Confetti mix (chopped broccoli, cauliflower, cabbage, carrots, celery)	Ready-Pac	7-oz. container
Diced onion	Ready-Pac	7-oz. container
Sliced peppers and onions for fajitas	Ready-Pac	7-oz. container
Diced tri-pepper	Ready-Pac	7-oz. container
Fruit glaze (Peach, Strawberry)	Marie's	18 oz. = 6 servings
PACKAGED		
Instant pudding and pie filling	Jell-O	3.8-oz. pkg. = 4 servings
Fat-free sugar-free instant pudding and pie filling	Jell-O	1 oz. = 4 servings

PRODUCT	NAME BRAND	PACKAGE SIZE/ SERVINGS
Sugar-free Jell-O	Jell-O	.6-oz. pkg. = 8 servings
Smart Start cereal	Kellogg's	17.5 oz. = 10 servings
Puffed kashi cereal	Kashi	7.5 oz. = 8.5 servings
Tortilla soup mix	Bear Creek	9 oz. = 8 servings
Herb-seasoned, Cool Herb Ranch, Cheese and Garlic, Onion and Garlic Fat-Free Croutons	Mrs. Cubbison's	5 oz. = 20 servings
Fruitlings: Apricot, Cranberry-Orange	Sunsweet	5 oz. = 3½ servings
Fat-free muffin mix (Apple Cinnamon, Blueberry, Banana, Cranberry Orange)	Krusteaz	19 oz. = 12 servings
Fat-Free Honey Cornbread mix	Krusteaz	14.5 oz. = 12 servings
Super Moist Cake Mix (German Chocolate, Vanilla, Devil's Food, Carrot, Yellow, Lemon)	Betty Crocker	18.25 oz. = 12 servings
Cake mix	Sweet Rewards	8 servings
Thin unsalted matzos	Manischewitz	10 oz. = 12 servings
Lahvosh crackers	Valley	8 oz. = 8 servings
Original Corn Thins	Real Foods	5.5 oz. = 13 servings
Turkey Gravy Dry Mix	McCormick	.87 oz. = 4 servings
Enchilada Sauce Dry Mix	McCormick	1.5 oz. = 8 servings
Chicken Dijon Sauce Blend Dry Mix	McCormick	1.37 oz. = 4 servings
Taco Seasoning Dry Mix	Schilling	1.0 oz. = 6 servings
Cajun-Style Fry Mix for Fish and Chicken	Golden Dipt	10 oz. = 30 servings
Bacon Crumbles	McCormick Produce Partners	1.3 oz. = 5 servings
Sun-dried tomatoes (regular, julienne-cut)	Bella Sun Luci	3 oz. = 6 servings
Spanish Rice Mix	Rice-a-Roni	6.8 oz. = 3.5 servings
Red Beans & Rice Mix	Grandma Maud's	6.2 oz. = 6 servings

PRODUCT	NAME BRAND	PACKAGE SIZE/ SERVINGS
Shake 'n Bake Coating for chicken or pork	Shake 'n Bake	5.75 oz. = 16 servings
Stove Top Stuffing	Stove Top	6 oz. = 6 servings
98% Fat-Free flour tortillas—8"	Mission	17.5 oz. = 10 servings
Herbed Chicken Couscous	Near East	6.09 oz. = 3 servings
Rice Pilaf Mix	Near East	6.09 oz. = 3 servings
Long Grain and Wild Rice Mix	Rice-A-Roni	4.3 oz. = 2 servings
Yakisoba Noodles with Sweet 'n Sour Sauce	Fortune Brand Stir-Fry Noodles	7 oz. = 2 servings
Rice pudding mix French Vanilla	Uncle Ben's	4.1 oz. = 3½ servings
Cinnamon & Raisin		5.5 oz. = 3½ servings
CANNED Cream of Chicken Soup	Healthy Request	10¾ oz. = 2.5 servings
Seasoned Tomato Sauce for Lasagna	Hunt's	15 oz. = 7 servings
Seasoned Diced Tomato Sauce for Tacos	Hunt's	14½ oz. = 7 servings
Seasoned Tomato Sauce for Pizza	Hunt's	15 oz. = 7 servings
Seasoned Diced Tomato Sauce for Chili	Hunt's	15 oz. = 7 servings
Seasoned Tomato Sauce for Meatloaf	Hunt's	15.25 oz. = 7 servings
Ready-Cut Italian Recipe Peeled Tomatoes Diced with Garlic, Oregano & Basil	S & W	14½ oz. = 3½ servings
Diced Tomatoes & Green Chiles	Ro-Tel	10 oz. = 2½ servings
Petite Diced Tomatoes with Green Chiles	Hunt's	14½ oz. = 3½ servings
Diced Tomatoes with Garlic and Onion	Del Monte	14½ oz. = 3½ servings
Petite Cut Diced Tomatoes with Roasted Garlic and Sweet Onions	S & W	14½ oz. = 3½ servings

PRODUCT	NAME BRAND	PACKAGE SIZE/ SERVINGS
Diced Tomatoes with basil, garlic & oregano	Del Monte	14½ oz. = 3½ servings
Italian Paste with Roasted Garlic	Contadina	6 oz. = 5 servings
Original Sloppy Joe Sauce	Hunt's Manwich	15½ oz. = 7 servings
Canned Sauce for Spanish Rice	Hatch	15 oz. = 7 servings
Quartered Artichoke Hearts	Maria	13¾ oz. undrained = 3 servings
Hearts of Palm	Maria	14½ oz. = 3 servings
Julienned Beets	S & W	15 oz. = 3½ servings
Sweet Corn Cream Style	Del Monte	14¾ oz. = 3½ servings
Mexicorn	Green Giant	11 oz. = 4 servings
Vegetable Garden 4-Bean Chili	Stagg or Hormel	15 oz. = 2 servings
Fat-Free Refried Beans (Regular, Green Chile & Lime)	Rosarita	16 oz. = 3½ servings
Chunk White Chicken in Water	Premium	10 oz. = 4 servings
Chunk Light Tuna in Water	Chicken of the Sea	6 oz. = 2½ servings
REFRIGERATED/DAIRY Diced Potatoes with Onion (precooked)	Simply Potatoes	1 lb. 4 oz. = 6 servings
Pre-cooked Hash Brown Potatoes	Purely Idaho	16 oz. = 4 servings
Pre-cooked Cubed Potatoes	Purely Idaho	16 oz. = 4 servings
Southwest Style Hash Brown Potatoes	Simply Potatoes	1 lb. 4 oz. = 7 servings
Sliced Home Fries	Simply Potatoes	1 lb. 4 oz. = 5 servings
Pre-cooked Roasted Onion Potato Cubes	Purely Idaho	16 oz. = 4 servings
Egg blends—Vegetable Garden, Southwestern	Egg Beaters	15 oz. = 7 servings
Fat-free single cheese slices (American, Cheddar, Mozzarella, Swiss)	Kraft	12 oz. = 16 servings

PRODUCT	NAME BRAND	PACKAGE SIZE/ SERVINGS
Fat-free crumbled feta cheese	Presidente	6 oz. = 6 servings

CONDIMENTS/SAUCES

PRODUCT	NAME BRAND	PACKAGE SIZE/ SERVINGS
Garlic Lemon Marinade	Garlic Survival Company	14 oz. = 40 servings
Fat-Free Lemon Butter Dill Sauce for Seafood or Chicken	Golden Dipt	8.7 oz. = 8 servings
30-minute Lemon-Pepper marinade for chicken, meat or fish	Lawry's	12 fl. oz. = 24 servings
Roasted Garlic Teriyaki Sauce	Kikkoman	10 oz. = 20 servings
Sweet Roasted Peppers	Dunbar	12 oz. = 12 servings
Hot Mango Chutney	Crosse & Blackwell	9 oz. = 13 servings
Seafood Cocktail Sauce	Crosse & Blackwell	12 oz. = 5 servings
Original Gourmet Sauce	Yoshida's	17 fl. oz. = 33 servings
Chili Sauce	Heinz	12 oz. = 20 servings
Fat-Free Tartar Sauce	Golden Dipt	8 oz. = 8 servings
Prepared horseradish	Morehouse	4 oz. = 20 servings
Fat-Free Dorothy Lynch salad dressing	Dorothy Lynch	16 fl. oz. = 16 servings
Pasta sauce: Fire Roasted Tomato & Garlic, Tomato & Basil, Portobello Mushroom	Classico	26 oz. = 6 servings

DESSERTS/DESSERT TOPPINGS

PRODUCT	NAME BRAND	PACKAGE SIZE/ SERVINGS
Cinnamon 'n Spice Apple Pie Filling or Topping	Comstock	21 oz. = 7 servings
Fat-free Caramel apple dip	T. Marzetti's	12 oz. = 6 servings
Fat-free loaf cake	Entenmann's	13.6 oz. = 8 servings
Fat-free chocolate loaf cake	Entenmann's	15 oz. = 8 servings
Light Fudge Brownies	Entenmann's	10 servings
Marshmallow Creme	Kraft	7 oz. = 17 servings
Ice cream (dessert) topping: Butterscotch, Caramel, Pineapple, Strawberry	Smucker's	12.25 oz. = 8 servings

PRODUCT	NAME BRAND	PACKAGE SIZE/ SERVINGS
Simply Fruit Spread (Strawberry, Apricot, Black Cherry, Raspberry, Blackberry)	Smucker's	10 oz. = 15 servings
MEAT, FISH, POULTRY		
Imitation Crab Meat	Captain's Choice	16 oz. = 5 servings
Reduced-fat Pepperoni slices	Gallo	6 oz. = 6 servings
Fat-free hot dogs	Oscar Meyer	14 oz. = 8 servings
Turkey/chicken breast slices (oven roasted, honey roasted)	Foster Farms	10 oz. = 10 servings
Smoked turkey breast slices	Butterball	6 oz. = 3½ servings
Low-fat turkey bacon	Jennie-O	12 oz. = 11 servings
White turkey breast tenderloin or boneless breast chops	Honeysuckle	4 oz. = 1 serving
Ahi tuna steak	Galletti Brothers	4 oz. = 1 serving
Alaskan cod fillet	Galletti Brothers	4 oz. = 1 serving
Mahi mahi fillets	Galletti Brothers	4 oz. = 1 serving
Boneless, skinless chicken breast fillets	Butterball	4 oz. = 1 serving
Extra-lean ground turkey	Jennie-O	4 oz. = 1 serving
Ground beef (4 grams fat per serving)	Laura's or Healthy Choice	4 oz. = 1 serving
BBQ shredded chicken or pork	Lloyd's	32 oz. = 16 servings
BBQ with sliced beef	Lloyd's	32 oz. = 16 servings
FROZEN		
Fat-free Cool Whip Topping	Cool Whip	8 oz. = 15 servings
Create a Meal—Stir-Fry Sweet & Sour	Green Giant	21 oz. = 3 servings
Frozen scallops	Contessa	12 oz. = 3 servings
Frozen chopped onions	Bird's Eye	12 oz. = 4 servings
Frozen pepper stir-fry	Bird's Eye	16 oz. = 5 servings

PRODUCT	NAME BRAND	PACKAGE SIZE/ SERVINGS
Frozen diced green peppers	Bird's Eye	10 oz. = 3½ servings
Frozen white bread dough	Rhodes	3 lbs. = 27 servings per package
Seasonings Lemon Pepper Seasoning	Lawry's	2.25 oz. = 91 servings
Mexican Seasoning	McCormick	2.75 oz.
Salt-free herb-and-spice blend	Mrs. Dash	

Index

❖ ❖ ❖

INDEX

INDEX

INDEX

265

INDEX